CHARTER SCHOOLS AT
THE CROSSROADS

CHARTER SCHOOLS AT THE CROSSROADS

Predicaments, Paradoxes, Possibilities

Chester E. Finn, Jr.
Bruno V. Manno
Brandon L. Wright

HARVARD EDUCATION PRESS
CAMBRIDGE, MASSACHUSETTS

Paperback ISBN 978-1-61250-977-8
Library Edition ISBN 978-1-61250-978-5

Library of Congress Cataloging-in-Publication Data

Names: Finn, Chester E., Jr., 1944– author. | Manno, Bruno V., author. |
    Wright, Brandon L., author.
Title: Charter schools at the crossroads : predicaments, paradoxes,
    possibilities / Chester E. Finn, Jr., Bruno V. Manno, Brandon L. Wright.
Description: Cambridge, Massachusetts : Harvard Education Press, [2016] |
    Includes bibliographical references and index.
Identifiers: LCCN 2016021200| ISBN 9781612509778 (pbk.) |
    ISBN 9781612509785
    (library edition)
Subjects: LCSH: Charter schools—United States. | Privatization in
    education—United States.
Classification: LCC LB2806.36 .F56 2016 | DDC 371.05—dc23
LC record available at https://lccn.loc.gov/2016021200

Published by Harvard Education Press,
an imprint of the Harvard Education Publishing Group

Harvard Education Press
8 Story Street
Cambridge, MA 02138

Cover Design: Ciano Design
The typefaces used in this book are ITC Legacy Serif and ITC Legacy Sans

For the children, parents, educators,
and visionaries who have shared this adventure

CONTENTS

ACKNOWLEDGMENTS

WE OWE A GREAT DEAL to many individuals and organizations for their help in making this book possible and improving its content. None, of course—least of all the organizations that employ us, the Thomas B. Fordham Foundation and Walton Family Foundation—bears any responsibility for our conclusions or for errors and omissions that we commit en route.

Both organizations blessed this project, however, and freed enough of our time to make it possible as well as supplying knowledgeable, incisive, and accessible colleagues who clarified our thinking, widened our horizons, and boosted our morale. Also enabling this endeavor were the Ewing Marion Kauffman Foundation and the Kern Family Foundation, whose financial support we deeply appreciate.

While it's impossible to list every organization and person who answered our questions, led us to sometimes-obscure sources, and lent us worthy insights, we must mention a few that proved indispensable. At the National Alliance for Public Charter Schools, we benefited hugely from the goodwill and resourcefulness of Susan Aud Pendergrass, Nina Rees, and Todd Ziebarth. At the Center on Reinventing Public Education, we owe much to Christine Campbell, Paul Hill, and Robin Lake, as well as their many colleagues over the years. At the Center for Research on Education Outcomes, we're particularly grateful to Macke Raymond and James (Lynn) Woodworth. We're also indebted to Meagan Batdorff, Jay Greene, and the other prolific and persistent scholars of the University of Arkansas's Department of Education Reform.

Earnest thanks, too, to the National Association of Charter School Authorizers, especially Greg Richmond; to David Osborne, now with the Progressive Policy Institute; to Brian Gill at the Rand Corporation; to Matthew Carr at the Kauffman Foundation; to Ted Kolderie, one of chartering's indispensable parents, now with Education Evolving; and to Lauren Morando Rhim at the National Center for Special Education in Charter Schools.

Our long-suffering spouses, Renu Virmani, Elena Vejarano, and Mary Gardner, tolerated and encouraged us through it all, including too many preoccupied evenings and interrupted weekends.

We've all had the pleasure of working more than once with the Harvard Education Press. Editor in chief Caroline Chauncey again provided superb editorial counsel—and managed to stay cordial and supportive even when recommending major changes in our evolving manuscript. Others at Harvard Education Press who have been invaluable in bringing this project to a successful conclusion include Patricia E. Boyd, Laura Cutone Godwin, Rose Ann Miller, and Sumita Mukherji.

America's great adventure in charter schooling may already have lasted a quarter century, but in many ways it has scarcely begun. We look to its future with optimism—and with the hope that these pages will inform and encourage those who carry it forward.

INTRODUCTION

A QUARTER CENTURY has passed since Minnesota passed America's first charter-school law in 1991. Today, forty-three states (including the District of Columbia) contain some sixty-eight hundred charter schools, serving nearly three million students, almost 6 percent of the US public school enrollment. Charter schools constitute the fastest-growing school-choice option in the land and are as close to a disruptive innovation as American K–12 education has seen in decades. They create a new market and an alternative delivery system that affords families and children access to public schools different from those they find within the traditional district structure. Together with the promulgation and strengthening of academic standards, the charter phenomenon is the most visible and substantial education reform of the modern era. At least ten other countries are also experimenting with kindred models of independent public schools, even (in England) putting them into practice on a vast scale.

How did this change come about? How is it working? What lies ahead? And what does all this mean for public education?

Up to this point, charters have performed spectacularly unevenly in many ways, sometimes succeeding wonderfully and other times faltering badly. They also remain the object of widespread misunderstanding as to what they are and how they work. They have fervent opponents as well as ardent supporters. The former tend to slight their accomplishments while the latter often turn a blind eye to their shortcomings. These persistent battles over chartering's legitimacy partly explain why such schools have only begun to fulfill their potential as an engine of change for American education.

Chartering today is pigeonholed by some (including many of its staunchest supporters) as an escape valve for low-income, inner-city, mostly minority students needing to exit poorly performing district schools and unable to afford private-school alternatives. This is an important role in American K–12 education, and the best charters—aided and advanced by single-minded philanthropy and public policies—are doing it well. Expanding and perfecting that role is a plausible, defensible path into the future.

Yet chartering has greater potential to tackle other problems within (and beyond) K–12 schooling. It can serve additional needy clienteles in more parts of the country. It can demonstrate US schools' capacity to produce more internationally competitive graduates. Charter schools can also pioneer new approaches to education, addressing the diverse and ambitious outcomes, both cognitive and otherwise, that educators seek for children. Finally, chartering can retool and even supplant the antiquated governance structures of public schooling.

Before peering into the future, we review some ways in which the much-needed reinvention of American K–12 education has been pioneered by the charter experiments of the past quarter century. We also show that the charter sector itself needs repairs and further development before it can deliver on its promise.

This book has four parts. Part I is historical and quantitative. Chapter 1 recaps the origins of chartering in both concept and statute, recognizing the diverse visions harbored by its theorists, policy shapers, and practitioners. This subject remains contentious, even polarizing. We hope that a recap of how it began will be valuable to all parties. In chapter 2 (and the appendix), we document the growth and evolution of charter schools over the past quarter century (though data from the early years are sparse).

In part II, we turn qualitative and more analytical. Chapter 3 reviews the charter sector's uneven track record in academic achievement. In chapter 4, we illustrate with this concrete examples of specific charter initiatives, both laudable and flawed. Chapter 5 moves beyond school performance and summarizes several noteworthy examples of charter-based accomplishments that, even when beset with imperfections of their own, are already helping to renew public education.

Part III addresses a host of troublesome, unresolved, and often unanticipated problems—some of them better described as tensions or dilemmas—that beset the charter sector in 2016. These challenges impede efforts to advance and enhance chartering, both in its own right and as a source of further educational revitalization. This part of the book discusses shortcomings in the charter marketplace (chapter 6); the precarious relationships among authorizing, governance, and leadership (chapter 7); the fiscal challenges facing these upstart schools along with the mixed blessings of philanthropy and private investment (chapter 8); the eternal balancing and rebalancing of freedom and regulation (chapter 9); and the ever-contentious political realm (chapter 10).

In the four chapters that constitute part IV, we examine the future of chartering and its place in the larger primary-secondary arena. Chapter 11 aims to extend and improve the no-excuses model of chartering as a source of opportunities for disadvantaged children, while recognizing the limits of that strategy. In chapter 12, we widen our focus on how chartering can tackle more problems and participate in larger reforms, including alternative structures for governing and delivering education. In chapter 13, we review a number of changes that would strengthen the marketplace and address significant shortcomings that chartering has surfaced. Finally, chapter 14 places chartering and its future into the context of public education in twenty-first-century America and the major challenges that it faces.

PART I

Looking Back

1

The Origins
of Chartering

THE DEBUT OF CHARTERING was no lightning bolt. By the late twentieth century, other currents flowing through American society and primary-secondary education were already disrupting the old circuits. In this chapter, we briefly review the charter concept, then trace its genealogy and the multifaceted context from which this reform and many other changes in the K–12 realm arose. We show that chartering is no single, coherent experiment but, rather, a multihued strategy that has taken numerous forms and incorporated diverse hopes. Its very flexibility has allowed for parallel experiments in the creation, operation, and rethinking of schools and school systems while giving needy children and families more options and helping to redefine local control.

A CHARTER PRIMER

Chartering allows for the creation of independent public schools of choice. They operate primarily beyond the authority of the school district and are free from many district rules, yet they're accountable to the public via state-approved authorities for agreed-upon results spelled out in a legally binding performance contract.[1] Such schools mix key features of both public and private education in ways seldom seen before in the United States.[2]

As a public school, a charter is ordinarily open to anyone who wishes to attend it and is paid for with tax dollars. It charges no tuition and generally adheres to state academic standards and testing regimes. Unlike a conventional public school, however, a charter school is not assumed to be permanent; indeed, authorizers can close (or decline to renew) it if it fails to produce the promised results or otherwise goes off track.

Charters also benefit from some features of private schooling. They are more autonomous in their operations than most district-operated schools and are freed from some state mandates and local regulations. Almost anyone, including educators, parents, nonprofit organizations, and private firms, can create such a school. An independent board of directors oversees the school, which enrolls only children whose families choose it.[3] Like the students, the educators employed in charter schools choose to work there of their own volition, not according to the mandate of a union contract or assignment by a district office.[4]

Charters can be single, stand-alone schools or parts of larger networks of kindred schools. Such networks may be nonprofit charter management organizations (CMOs) or profit-seeking education management organizations (EMOs). Most charters are new, start-from-scratch schools, but district schools may convert to charter status if a significant number of teachers (and, sometimes, parents) vote to do so or if a conversion is part of efforts to turn around troubled district schools.

MANY FOREBEARS

Chartering (and other forms of school choice) can trace its ancestry to the era before Horace Mann began to gather public education into government-run systems. As historians David Tyack and Elisabeth Hansot explain, in colonial times and the early days of the republic, "many forms of schooling deserved the favor of government [and] citizens tended to have an attitude toward education that Americans today have toward religion: attend the school of your choice."[5]

This "thousand flowers" approach to public schooling gradually gave way to the "common school" ideas of Mann and other nineteenth-century reformers who, in the words of Tyack, Hansot, and Michael Kirst, favored an education system that was "public in political control and economic support, to include children of all classes, sects, and ethnic groups, and existed to produce literate, numerate, and moral citizens."[6] With the passage of time and the influence of progressive reformers of the early twentieth century, this approach evolved into what Tyack has famously termed the "one best system," one that "glorified expertise, efficiency, and the disinterested public service of the elites" and shielded schools from municipal politics and corruption.[7] As additional reformist impulses kicked in, states also legislated such standardizing features as compulsory attendance, graduation requirements, and teacher qualifications, gradually tightening the state's grip on the delivery of K–12 education while also shouldering more of its costs. In time, the federal government added more carrots and sticks, primarily starting in 1965, when Lyndon Johnson signed the Elementary and Secondary Education Act. Twenty-four years later, the late Albert Shanker, a lifelong teachers union leader and visionary education reformer, bitingly criticized the result of these accreting layers of government control: "It's time to admit that public education operates like a planned economy, a bureaucratic system in which everybody's role is spelled out in advance, and there are few incentives for innovation and productivity. It's no surprise that our school system doesn't improve. It more resembles the communist economy than our own market economy."[8]

Alongside this centralizing, standardizing trend, K–12 education in the United States has retained an independent sector of schools, often with religious affiliations, for families with the wherewithal and inclination to patronize them. For many decades, private schools chiefly served well-to-do families and those who viewed the religious and character development of their children as central to their education as skills and knowledge. Policy mechanisms such as vouchers and tax credits have given more families access to such options in recent decades. This independent sector today enrolls about 10 percent of US students in some thirty-one thousand schools and incorporates a key approach that charter schools also now embrace: self-governing and diverse educational institutions that serve children, with little government control or industrial-style management.[9]

Several other wellsprings of chartering—and other education reforms—are more recent.

QUESTIONING THE LINK BETWEEN
RESOURCES AND RESULTS

The 1965 Elementary and Secondary Education Act rested on the premise that schools serving poor kids were generally under-resourced. Supplying their schools with more money—in this case, unprecedented sums of federal tax dollars—would produce better academic outcomes for these children and help lift them out of poverty.

The very next year, however, the eminent sociologist James S. Coleman produced the massive study, titled *Equality of Educational Opportunity*, which failed to find a reliable relationship between the resources going into schools and their results.[10] In Coleman's words, "the major virtue of the study [was] shifting policy attention from . . . inputs (per pupil expenditure, class size, teacher salaries, and so on) to a focus on outputs."[11]

Consider the irony: as the Great Society was adding resources to public schools on the assumption that doing this would yield better results, Coleman was raising profound questions about the efficacy of that strategy, indeed about the entire basis on which judgments of school quality had long rested. Though he was widely ignored for years by much of the education establishment, his core findings were replicated by other scholars, and his central message—the weak link between school inputs and outcomes—has never been disproved.[12]

If inputs didn't explain differences in achievement, then what did? And could these differences be bridged? How best to boost the achievement of disadvantaged children? Answering such questions was not going to be easy. As Coleman himself wrote, "overcoming . . . inequities in the opportunity for educational achievement . . . [is] far more ambitious than has ever been attempted by any society."[13]

The respected Harvard psychologist John B. Carroll suggested that outcomes might be more similar if instructional practices were better tailored to the differing needs of children.[14] Others sought to understand which school practices worked best, particularly with poor and minority youngsters. This scholarship gave rise to a line of inquiry that became known as *effective-schools research*, which focused on the "alignment" of all elements of the education delivery system.[15] Still other analysts proposed different possibilities.

PURSUING EQUITY THROUGH
HIGHER STANDARDS

Kenneth B. Clark, an iconoclastic and influential African American psychologist whose work the Supreme Court approvingly cited in *Brown v. Board of Education*, wrote extensively to refute the view that minority students require a watered-down approach to schooling. For him, this patronizing attitude fostered a "racism of double standards [caused by] . . . the sloppy, sentimentalistic good intentions of educators."[16] He argued that K–12 public education did not have to be seen only in terms of the existing district system and that schools should ultimately "be judged in terms of performance, not opportunity alone." In this argument, he echoed Coleman while also tying his insight to the idea of common expectations for all children, thus foreshadowing what became known as the *standards movement*, including its evolution into today's Common Core State Standards. Clark saw shared expectations as a way to ensure equity.[17] His conviction that excellence and equality were complementary goals would become another key component of the charter idea.

The insights of Coleman, Clark, and others offering ideas for boosting achievement also anticipated today's *accountability tripod* of standards, testing, and consequences. After all, if inputs don't reliably produce better outcomes, then it's crucial for policy leaders to specify the education outcomes that are sought, devise a means of measuring performance in relation to them, and install mechanisms for stimulating and rewarding progress toward them.

THE RISE OF THE EXCELLENCE MOVEMENT

What education writer Tom Toch termed the *excellence movement* emerged from *A Nation at Risk*, the much-discussed 1983 report of the National Commission on Excellence in Education, which characterized the United States as awash in "mediocre educational performance [amounting] to an act of unthinking, unilateral educational disarmament."[18] State governors took up this challenge and, beginning in 1986, issued a series of reports called *Time for Results*. They were led by a group of mostly Southern governors who would later emerge as national figures in their own right, including Democrats Bill Clinton of Arkansas (future president) and Richard Riley of South Carolina (future secretary of education), and Republican Lamar Alexander of Tennessee (future secretary of education, now a senior US senator). Their immediate goal was to boost their impoverished states' economic prospects in an increasingly competitive world. They understood that, in Alexander's oft-repeated slogan, "better schools mean better jobs for Tennesseans" and for every other state.

The initiatives undertaken by the governors and their colleagues, first via the Southern Regional Education Board and then the National Governors Association, led to a 1989 invitation to all the governors from President George H. W. Bush to join him at an education summit held in Charlottesville. The conclave yielded six ambitious national education goals. The objective of summit participants was, in their words, "to swap red tape for results."[19] This swap, too, became a key part of the charter idea as well as numerous other contemporary reforms.

CREATING NEW SCHOOLS

Tyack's "one best system" proved less and less workable as the country and many of its communities grew more diverse and as Americans grew more accustomed to variety and choices in other aspects of their lives. The industrial model of schooling also appeared archaic in an era that was reinventing everything from communications to transportation to health care. This changing technological and organizational environment prompted efforts to create new education models better suited to the needs and preferences of a changing population.

Thus arose the nonprofit New American Schools Development Corporation (NASDC, later New American Schools), established in 1991 (the year of the first charter law) by major corporate executives and tasked with devising innovative school models. Led by David Kearns, former CEO of Xerox and then Alexander's deputy at the US Department of Education, NASDC ran a design competition and eventually funded eleven "break the mold" teams with differing ideas about how new-style schools should function.[20] Concurrently,

Chris Whittle's Edison Project, co-led by former Yale president Benno Schmidt, set out to reinvent the school via the private sector.[21]

FOSTERING CHOICE AND COMPETITION

Although school choice has the colonial roots noted above, as well as the blessing of early theorists such as John Stuart Mill, it got a modern boost in 1962 when Nobel Prize–winning economist Milton Friedman published *Capitalism and Freedom*. In the book, Friedman described (along with the right of parents in a democracy to choose their children's schools) the potential of market forces to strengthen educational quality, efficiency, and productivity.[22] He favored a competitive, private-sector model and did not think government should deliver education directly. Rather, it should provide needy families with vouchers that could be redeemed for education at any state-approved school. He expected market forces to cause bad schools to improve or close, motivate decent schools to get better, and induce individuals and organization to open new ones.

The suggestion that choice would boost education quality and empower families had early advocates on the left as well. Indeed, Yale law professor James Forman, Jr. contended "that [school] choice has deep roots in liberal education reform movements, the civil rights movement, and black nationalism . . . [and] that the left has . . . seen a role for choice in promoting educational opportunity for poor and minority children."[23] Sociologist Christopher Jencks argued for giving families tuition grants to opt out of failing public schools.[24] Harvard education dean Theodore Sizer and Philip Whitten (then a Harvard graduate student and later an author, an editor, and a film producer) called for a similar approach, dubbing it the "poor children's bill of rights."[25]

This argument gained additional force in 1990, when the Brookings Institution published an influential analysis by political scientists John Chubb and Terry Moe, who concluded that a lively market of private choices should replace public education's faltering monopoly.[26] Their conclusions led Harold Howe II, who had served as Johnson's commissioner of education, to call for the creation and testing of some new forms of education choice.[27] Later that decade, economist John Brandl, a state legislator (D-MN) and the dean of the University of Minnesota's Humphrey Institute, took a somewhat different approach in another Brookings publication. He called for the creation of "social markets": "government-designed competitive arrangements for fostering innovation, efficiency, and self-policing in the production of services . . . [especially in] elementary and secondary education."[28]

MORE RUMBLINGS

Along with these sea changes in education, developments in other domains of American life helped pave the way for chartering as well as a number of district-based reforms. In the corporate sector, bureaucratic structures and top-down management were absorbing concepts of continuous improvement and leaner, more flexible operating systems. Today, people commonly refer to a *tight-loose strategy* for managing organizations: tightly specify the results to be achieved and the metrics by which these are monitored, but loosen the means by which results are produced and encourage those on the ground to innovate, improvise, and operate their units as they think best. In the public sector, meanwhile, discontent with the efficacy and efficiency of large bureaucracies fed the idea that government should try steering rather than tugging the oars and should outsource many functions to external providers that would then be held to account (and paid) for delivering the prescribed results.[29] Columbia law professor Charles Sabel terms this large shift in public-sector governance "democratic experimentalism" and has documented its spread in many countries.[30]

Concurrently, America saw renewed interest in "civil society" and "mediating institutions," everyday organizations that people join voluntarily—from churches and schools to fraternal organizations and professional associations—and that intercede between the individual and the state.[31] These value-centered, voluntary entities support the pluralistic inclinations of a diverse society while cushioning the impersonality of large public bureaucracies. Seeing schools as mediating institutions and having the opportunity to choose one that aligns with a family's values and preferences becomes an issue of personal empowerment and community renewal.

We have identified seven ancestors of the charter idea:

- an enduring sector of self-governing schools, and families' ability to select the ones that best suit their children
- gradual but profound shifts in emphasis from school resources and programs to educational outcomes and how to strengthen them
- a dual emphasis on both educational equity and excellence through higher standards
- the diversification of school models for a changing society and the creation of new designs from scratch
- the impetus to replace a bureaucratic quasi monopoly with a competitive marketplace of multiple providers
- the decentralization of large organizations' management and the reinvention of government into a tight-loose model
- the role of schools as mediating institutions that strengthen civil society by engaging people voluntarily with organizations that can be adapted to their circumstances

As these shifts roiled the American K–12 system, they also formed the complex genetic map of the infant idea that was born in Minnesota twenty-five years ago.

FROM BIRTH TO TODDLER

The first significant formulation of chartering was a 1974 paper by Ray Budde, a teacher, a school principal, and an eventual faculty member at the University of Massachusetts.[32] It focused on district organization and argued that teachers should play a key role in this. At the outset, however, Budde's idea was limited to *existing* schools and the idea that school boards ought to issue charters to teachers to create new programs or departments within their schools.

His initial paper was provocative but got little response. Budde later recalled that in the mid-1970s, "no one felt that things were so bad that the system itself needed to be changed. . . . So I put the idea of 'education by charter' on the shelf and went on to other things."[33]

A few years later, however, after *A Nation at Risk* and myriad other studies and reports called for sweeping K–12 reforms, Budde decided to try again with *Education by Charter: Restructuring School Districts*.[34] This 1988 treatise reached American Federation of Teachers (AFT) president Albert Shanker, who credited it as inspiration for an influential speech he gave at the National Press Club in March of that year.[35] There, Shanker introduced his version of the charter idea, which soon reemerged as a *New York Times* column titled "A Charter for Change."[36]

Shanker expanded Budde's focus, viewing chartering as a way to foster teachers' professionalism by allowing them to start *new* schools. He suggested—and union delegates to the 1988 AFT convention endorsed—what he described in the *Times* as "a procedure that would enable teams of teachers and others to submit and implement proposals to set up their own autonomous public schools within their schools [*sic*] buildings." Shanker saw this leading to a quasi marketplace in which "a school system might charter schools distinctly different in their approach to learning. Parents could choose which charter school to send their children to, thus fostering competition."[37]

These ideas caught the attention of a group of Minnesota educators and policy innovators, notably including Joe Nathan, Ted Kolderie, Curtis Johnson, and Ember Reichgott, a Democratic state senator who would introduce and eventually pass that state's pathbreaking charter law.[38] Nathan, the founder of an innovative "open school" in Saint Paul, believed that public education should offer parents and teachers opportunities to create new kinds of public schools.[39] After working for two years at the National Governors Association at the behest of Lamar Alexander, he drew a link between the charter concept and the governors' push to deregulate schools that produce better results.

Kolderie and Johnson, under the aegis of the Citizens League, a good-government group based in the Twin Cities, served on a study committee that probed the chartering idea. The league's December 1988 report, "Chartered Schools = Choices for Educators + Quality for All Students," built upon initiatives that had already made Minnesota a pioneer in school choice.[40] These programs established a policy foundation for chartering and, combined with the Citizens League report, became the basis for the bill that Reichgott introduced in January 1989.[41]

She encountered fierce opposition, led primarily by Minnesota's two teachers unions, and her bill twice failed to clear the legislature. The following year, however, her proposal got a boost when the Washington-based Progressive Policy Institute published "Beyond Choice to New Public Schools: Withdrawing the Exclusive Franchise in Public Education."[42] Kolderie, who wrote it, summarized its message this way: "The proposal outlined in this report is designed to introduce the dynamics of choice, competition and innovation into America's public school system, while at the same time ensuring that new schools serve broad public purposes."[43] His (and other people's) conception of innovation included a role for chartering as an R&D sector for public education—what education consultant Bryan Hassel has called the "laboratory thesis."[44]

By 1991, Reichgott had enlisted more legislative allies from both sides of the aisle and succeeded in passing her plan, which enabled GOP governor Arne Carlson to sign the nation's first charter-school law on June 4 of that year.[45]

California passed the second such measure in 1992, thanks to the efforts of Democratic state senator Gary Hart with the support of Republican governor Pete Wilson. The following year, six more states climbed aboard: Colorado, Georgia, and New Mexico (with Democratic governors) and Massachusetts, Michigan, and Wisconsin (with Republican executives). Thus began a nonstop process in which various states modified the Minnesota and California versions of chartering, thereby blurring and diversifying both the mechanism to be used and the kinds of schools to which it might give rise. For example, Michigan and Massachusetts allowed nondistrict authorizers to start new schools, whereas Colorado introduced a state-level appeals process to be used when a district denied a charter application.

Shortly after passage of the Minnesota law, David Durenberger (the state's Republican senator and a longtime Citizens League member) and policy aide Jon Schroeder brought the chartering idea to Congress. Durenberger teamed up with Senator Joseph Lieberman (D-CT) to propose a new federal support program for charter schools. This measure was signed into law in 1994 by President Bill Clinton and continues to enjoy wide support and increased funding today.[46]

As chartering gradually spread, a state and national support system also emerged. At first, individual state groups (e.g., the Colorado

League of Charter Schools and today's California Charter Schools Association) focused mostly on improving their own states' laws. In 1996, Schroeder helped organize the Charter Friends National Network to facilitate conversation and cooperation among such groups. In 2004, it morphed into today's National Alliance for Public Charter Schools.[47] Other groups have arisen along the way, including (in 2000) the National Association of Charter School Authorizers, which is focused on improving authorizer practices.[48]

Today's state charter programs contain as many policy differences and priorities as similarities. A 2005 analysis of forty-one laws found thirty-two with preambles or "purposes" sections describing what legislators hoped to accomplish.[49] Eighteen reasons appeared in these, often with further differences in wording. The most common goals, found in more than half the laws, relate to improving the achievement of *all* students and providing more options to *all* families. But ten other missions turned up in many statutes: provide teachers more professional options; give them greater ownership of schools; encourage classroom innovation; foster greater accountability; increase options for targeted students (especially low-income and at-risk youngsters); create new academic programs; develop novel measures of student achievement; increase school autonomy; create performance-based schools; and boost parental involvement. Other, albeit less widespread, goals were increased community collaboration; the spurring of competition; the replication of school successes; bolder uses of technology; and improved financial efficiency.

Such a plethora of goals and purposes helps explain why charter schooling across America today resembles the proverbial blind men and the elephant, with disparate perceptions of what exactly this innovation is and is meant to do. But we shouldn't be too surprised, considering that chartering is a reform that incorporates so many visions, refracted through the hopes and beliefs of Democrats and Republicans and tailored to the needs and political realities of many states. Yet that elastic quality also made it easier for the idea to spread. Philanthropy boosted it—though mainly in narrow directions—as did federal incentive payments. So, too, did rivalry and copycat tendencies among state leaders. And the fact that charter schools are not the same as vouchers made them more palatable politically.

(In several cases, teachers unions' strong allergic reaction to vouchers led them to tolerate charters.)

Many lessons might be drawn from this history, but three strike us as especially salient.

1. *The states' crucial role*: States were the critical agents in creating the charter sector as they withdrew their districts' exclusive franchises to create and operate schools. As Kolderie wrote in 1990, "only the state can do this, for districting is created by state laws."[50] In weakening the districts' monopoly, however, states were also reinventing and reinvigorating local control of education down to the building level.

2. *Not just one idea*: There is no single founding legend for charter schooling, no matter how hard some people search for a unique story line. Ray Budde, Albert Shanker, and Ted Kolderie were all part of it, but so were Milton Friedman, James Coleman, Lamar Alexander, Bill Clinton, Kenneth Clark, David Osborne, Ember Reichgott, and innumerable others. Consequently, chartering has not been a single experiment or the product of a single vision, theory, or doctrine. Rather, it's a fine illustration of what Justice Louis Brandeis termed "laboratories of democracy" and perhaps what Daniel P. Moynihan dubbed "maximum feasible misunderstanding."

3. *Bipartisanship*: Much of this history flies in the face of today's widespread sense that Republicans and Democrats are hopelessly and permanently at loggerheads. In every state with a charter law, governors and legislators on both sides of the aisle have favored this innovation, and most such statutes (and later revisions of them) happened through bipartisan effort.

The presence of bipartisan sailors does not, however, mean that the seas have been smooth for chartering. Later chapters discuss the political battles that have raged over the enactment and revision of charter laws and some of the constraints placed on these upstart schools. As we began writing, the Washington State Supreme Court voided that state's new charter law—whose passage had taken twenty years of political struggle—on grounds that such schools don't qualify as "common schools." (It has since been revised and reenacted.)

Chartering, in other words, is a story still being written. Yet the mixed motives and interpretations within it, as well as the battles and compromises around it, have undeniably caused charter programs across the United States to take very different forms in different places. Laboratories of democracy, indeed!

2

What's
Happened Since

MUCH HAS CHANGED since chartering began to toddle about the education landscape. In this chapter, we recap key developments and offer a quantitative snapshot of today's charter scene. (For detailed figures that supplement the analysis in this chapter, see the appendix.)

SINCE 1991

States

Forty-four states have passed charter-enabling legislation since 1991.[1] By 1999, just eight years after Minnesota made the first move, the number of charter-friendly states had already reached thirty-six. Statutory expansion slowed thereafter. Just one wholly new charter law was passed since 2012 (Alabama in 2015), while another was declared unconstitutional (Washington State, also 2015) and subsequently replaced (2016). Seven jurisdictions have never had charter statutes on their books.

State laws differ widely, however, in their receptivity to the creation, financing, governance, and autonomy of these novel schools. The National Alliance for Public Charter Schools (NAPCS)—the lead advocacy organization of the charter movement—has created a model law with twenty elements that, in their view, would best "support more and better public charter schools."[2] The alliance then ranks state laws according to how well they align with its model, using a

228-point scale. Table 2.1 shows these rankings as of 2016. On this metric, Indiana comes in first, although its 177 points suggest that even the charter-friendliest state has room to improve. Trailing at the back is Maryland with a meager 49 points, suggesting that the Old Line State's fifty-three charter schools must operate in an unusually hostile environment.

Schools and Students

As enactment of new charter laws tapered off, the number of schools soared. Figure 2.1 shows their increase since 1999, an average net annual rise (schools opened minus schools closed) of about 330.[3] In the autumn of 2015, charters numbered more than 6,800, compared with the country's 90,000 district-operated public schools.

Figure 2.1 also displays annual school openings and closings since 2005 (the earliest year for which such data are available). Although openings have always trumped closings, they've slowed a bit since 2013, whereas closures have seen an uptick, potentially pointing to convergence in the next few years. This could portend a steady state in the total number of US charter schools—a very different picture from the rapid expansion of the past quarter century. Possible causes

TABLE 2.1   National Alliance for Public Charter Schools ranking of state charter laws, 2016

1 Indiana	12 District of Columbia	23 Ohio	34 Tennessee
2 Alabama	13 South Carolina	24 Delaware	35 Rhode Island
3 Minnesota	14 North Carolina	25 Texas	36 New Jersey
4 Louisiana	15 California	26 Hawaii	37 Wisconsin
5 Colorado	16 New Mexico	27 Pennsylvania	38 Wyoming
6 Maine	17 Mississippi	28 Oregon	39 Virginia
7 New York	18 Georgia	29 Arkansas	40 Alaska
8 Nevada	19 Oklahoma	30 Missouri	41 Iowa
9 Florida	20 Utah	31 Connecticut	42 Kansas
10 Arizona	21 Michigan	32 Illinois	43 Maryland
11 Massachusetts	22 Idaho	33 New Hampshire	

Source: National Alliance for Public Charter Schools, "Measuring Up to the Model: A Ranking of State Charter School Laws," January 2016, www.publiccharters.org/wp-content/uploads/2016/01/Model-Law-Final_2016.pdf.

FIGURE 2.1   Changes in the number of total, new, and closed charter schools, and in charter enrollment nationwide, 1999–2015

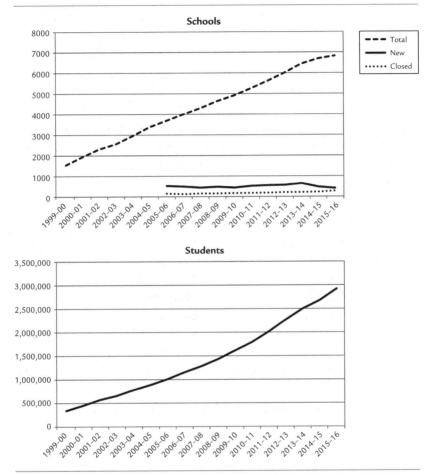

Sources: National Alliance for Public Charter Schools, "The Public Charter Schools Dashboard," accessed November 12, 2015, www.publiccharters.org/dashboard/home; National Alliance for Public Charter Schools, "Estimated Number of Public Charter Schools & Students, 2013–2014," February 2014, www.publiccharters.org/wp-content/uploads/2014/02/New-and-Closed-Report-February-20141.pdf; and National Association for Public Charter Schools, "A Closer Look at the Charter School Movement: Schools, Students, and Management Organizations, 2015–16," February 2016, www.publiccharters.org/wp-content/uploads/2016/02/New-Closed-2016.pdf.

include more rigorous authorization practices, state accountability systems that require the automatic closure of faltering schools, states and districts whose caps on the number of charters permitted have been reached, and the likelihood that some charter markets have become saturated, even as other places have waiting lists.

Charter schools close—over 1,200 of them between 2010 and 2015—for various reasons, most commonly financial hardship. In 2011, for example, money problems were to blame for 41 percent of closings, followed by mismanagement (24 percent), then poor academic performance (19 percent).[4] There's some evidence, however, that authorizers' moves to shut or not to renew schools on grounds of weak academics have been increasing.

As we also see in figure 2.1, charter enrollments have risen steadily, averaging about 160,000 more students each year between 1999 and 2015. But that doesn't tell the whole story, for these numbers have grown at an increasing *rate*—visible in the steepening slope of the trend line. Between 1999 and 2000, for example, the charter sector added just over 100,000 pupils. Between 2012 and 2015, however, the average annual increase in student numbers exceeded 210,000, in part because some of the newer schools are virtual, which can enroll large numbers of kids from almost anywhere within their states (see chapter 4).

Charters average about 430 students apiece, compared with 525 in the average district school. But the enrollment at most charters is even smaller, because of the number (about 200,000) of students who attend some 200 virtual schools, which—obviously—tend to be larger. If we look only at brick-and-mortar charters, the average enrollment drops closer to 400 for 2013–2014, the most recent year for which data are available.

An important reason for enrollment growth in the charter sector is that children are switching sectors, notably in a handful of charter-rich states. Except for 2007, the charter population has risen every year since 1999 (figure 2.2). Yet enrollments in *district* schools have fallen since 2006. The top line in figure 2.2 tracks all students, the bottom line shows those in district schools, and the dotted lines in between represent students attending charter schools. Those lines have lengthened steadily while the number of children in district schools has shrunk. Simply put, charters have accounted for the *entire increase* in US public school enrollments since 2006, suggesting, at minimum, the presence of considerable demand for such options.

Sectors Within the Sector

Charters started as individual (one-off) schools, but entrepreneurs, philanthropists, and ambitious school leaders soon realized that small,

FIGURE 2.2   Number of students by type of public school, 1999–2013

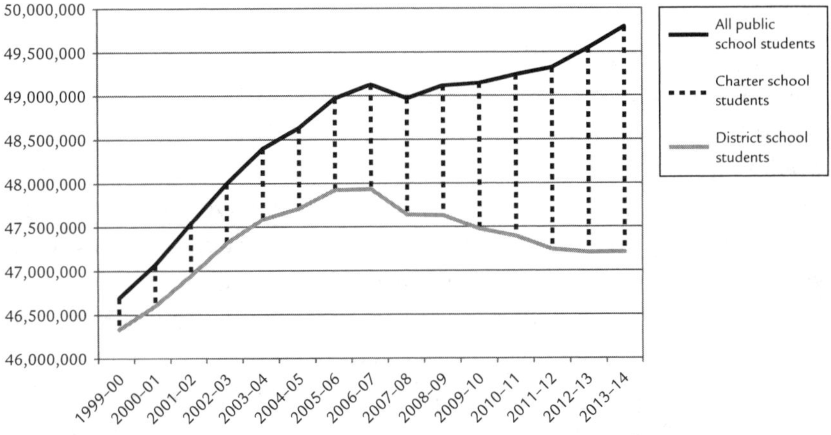

Source: National Alliance for Public Charter Schools, "The Public Charter Schools Dashboard," accessed November 12, 2015, www.publiccharters.org/dashboard/home.

isolated schools encounter numerous challenges—beginning with finances, back-office services, and special education—that might be better addressed via networks or clusters of schools. Creating such networks also looked like a reasonably efficient way to replicate successful models and to scale this emerging sector of public education. For example, the California-based Aspire Public Schools network opened its first two schools in 1998 and now comprises thirty-eight, with a total enrollment exceeding fourteen thousand.

Today, 60 percent of charter schools are still the one-off kind, but the other 40 percent are parts of larger networks. The network schools take two forms: nonprofit entities called charter management organizations (CMOs) and for-profit education management organizations (EMOs). EMO schools outnumbered CMO schools until 2006, but today, there are almost twice as many CMO schools, though total enrollments in the two subsectors are similar.[5]

THE PRESENT PICTURE

Unsurprisingly, California and Texas, the two most populous states, have the most charter schools.[6] Seven states (California, Texas, Florida, Arizona, Ohio, Michigan, and New York) have more than 250 apiece, and the top four exceed 500 schools each.[7] Yet twenty-five states have fewer than 100 schools apiece, and fifteen states have fewer than 50. (Eight states still have none; see the appendix.)

The picture is broadly similar for student numbers. In a nation with almost three million charter pupils, over half a million of them are found in California alone (as of 2013–2014). Another eight hundred thousand live in the four states with the next-highest enrollments (Texas, Florida, Arizona, and Michigan). In other words, almost half of all charter pupils are found in five of the forty-three states with such schools. But while about 6 percent of US students attend charter schools, the statistical mode of the charter share (spanning seven states) is close to 5 percent, showing that, although charters and their pupils are concentrated in only a few states, there's slightly less variance across states in terms of market share.[8]

Local Differences

Tightening the geographic focus and looking at district data, there are fourteen locales—spread across nine states and the District of Columbia—where more than 30 percent of public school pupils attended charters in 2014–2015. New Orleans topped the list, with a 93 percent market share. Detroit was second, with 53 percent, followed by Flint, Michigan; Washington, DC; Kansas City, Missouri; and Gary, Indiana. In all of these places, charters enrolled at least 40 percent. Such communities vary widely in size, however, from the 12,000 pupils in Flint's public schools to almost 200,000 in Philadelphia (including 64,000 charter-goers).

Reversing the lens, we see that charters have little or no presence in many of the country's largest districts, including some that adjoin places with huge charter market shares. For example, neither Fairfax County, Virginia, nor Montgomery County, Maryland, has any charters, although these big counties lie just across the border from charter-heavy Washington, DC. Suburban Gwinnett County, Georgia, has less than a 1 percent market share, although Atlanta itself has over 10 percent. As these figures suggest, charter schooling today is primarily an urban phenomenon. More than half of all such schools are located in cities, and only 16 percent are found in rural areas. For district schools, the story is flipped; less than a quarter are in cities, and more than a third are rural.[9]

Why the urban concentration for charters? In some states, they're permitted only in cities, which is also where parents create the heaviest demand for them. For the most part, low-income, inner-city children in need of better school options are also the focus of charter-related philanthropy and reformer passion. Suburban families typically don't express the same level of dissatisfaction, and many suburban lawmakers oppose this kind of structural disruption in the public schools of their comfortable constituents.

As for small-town and rural America, the population is generally not dense enough for multiple schools (except the virtual kind) to operate within reasonable travel distance. Yet even here, from the Arkansas delta to northern Idaho and the Colorado Rockies, chartering has gained a toehold. A recent report from Bellwether Education Partners found 785 rural charters, 111 of them located in "remote" rural areas.[10]

As noted earlier, the United States also contains some 200 virtual charter schools, operating in twenty-six states.[11] California has the most—46—but Ohio's virtual schools enroll the most students: 37,000 in 2013, representing over 30 percent of Ohio's charter pupils.[12]

School Types

What approaches to educating children can be found in charter schools? This sector offers greater variety than one might expect, since public attention has generally focused on the no-excuses model (discussed in several places later in the book). In a study examining seventeen cities with 1,151 charters enrolling more than 471,000 students in 2012–2013, about half of these schools were deemed "general"—that is, with no stated "mission, vision, educational philosophy, academic model, or curriculum." The other half were termed "specialized" (figure 2.3).[13]

Figure 2.3 sorts the specialized half into thirteen categories and shows the percentages of schools employing each approach and the percentages of pupils that they enroll. No-excuses and progressive schools (e.g., Montessori or other "child-centered" schools) top the list for number of schools, but no-excuses schools are alone at the top of the enrollment numbers. Hybrid, or blended-learning, schools (with instruction time divided between flesh-and-blood educators and technology-based learning) and STEM schools (specializing

FIGURE 2.3   Specialized charter schools in seventeen cities by type, showing percentages of schools and student enrollment, 2012–2013

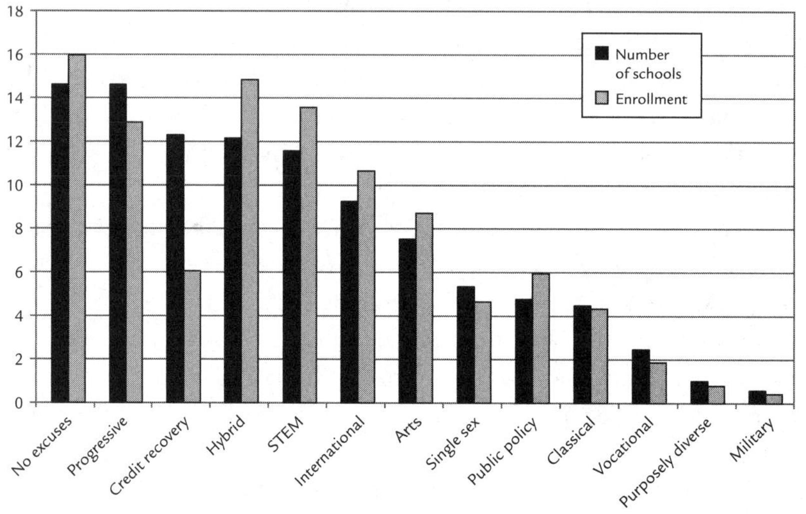

Source: Michael Q. McShane and Jenn Hatfield, "Measuring Diversity in Charter School Offerings," American Enterprise Institute, July 2015, www.aei.org/wp-content/uploads/2015/07/Measuring-Diversity-in-Charter-School-Offerings.pdf.
Note: STEM = science, technology, engineering, and mathematics.

in science, technology, engineering, and mathematics) had the second- and third-highest enrollments, respectively.

Authorizers and Grade Levels

Every charter school has an *authorizer* or *sponsor*, the entity that approves it and determines, on the basis of performance, whether to extend or terminate its license to operate. Authorizers take many forms (figure 2.4). Most common is the district itself, that is, the local education agency. Districts oversee 39 percent of charter schools—often just one or two apiece—while representing 89 percent of all authorizers. The picture gets more complicated thereafter, as some authorizer types—such as state education agencies (SEAs) and independent charter boards (ICBs)—are few in number but typically responsible for many schools. SEAs sponsor 28 percent of all charter schools while making up less than 3 percent of all authorizers. ICBs handle 15 percent of all charters but account for just 1 percent of authorizers.[14]

FIGURE 2.4   Charter authorizers by type and schools by authorizer type, 2014

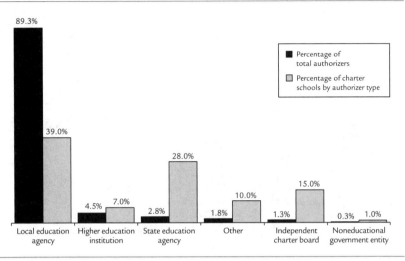

Sources: Ted Rebarber and Alison Consoletti Zgainer, eds., "Survery of America's Charter Schools 2014," Center for Education Reform, Washington, DC, February 2014, www.edreform.com/wp-content/uploads/2014/02/2014CharterSchoolSurveyFINAL.pdf; and US Department of Education, Institute of Education Sciences, National Center for Education Statistics, "Elementary/Secondary Information System," Institute of Education Sciences, accessed January 1, 2015, https://nces.ed.gov/ccd/elsi.

Collectively, charter schools span all the primary and secondary grades. Some offer preschool, too, and the early-college model enables students to dual-enroll in university courses while still attending high school.[15] But charter and district schools often display different grade configurations. For example, schools that combine elementary and middle grades—or even extend all the way through high school—make up almost 20 percent of charters, but fewer than 6 percent of district-operated schools. Consequently, there are fewer elementary-only charter schools (55 percent) than in the district sector (69 percent).

Demographics

Because most charters are urban, it's no surprise that they serve disproportionate numbers of black and Hispanic students. As figure 2.5 shows, each of those groups accounts for more than a quarter of charter enrollees, although they constitute 15 and 24 percent, respectively, of district school students. White children outnumber both groups

FIGURE 2.5   Racial makeup of charter and district schools by enrollment
              percentage, 2012–2013

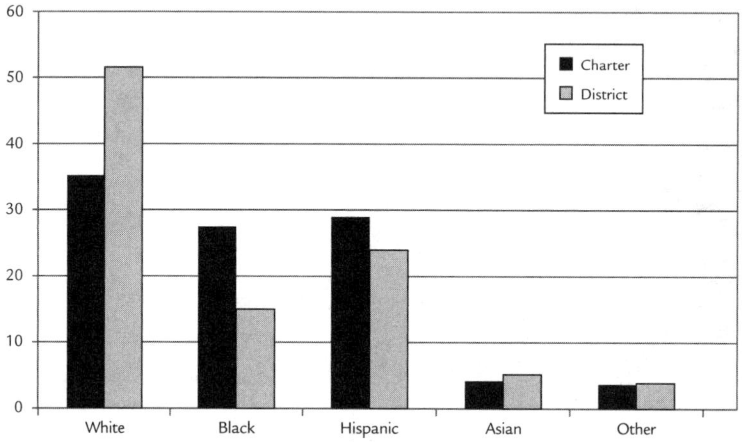

Source: US Department of Education, Institute of Education Sciences, National Center for Education Statistics, Digest of Education Statistics, 2014 tables and figures, table 216.30, http://nces.ed.gov
/programs/digest/d14/tables/dt14_216.30.asp.

but make up only 35 percent of charter-goers, compared with 52 percent of the country's district population. Moreover, the proportions
of white and black students within both charter and district schools
have fallen in recent years as Hispanic enrollees have increased their
numbers.[16] Asian students represent a small slice of charter enrollments, but their numbers have also been rising and their proportion
now approaches that found in district schools.[17]

Pupil demographics vary considerably by district. For example,
charters in both New York City and Washington, DC, serve disproportionately large percentages of black students and small percentages of white and Asian students. But the enrollment picture in the
two cities is very different.

In New York, black students make up 60 percent of charter-goers,
despite constituting less than 30 percent of district pupils. In the District of Columbia, the proportions of black students are closer in the
two sectors: a little over 80 percent in charters, a little over 70 percent
in district schools. Hispanic numbers also differ. In New York, they
make up a larger percentage of non-charter-goers (over 40 percent)
than charter pupils (33 percent), while in Washington, the two sectors

serve the same proportions of Hispanic kids. In both cities, white and Asian students are mostly absent from charter schools.

A more sensitive issue is how charter and district enrollments compare in at-risk populations, notably, children with disabilities, English language learners, and students from poor families (figure 2.6). In district schools, special education students make up almost 13 percent of the enrollment, compared with more than 10 percent in charters. (Chapter 9 delves deeper into the issue of special education and shows the wide variation from state to state.) For English language learners, the percentages are a little closer. For low-income children, charter percentages exceed those in district schools. The percentage of charter schools and district schools where less than 25 percent of pupils qualify for free or reduced-price lunches is about the same

FIGURE 2.6   Percentages of at-risk students in charter and district schools, 2012–2013

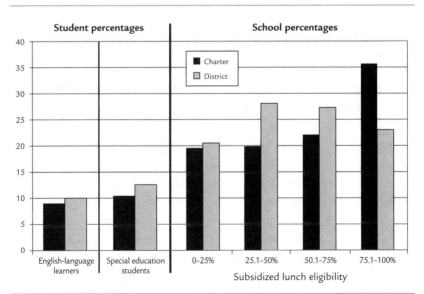

Sources: Public Agenda, *Charter Schools in Perspective* (New York: Public Agenda, 2015), www.in -perspective.org/pages/download-the-guide; Lauren Morando Rhim, Jesse Gumz, and Kelly Henderson, "Key Trends in Special Education in Charter Schools: A Secondary Analysis of the Civil Rights Data Collection 2011–2012," National Center for Special Education in Charter Schools, 2015, http://static1.squarespace.com/static/52feb326e4b069fc72abb0c8/t/564109d3e4 b027fb791d1964/1447102931798/crdc_full.pdf; and US Department of Education, Institute of Education Sciences, National Center for Education Statistics, 2014 *Digest of Education Statistics*, November 2014, table 216.30, http://nces.ed.gov/programs/digest/d14/tables/dt14_216.30.asp.

(20 percent). In contrast, schools where more than three-quarters of students are eligible for subsidized lunches make up 36 percent of charters and only 23 percent of the district sector—not very surprising, actually, when one recalls how many charter schools are located in inner cities.

Teachers

Charters employ slightly more than 3 percent of all public school teachers, but represent nearly 6 percent of all pupils and 7 percent of all schools. This disproportion is caused, of course, by the charter sector's smaller schools and larger classes. Regardless of whether a charter instructor works in a self-contained classroom or a departmentalized structure, he or she operates with a student-teacher ratio substantially larger than that of district counterparts.[18]

The charter-sector's teaching cadres tend to be more racially diverse, younger, and less experienced. On average, they work a bit longer each week, teach more students, and are likelier to get performance pay. Yet they're somewhat less apt to possess advanced degrees, perhaps because they're younger or because traditional districts often cover the costs of obtaining such degrees and pay more to those who obtain them. Charter teachers also earn about $9,000 less annually than do their district counterparts, which may be attributed to their lack of union protection and the fact that they're younger, have less experience, and hold fewer degrees.

Because charter pay varies widely by state, district, and even school, it's impossible to get usable, comparable nationwide data beyond simple salary averages, which don't take into account years of experience or other pertinent variables. We do know, though, that in relatively well-financed Washington, DC, in 2011–2012, the minimum, maximum, and average salaries at the city's charter schools were considerably lower than in the District of Columbia Public Schools (DCPS), where the minimum salary was $51,539, the average was $78,095, and the maximum was $106,540. Of the sixty DC charters that provided data for that year, only one had a higher minimum salary than DCPS and none had higher average or maximum pay.[19]

Some charters are experimenting with more generous compensation, although few can afford much of this. The Equity Project, a small New York City school that opened in 2009, pays its teachers nearly double the average salary at the city's conventional public schools. A 2014 study found that Equity Project pupils made more academic progress than did similar peers in district schools, with eighth graders exhibiting an extra year and a half of learning in math.[20] These results are probably not *because* the teachers are better paid, but because greater pay draws better teachers. Meanwhile, charter teachers around the United States are slightly likelier to change jobs and to report a bit less satisfaction with their work. Teacher turnover is running about 18.4 percent in this sector, compared with 15.7 percent in district schools. Yet 90 percent of charter teachers (93 percent in the district sector) say they're at least somewhat satisfied with their jobs.

As we've seen, the charter sector has grown steadily, from one school educating a few hundred children in Minnesota to over sixty-eight hundred operating in forty-three states and enrolling nearly three million students. The sector remains small when placed alongside the behemoth of American public education, but its influence (and the momentum behind it) exceeds its size—and it's markedly more consequential in some places than in others. Notable examples are New Orleans, where over 90 percent of schools are charters, and California, home to more than one-seventh of all such schools and nearly one-fifth of charter pupils. Nebraska, Montana, and the Dakotas, by contrast, are untouched by the charter phenomenon. That's related to the fact that charters tend to be urban and to serve minority and low-income children. Yet the schools themselves are more variegated and wide ranging than many people (even within the charter movement) realize. They operate in suburbs and towns and even some remote rural areas as well as cities. They have accounted for the entire increase in public school enrollment since 2006. And perhaps most consequentially, they have captured the imagination and support of reformers and philanthropists in nearly unprecedented ways, as we'll show in subsequent chapters.

PART II

How's It Going?

3

Mixed Achievement: Down and Up with Scores and Methods

NOW TO ACADEMIC ACHIEVEMENT, the primary coin of the modern education-reform realm, one where the charter track record can best be described as stunningly uneven, although gradually improving. Some of America's highest-achieving schools are charters, but so are some of its worst. We can average it out and conclude that charters are producing results that roughly equal those of the district schools to which they're alternatives. But that glib summary doesn't begin to do justice to a galaxy of education institutions that range from dismal to superb. Indeed in *U.S. News & World Report*'s 2016 list of the nation's hundred best high schools, more than one-third are charters.[1] Nor does any simple statement encompass the differing effects that charters—and different kinds of charters—have on different student populations, or the notable disparities we find from one city or state to the next, as well as within individual jurisdictions. Our challenge in this chapter is to clarify this tangled tale as much as possible while respecting the complexity of the data, the variability of schools, the lively debates over evaluation methods, and the competing motives of not-always-disinterested analysts.

THE BACKDROP

Before 2004, studies of charter school student achievement were nearly all conducted within individual states.[2] The first attempt at a national analysis of charter performance was conducted by the American Federation of Teachers (AFT) and used 2003 data from the federal government's well-regarded National Assessment of Educational Progress (NAEP).[3] That study, which triggered a front-page item in the *New York Times* in August 2004, provoked a multimonth firestorm in education and policy circles and launched a sequence of events that in the end proved useful.[4]

The 2003 NAEP tests made possible for the first time a multistate comparison of pupil academic achievement in some 167 charters with that of students in district schools.[5] As reported in the *Times*, fourth graders attending charter schools performed about half a year behind district pupils in reading and math. When demographic differences were controlled for, the students scored about the same.[6]

The No Child Left Behind Act was barely three years old at the time, and its clear intent—closing gaps and boosting achievement, particularly for the poor and minority youngsters most likely to attend charters—was widely agreed upon. Moreover, schools across America were beginning to be judged on their academic success as gauged by test scores. This was the hopeful yet anxious (and narrowly focused) environment into which the AFT study landed.

Criticism of it came fast and furiously, including a full-page *Times* advertisement signed by thirty-one academics who faulted the union's analysis on grounds that it drew on far too small a sample of schools, enrolling barely 1 percent of charter students. Moreover, noted the ad's authors, the study failed to distinguish between long-established charters and fresh start-ups and was a single snapshot of attainment and not a measure of growth or change over time. Above all, the signers argued, the study didn't take into account the likelihood that charter schools begin with lower-achieving pupils—those whose families are most inclined to leave their current school for a promising alternative.

The debate surrounding this study, however, was scarcely the end of the matter. Around the time the AFT issued its report, another emerged, this time a more sophisticated analysis that would be published in a bona fide academic journal.[7] Based on an examination of six years of test scores for six thousand North Carolina students enrolled in regular and charter schools, it buttressed the union's conclusion, finding that achievement gains in charters were smaller than those made by district pupils.

A few months later, the federal government's National Center for Education Statistics released its own analysis of the same NAEP data that the AFT had examined, this time concluding that the "picture is not so easily discerned."[8] For example, among charter and district pupils from the same racial and ethnic backgrounds, there were no major differences in reading and math performance. But among all students from the two sectors, charter pupils scored lower in math than their district counterparts. On the other hand, reading showed no measurable difference.

None of this could be termed good news for the charter movement, but these were just the opening skirmishes of achievement wars that continue to this day. The polarized context means that little research in this realm is viewed as wholly objective by all parties. Generally, however, the analytical quality has improved and, with the passage of time, there have been more data to analyze and more analysts attempting to do so. There's also some evidence of gains in charter school effectiveness—though the reasons for those gains are themselves subject to debate.

STRIVING FOR COMMON GROUND

A worthwhile early development was the creation of the Charter School Achievement Consensus Panel by the University of Washington's Center on Reinventing Public Education (CRPE) in 2005. Composed of nine highly regarded analysts who came from different disciplines and had divergent views on charter schools, the panel had a mandate to evaluate existing research on school effectiveness and to develop standards for future studies to improve their quality.[9] The principal drafters of its report were CRPE director Paul T. Hill and Julian Betts, professor of economics at the University of Southern California. Betts and his colleagues summarized several key panel conclusions:

> [Studies that use] average test scores across schools . . . are doomed to fail because they . . . mostly reflect selectivity bias. That is, the initial achievement of students before they enter charter schools

explains most of the differences. Similar problems arise when one studies trends in average test scores across schools, which can paint a quite misleading picture of trends in the relative quality of instruction provided at the two types of schools.

. . . [M]odeling *gains* in achievement . . . rather than *levels* . . . is clearly an improvement because it takes into account the past achievement of the students. But almost as important, adding student fixed effects to account for unobserved variations among students in test-score growth increases the estimated effectiveness of charter schools, and indeed often produces a statistically significant gap favoring charter schools.[10]

The panel's methodological recommendations were embraced by a number of groups, including the National Alliance for Public Charter Schools (NAPCS), which over the next several years released six editions of *Measuring Charter Performance: A Review of Public Charter School Achievement Studies*. These compilations reached back to 1992 and eventually—the final edition was in 2010—incorporated more than two hundred studies that met the consensus panel criteria.[11] The NAPCS is no neutral party—it's the primary national advocacy organization of the charter movement—but its reviews intentionally included both positive and negative findings, allowing the debate to continue while advancing its own agenda for "quality charter schools."

The NAPCS reported that studies using longitudinally linked student-level data to look at changes in achievement—that is, *panel studies*—usually found that charter students across all grade levels experience similar or greater gains than students in district schools: in math, there were forty-one instances of larger gains, twenty-three instances of comparable gains, nine of mixed gains, and forty-four of lesser gains. (The results for reading were similar.) The Alliance also reviewed studies of students who remained in charter schools for multiple years. Of thirty-three studies examining their attainments, twenty-one showed larger gains for children the longer they were enrolled in charters, while just one study showed lesser gains. The bottom line was balanced yet inconclusive: "no single study should be considered definitive for answering the question of how charter schools are performing in a district, state or at the national level."[12]

Betts and his colleagues also published several meta-analyses using consensus panel criteria.[13] They concluded that "it is wrong to say that charter school performance is simply 'mixed' or on par with traditional public schools."[14] After poring over the wide variation among schools, usually associated with factors like location (e.g., the state where the school is located), grade level, and subject, the Betts team declared that charters "typically outperform rather than underperform their traditional public school counterparts."[15] But not always:

- Charters frequently outperform other public schools in elementary reading and middle school math.
- Charters frequently underperform in elementary math and middle school reading.
- Charters consistently underperform in high school reading and math.

ENTER CREDO

The most thorough and rigorous series of large-scale, multistate analyses has been conducted by Margaret Raymond and her team at Stanford's Center for Research on Education Outcomes (CREDO) and builds on the work of the consensus panel. Raymond is a research fellow at Stanford's Hoover Institution and CREDO's director. Because of Hoover's reputation as a conservative think tank that favors market-based policies, Raymond has had to work to demonstrate her objectivity regarding charters. Despite some critics doubting her impartiality and methodology (see below), we regard her as scrupulous in her approach to charter-school performance, letting the chips fall where they may.

CREDO's first charter study (in 2009) examined pupil achievement in fifteen states and the District of Columbia between 2001 and 2008, using math test results spanning at least three years. The study included 1.7 million students and more than twenty-four hundred schools, encompassing over 70 percent of the nation's charters. It was the first truly large-scale, multistate appraisal of charter effectiveness. Analysts fashioned a comparison group by creating a "virtual twin" for each charter student, that is, a district-school pupil matched on seven characteristics—including test scores from the previous year—that were very close to those of the charter student.[16]

CREDO summarized its findings in this press-release headline: "Report finds serious quality challenge in charter school sector." On average, charter students were learning less in reading and math than were their classmates in district schools—the equivalent of seven days a year less in reading and twenty-two in math.[17] Just 17 percent of charters showed academic gains significantly stronger than district schools, while 37 percent showed lesser gains and 46 percent displayed no significant differences. Disaggregated by state, charter performance was superior to that of district schools in six jurisdictions (Arkansas, Colorado, Illinois, Louisiana, Massachusetts, and Missouri), worse in another six (Arizona, Florida, Minnesota, New Mexico, Ohio, and Texas), and mixed in four (California, District of Columbia, Georgia, and North Carolina).

For charter advocates, this initial CREDO study was another chilly shower, yet it also surfaced some warmer findings. For low-income children, charters had stronger positive effects on achievement than did district schools. Significantly higher gains were also reported for English language learners, although not for special education students. And again, charter pupils did better over time, showing achievement declines during the first year but significant gains during years two and three.

There's no one way to evaluate school effects, and the CREDO methodology has its critics, including some who generally support choice-oriented education reforms. For example, Stanford economist Caroline Hoxby, who had published her own analyses showing positive achievement outcomes for charters (see chapter 4), claimed that the virtual-twin approach "contains a serious statistical mistake that causes a negative bias in its estimate of how charter schools affect achievement . . . [that is] substantially biased downward from the truth."[18] Raymond's tart response characterized Hoxby's critique as "misleading in the extreme, even had the supporting logic been correct."[19] Other skeptics—both advocates and foes of charters—would level additional criticisms at this (and future) CREDO reports. Their concerns spanned matching procedures, statistical assumptions, the estimates of growth (especially when translated into days of learning), the analytic choices made, and the extent to which causal inferences can legitimately be drawn.[20]

FROM QUANTITY TO QUALITY

The accumulating evidence of weak charter-school performance had two effects. Although it fueled opponents' criticisms, it also dampened boosters' enthusiasm for simple, rapid sector growth. While some in the charter community sought ways to excuse the bad news, others engaged in genuine soul-searching regarding school effectiveness. This led to both state and national initiatives to bring quality rather than quantity to the forefront of chartering.

Ohio's early history of community schools—as charters are termed in the Buckeye State—illustrates what became a growing tension between advocates for unconstrained growth and those pushing for quality and accountability. Ohio's original charter law was signed by Republican governor George Voinovich in 1997. Within a decade, the state's charter sector—initially limited to one county but soon expanded to the state's eight largest urban districts—grew to more than 330 schools, enrolling nearly 5 percent of Ohio public school students (but much larger portions in cities where start-up charters were permitted). As early as 2000, Ohio newspapers included headlines such as "Charters Fail to Deliver, Analysis Shows" and "State Auditor Says Charter School Company Owes Thousands."[21] In June 2000, the *Cleveland Plain Dealer* wrote that "charter school students did worse on mandatory exams than youngsters in the academically distressed districts from which they fled. . . . Statewide, only 5 percent of charter school students who took the fourth grade proficiency test in March passed all five parts, compared to a 31 percent passage rate for public schools. Just 3 percent passed the sixth grade test, compared to 35 percent for public schools."[22]

Such negative publicity fed a spirited and increasingly acrimonious debate within Ohio's charter sector between those favoring a wide-open marketplace and rapid school growth and those pressing for a more rigorous, quality-centered approach to authorizing and accountability. The division was evident in the establishment of two separate statewide charter organizations, which managed to merge in 2003 but split again two years later.[23] Variations of this story oc-curred all over the country.

In 2009 (after CREDO's first report), the quantity-versus-quality debates led to the launch of a promising project.[24] Called Building Charter School Quality, the initiative was funded by the US Department of Education and was a joint undertaking of the Colorado League of Charter Schools, the NAPCS, the National Association of Charter School Authorizers (NACSA), and CREDO itself. All participants agreed that the primary challenge to the charter movement was "the wide range in charter school quality ... [from] schools [that] rank among the country's best . . . [to] a notable minority [that] are chronically poorly performing." The project sought to be "a force for improving the performance of charter schools nationwide." Over four years, it worked to align school operators, service providers, authorizers, policy makers, and others around quality, producing numerous tools and holding workshops around the country to assist charter leaders in improving school performance. The group published documents in 2008 and 2009 that set forth key elements of charter quality.[25] In 2012, NACSA revised its own standards for charter schools, and two years later, the NAPCS updated its manifesto on the issue, which was signed by many leaders of state charter groups.[26]

CREDO REDUX

Early evidence that this attention to quality was paying off turned up in 2013, when CREDO issued two more studies, both showing a considerably brighter achievement picture. The first analyzed school growth and replication in twenty-three states, New York City, and the District of Columbia.[27] The second updated and expanded the 2009 academic achievement report, matching charter pupils in twenty-five states (plus the District of Columbia and New York City) with similar students in district-operated schools, thus covering more than 95 percent of US charter pupils and examining their achievement growth on state tests from the 2006–2007 school year through 2010–2011.[28]

As table 3.1 shows, the magnitude of the impact—and whether it was positive or negative—varied considerably by jurisdiction. In the District of Columbia and Rhode Island, for example, charter students gained more than one hundred days of learning in math in a single

TABLE 3.1   Charter schools' average one-year impacts on reading and mathematics achievement, expressed as days of learning, by state or other jurisdiction, 2006–2007 through 2010–2011

	Reading	Mathematics		Reading	Mathematics
Arizona	–22	–29	Nevada	–108	–137
Arkansas	–22	–22	New Jersey	43	58
California	22	–7	New Mexico	0	–29
Colorado	7	–7	New York State	36	79
District of Columbia	72	101	New York City	0	94
Florida	–7	0	North Carolina	22	–7
Georgia	14	–14	Ohio	–14	–43
Illinois	14	22	Oregon	–22	–50
Indiana	36	14	Pennsylvania	–29	–50
Louisiana	50	65	Rhode Island	86	108
Massachusetts	36	65	Tennessee	86	72
Michigan	43	43	Texas	–22	–29
Minnesota	14	–7	Utah	–7	–43
Missouri	14	22			

Source: Center for Research on Education Outcomes (CREDO), "National Charter School Study 2013," CREDO, Stanford, CA, 2013, http://credo.stanford.edu/documents/NCSS%202013%20 Final%20Draft.pdf.

Note: According to the source, "there are three states missing at least one year of data. New Jersey and Pennsylvania did not have growth data for the 2006–07 year, and CREDO does not have Illinois growth data from 2006–07 through 2008–09."

school year, compared with matched pupils in district schools.[29] In Nevada, on the other hand, charter-goers *lost* 137 days of math learning. In reading, Tennessee and Rhode Island enjoyed the largest gains, with 86 days each, whereas Nevada charter students again performed the worst, on average losing 108 days.

Another CREDO analysis, this one published in 2015, examined charter school achievement in forty-one cities across twenty-two states.[30] The analysis, which included more than 80 percent of all charter pupils in those jurisdictions, found that these students annually achieved, on average, 40 added learning days in math and 28 in reading, compared with their matched peers in district schools. This benefit did not hold everywhere, however, as CREDO found that charters in eleven communities posted smaller gains in math than did district schools—as also happened with reading results in ten locales.[31]

There were also significant differences by race. Black and Hispanic children—who, as described earlier, make up disproportionately large percentages of charter school enrollees—enjoyed the greatest gains. They gained between 6 and 36 more days of learning in reading and math than did their virtual twins in district schools. Asian charter-goers neither gained nor lost, whereas white students lost 14 days in reading and 36 in math (see appendix table A.3).[32]

Achievement also varied significantly with the duration of students' enrollment in charter schools. The 2015 CREDO study found (as had the original 2009 analysis) that the longer a child studied in a charter school, the greater the annual achievement boost, again represented as days of learning gained or lost in comparison with district schools. During a student's first year at a charter, he or she gained, on average, 7 days of learning in math. By year four or later, the gain was 108 days. In reading, first-year charter students actually lost 7 days of learning (akin to a 2009 finding), but by year four or later, they were gaining 72 days (appendix table A.4).

In a study yielding far bleaker results, 2015 also brought CREDO's—and the country's—first serious evaluation of *online* charter schools. This time, Raymond teamed up with two other research organizations to examine such schools' impact on pupil achievement, as well as school operations and policy. They found that most online charter-goers made markedly less academic progress than did their peers in district schools. In just two states did online charters yield stronger academic results. (We return to online charter schools—and this study—in the next chapter.)

OTHER ANALYSES

While CREDO's studies have dominated recent discussions of charter effectiveness, there have been many others. On the inconclusive front, June 2010 brought results from the first large randomized trial, conducted with 2,330 charter pupils from fifteen states in thirty-six middle schools that conducted admission lotteries.[33] This federally funded study was conducted by Mathematica Policy Research[34] The primary outcome measure was performance on state tests, but analysts also used school records and student and parent surveys to examine outcomes such as pupil behavior and attitudes, as well as parent involvement and satisfaction. This summary comes from the report:

- Although there were wide variations in performance, on average the [charter] schools did not have a statistically significant impact on student achievement.
- The schools did not significantly affect most other outcomes that were examined, either, save for parent and student satisfaction where charter students and their parents were more satisfied with their schools.
- Charter schools were more effective in math (though not reading) for lower income and lower achieving students and less effective for higher income and higher achieving students. There were no other significant school impacts for other student sub-groups such as gender.[35]

Two centers have emerged as hubs for research-based criticism of charters: the Great Lakes Center for Education Research and Practice, housed at Western Michigan University, and the National Education Policy Center (NEPC), based at the University of Colorado, but comprising a large network of academics and analysts.[36] (As with CREDO, though for opposite reasons, these two outfits have their share of detractors and dissenters.)

Both groups examine a range of education topics, including charters and school privatization. For example, the Great Lakes Center reviewed charters' impact on pupil achievement in the region. The project, led by Gary Miron of Western Michigan University, analyzed math and reading outcomes in grades four, seven, and ten over a five-year period. Released in 2007, the findings showed that although every state in the area had some successful charter schools, charter achievement was lower on average than in demographically similar district schools (although it was improving over time).[37]

NEPC has produced its own analyses as well as critical reviews of selected think-tank publications.[38] Its reports often discuss the hazards of accepting positive findings prima facie (a reasonable admonition in commenting on all research). For example, NEPC said about the Betts and Tang meta-analysis: "The report does a solid job of describing the methodological limitations of the studies reviewed, then seemingly forgets those limits in the analysis."[39] NEPC also declared that in CREDO's 2015 study, "there are significant reasons to exercise caution ... and concerns over analytic methods. ... [T]he actual effect sizes reported are very small, explaining well under a tenth of one percent of the variance in test scores. To call such an effect 'substantial' strains credulity."[40]

Other analyses tend to affirm or add to CREDO's findings that charters boost achievement for low-income and minority children, although some of these studies are limited in scope and represent little more than the specific schools or children whose performance was examined. For example, Harvard's Roland Fryer and Princeton's Will Dobbie have studied the Promise Academy Charter Schools in New York's Harlem Children's Zone, which serves children and families in central Harlem via a comprehensive set of social and health programs.[41] The Promise Academy began in 2004 under the Zone's umbrella and is now a network of eight schools enrolling nearly sixteen hundred students.[42]

The effects of attending the Promise Academy middle school were enough, reported Fryer and Dobbie, to close the black-white achievement gap in math by ninth grade, while elementary pupils experienced enough gains to close the racial gap in both math and English by third grade.[43] Another study of the same two schools by the same duo went beyond academic achievement: "Admitted females are 10.1 percentage points less likely to be pregnant in their teens, and males are 4.4 percentage points less likely to be incarcerated. ... These effects are larger than those expected from test score increases alone, implying that high achieving charter schools alter more than cognitive ability."[44]

In yet another study, released by the National Bureau of Economic Research in 2014, Patrick L. Baude and his colleagues tracked the evolution of charter quality in Texas from 2001 to 2011.[45] They found that quality improved over time, because of three related factors: the schools closed by authorizers during that period were among the least effective; the schools that opened far outperformed those that closed; and those that remained open typically got better.[46] In contrast, an examination of Arizona charters by Martin West of Harvard and Matthew Chingos, then at Brookings, reached a more sobering conclusion: The schools' overall performance was "uneven" and "mediocre," varying more than in district schools. At every grade level, they found that Arizona charter schools, especially those outside the metro areas, were moderately less effective than district schools at improving achievement in some subjects. On the other hand, no-excuses charters in the Grand Canyon State were more effective in raising math achievement than were schools with more generic missions. And, as in Texas, the Arizona charters that closed were weaker than those that stayed open, a process that naturally leads to sector-level gains over time.[47]

OTHER OUTCOMES

While the primary focus in this chapter has properly been charter schools' effects on pupil achievement—what Notre Dame sociologist Mark Berends calls "the horse race between sectors"—all schools, including charters, should be judged on more than this one dimension.[48] What happens to children after they exit twelfth grade is also important, as are the aspirations, behavior patterns, and character traits that young people emerge with. Because such outcomes are harder to gauge and compare than test scores, they have been much less studied. But we see hints of their significance.

For example, a RAND study examined the effects of charters on long-term student attainment (and other issues) in Florida and Chicago, among other places. The sample included more than forty-two hundred Florida students and nearly one thousand in Chicago. Using multiple methods to control for selection bias, the analysts concluded that attending a charter high school substantially increased the probability of graduating and enrolling in college. In Florida, 57 percent of students who went from a charter school in grade eight to a traditional public high school received a diploma in four years compared to 77 percent who entered a charter high school. As for college attendance, 57 percent of students who attended both middle and high school in the charter sector went on to two or four year postsecondary institutions within five years of starting high school, compared with 40 percent who moved from a charter middle school into a district-operated high school.

In Chicago, 75 percent of charter eighth graders who went on to a charter high school graduated, compared with 68 percent of those who proceeded into district-operated high schools. And 49 percent of those attending charter high schools went on to college, compared with 38 percent in the district sector.[49] Nobody should rest content with 49 percent, of course, but it beats 38!

Although place-specific, such findings open up additional questions about the effects of charter schools. What aspects of these schools might boost noncognitive outcomes that, in turn, may foster stronger academic achievement? Figuring this out, according to Berends, entails "looking inside schools, pointing to the importance of detailed information about curriculum, instruction, organizational conditions that promote achievement, and teacher characteristics and qualifications."[50] Such findings also lead us to ask whether the single-minded focus on test scores that resulted from No Child Left Behind has blinded us to school effects that may well be at least as consequential—for example, persistence, creativity, character, and citizenship.

BOTTOM LINE

What can we make of so many studies and conflicting findings on the effectiveness of charter schools? We venture five observations:

- *The urban achievement effect*: As with most studies of school results, the phrase *on average* masks truly wide variation in the charter sector. Broadly speaking, charters show positive effects for poor children (especially black and Hispanic students), often for English language learners, and sometimes for special education students. For white and Asian students, however, the effects are generally neutral or negative. As University of Michigan economist Susan Dynarski put it in the *New York Times* in November 2015, "a consistent pattern has emerged from this research. In urban areas, where students are overwhelmingly low-achieving, poor and nonwhite, charter schools tend to do better than other public schools in improving student achievement. By contrast, outside of urban areas, where students tend to be white and middle class, charters do no better and sometimes do worse than public schools."[51]
- *Achievement trends*: These are headed in the hoped-for direction. Newer (and more sophisticated) studies mostly show better outcomes than older ones. The push for quality appears to have

yielded some gains, although other education reform efforts under way in the past decade or two (e.g., higher standards, stricter accountability, and more-exacting teacher evaluations) affect both charter and district schools. Moreover, as more charters get more years of experience under their institutional belts and as more pupils spend more consecutive years in them, achievement generally increases.

- *Nonachievement outcomes*: Test scores aside, charters tend to show positive effects on indicators such as graduation rates, the odds of attending college, and college persistence, as well as student behavior and later earnings. As one analyst concludes, "it is possible that charter schools' full long-term impacts on their students have been underestimated by studies that examine only test scores."[52]

- *Authorizing*: Study after study either demonstrates or strongly implies that authorizing matters. Student achievement improves when authorizers are rigorous in determining who should get charters, monitoring schools' performance, holding them accountable for results, and closing those that fail.

- *Research methodology*: There's widening consensus on the strengths and weaknesses of the methods used for evaluating the effects of charter (and other) schools. When it comes to pupil achievement, assessment of gains over time (panel studies), rather than absolute levels at a specific point in time, is superior because it takes past achievement into account. And studies of schools that enroll students by lottery are optimal because, as with serious medical research, they allow for the random assignment of "treatment" and "control" groups.

What does this review of charter schools' uneven track record mean? We cannot claim today that the word *charter* is any more determinative than *district* when it comes to analyzing or explaining school performance—an important point that we illustrate in the next chapter.

4

Charter Schools in Action: Solid and Sketchy Examples

IN THIS CHAPTER, we sketch five real-world examples of charter performance and its variability across policy settings, places, and school types. We include both strong positive findings and troubling failures. The first two cases document how charters in a prominent nonprofit network and in a huge city are producing good results for many of the children they serve. The third examines the generally shabby performance of online charter schools. Number four contrasts Massachusetts and Ohio, states at opposite ends of the quality spectrum. Finally, an example drawn from the District of Columbia sketches a well-developed performance management system that can contribute to the winnowing of weak charter schools and the development of more good ones.

THE NATION'S LARGEST CHARTER MANAGEMENT ORGANIZATION

The Knowledge Is Power Program, universally known as KIPP, began in 1994 when Michael Feinberg and David Levin, two Teach For America alumni, launched a fifth-grade program within the Houston Independent School District. A year later, Feinberg opened the KIPP Academy Middle School as a charter in Houston while Levin moved to New York City to launch a second one. In 2000, they established the KIPP Foundation, in cooperation with (and greatly aided by) Doris and Don Fisher, founders of The Gap clothing store empire. Their goal was to create more schools in the KIPP mold.

KIPP is perhaps the paradigmatic no-excuses model, as well as the biggest, best-known, and most acclaimed of these school networks, with some 183 charters in twenty states and the District of Columbia, serving nearly seventy thousand students. (If it were a district, KIPP would rank about fiftieth in enrollment.) Although KIPP began with middle schools only, its network now includes pre-K, elementary, and high schools, too. More than 87 percent of "KIPPsters" are poor, and 96 percent are African American or Hispanic. As of fall 2014, among students who either completed eighth grade at a KIPP middle school or graduated from a KIPP high school, 82 percent had entered college, 45 percent had earned four-year degrees, and another 6 percent had earned associate's degrees.[1]

In 2008, Mathematica Policy Research began a multistage examination of KIPP middle schools.[2] The 2013 report probed student demographics, including the allegation that KIPP cherry-picked its pupils. Analysts found that KIPP schools overall had higher concentrations of black students than did the district elementary schools that feed them (65 versus 45 percent) and a slightly smaller proportion of Hispanic pupils (31 versus 34 percent). KIPP enrolls more low-income students (83 versus 75 percent) but fewer special education pupils (9 versus 13 percent) and limited English proficiency students (13 versus 15 percent). KIPPsters enter with lower math and reading scores than those of other pupils in the feeder schools. The Mathematica team concluded that "these results provide little evidence to support the claim that KIPP 'creams' or selectively enrolls higher-performing students."[3]

On the achievement front, Mathematica found that three years after enrolling, KIPP students had achieved eleven months of additional learning in math, and eight additional months in reading, beyond what they would have accomplished had they not moved to KIPP.[4] The authors concluded that "KIPP is among the highest-performing charter networks in the country."[5]

Mathematica's 2015 report measured both longer-term impacts and, for the first time, the outcomes of KIPP elementary and high schools.[6] Key findings include the following:

- At the elementary school level, positive and significant impacts on students' reading and math achievement.
- At the middle school level, positive and significant impacts on reading and math achievement, although somewhat smaller impacts than were reported in 2013.
- At the high school level, positive impacts on college preparation, including increased likelihood of applying to college and more advanced course taking.
- Across all grade levels, a positive impact on parental satisfaction with their children's schools, but scant impact on student motivation, engagement, educational aspirations, and behavior.

PROMISING RESULTS IN THE BIG APPLE

Caroline Hoxby and colleagues undertook a multiyear experimental study of sixty New York City charters and their students in grades three through twelve, examining achievement and other data from the school year 2000–2001 through 2007–2008. The lottery-based analysis compared those who wanted to attend charters and were randomly selected to do so with those who wished to attend but were not selected and remained in district schools.

Charter applicants were much likelier than New York students overall to be black (64 versus 32 percent) and poor (93 versus 74 percent); much less likely to be white or Asian (7 versus 28 percent); somewhat less likely to be Hispanic (27 versus 39 percent); much less likely to be English language learners (4 versus 14 percent); and similarly likely to need special education (11 versus 12.5 percent). The male-to-female division was approximately equal, as in the district overall.

The review of academic effects was based on state math and reading tests. Analysts scrutinized thirty-two schools enrolling students in grades three through eight. (The number of high school students was too small to produce significant results.) Among the most striking findings: by the end of eighth grade, charter pupils scored about thirty points higher in math and twenty-three points higher in reading than if they had remained in regular district schools. The authors offer this perspective: "Students in Scarsdale, New York, one of the most affluent suburbs of New York City, routinely score between 35 and 40 points higher than students in Harlem, where most of the city's charter schools are located. So, let's call 35 points the 'Scarsdale-Harlem achievement gap.' . . . If charter schools in New York City improve their students' scores by 30 points, then their students will have made up about 86 percent of the Scarsdale-Harlem achievement gap [in math] and 66 percent [in reading]."[7]

The variation in achievement effects between the lottery students who enrolled in charters and those who stayed in district schools is positively associated—though not definitely established—with practices such as a longer school year, day, and week. (This connection comes as no surprise to anyone familiar with time-on-task literature.) Other factors like class size and afterschool programs seem to have no relationship.[8]

In the years examined by Hoxby and colleagues, New York City was arguably the largest *portfolio district* in the land. (For a discussion of portfolio districts, see chapter 12.) Although only about 10 percent of the city's public schools are charters, during Michael Bloomberg's three mayoral terms (2002–2013) the creation of high-quality charters was a key element of his and school chancellor Joel Klein's education-reform strategy. Equally important were the encouragement of choice, the empowerment of effective principals, and the establishment of a competitive market in school services. (Mayor Bill De Blasio has not sustained this strategy, but the charters remain—and there are more every year, sponsored by state-level authorizers.)

ONLINE CHARTER SCHOOLS: A DREARY PICTURE

Although correspondence schools and home-study alternatives have long been available for families in unusual circumstances (e.g., residents of remote locations, children with medical issues, and Foreign Service families with overseas postings), full-time online K–12 schools are a recent phenomenon that's almost entirely confined to the charter sector. Such schools can take many forms: large or small, localized or multistate, nonprofit or for profit.

They're different enough from brick-and-mortar charters to deserve their own performance analysis, but the first such national appraisal did not appear until late 2015 in the form of a three-part evaluation by Mathematica Policy Research, the Center on Reinventing Public Education (CRPE), and the Center for Research on

Education Outcomes (CREDO). Each organization focused on a different aspect of online chartering.[9]

Mathematica studied the schools' operations and instructional strategies, included a survey of principals, and supplemented its sources with federal data.[10] CRPE analyzed how state policy shapes online schools.[11] These two reports found about two hundred such charters operating in 2013–2014 in twenty-six (soon to be twenty-seven) states, serving about two hundred thousand pupils, which was about 8 percent of charter students nationwide.[12] Three states—Ohio, Pennsylvania, and California—accounted for about half of the online enrollment. Nearly 90 percent of these schools reported serving a general population, while most of the rest focused on dropouts or young people lacking graduation credits. Almost a quarter of the schools enrolled more than a thousand students apiece, accounting for more than three-fourths of total online enrollments. (Seven schools enrolled more than five thousand students each.) Exceptionally large enrollments in Ohio and Pennsylvania were related to relatively generous funding levels and unlimited school growth (though Ohio eventually slowed the increase of virtual charters and their enrollments).[13] Shrewd political action on the part of school operators was also a likely factor.[14]

Nearly all states that permit online charters allow the schools to draw students from the entire state rather than individual districts, though fourteen jurisdictions limit either the number of schools or their total enrollments. Just six require that school operators have a physical presence within the state. As in the brick-and-mortar charter sector, most states allow authorizers to charge enrollment-based oversight fees to the schools they oversee, creating a potential disincentive to enforce quality and close weak schools. In twenty-two states, online schools are funded on par with brick-and-mortar charters; elsewhere they receive less.

More than half of online charters are affiliated with for-profit EMOs, and half of those schools are linked to the two largest such firms, K12 and Connections Academy.[15] Technology enables such operators to have a multistate presence, but key details (e.g., funding, standards, governance, accountability, and authorizing) vary by state. So instead of a single vast national (or international) virtual school, these firms typically hopscotch state by state, which is quite different from online operators at the postsecondary level, such as Coursera and EdX.

White students are significantly overrepresented in online charters (71 percent versus 49 percent in all public schools); Hispanic youngsters are significantly underrepresented (12 versus 31 percent), as are children from low-income families (35 versus 53 percent). Students with disabilities, however, enroll at nearly the same rates (14 percent). The average length of enrollment for a typical student is about two years, with 22 percent of these children eventually returning to traditional schools.

CREDO investigated the progress of online charter pupils in seventeen states and the District of Columbia, examining three years of data from 158 schools that enrolled thirty-five thousand students in 2009–2010 and more than sixty-five thousand in 2012–2013.[16] The study gauged academic impact from state test scores and comparisons of the achievement gains of online students with "virtual twins" enrolled in district schools (and, sometimes, in brick-and-mortar charters).

Students in online charters made markedly less academic progress than did their counterparts in traditional schools. More than two-thirds of the online schools showed weaker overall growth. On average, students achieved 180 fewer days of learning in math and 72 fewer days in reading each year than did similar pupils in district-run schools.[17] Online students in Florida, Louisiana, and Texas fared worst. Only in Georgia and Wisconsin did online charters show stronger results.[18]

Weak academic performance in online charters was fairly consistent across student categories and demographic groups and across differing instructional and management models. The CREDO analysis soberly concluded that "online charters don't serve very well the . . . set of students that currently attend these schools, much less the general population. . . . Current oversight policies in place may not be sufficient for online charter schools. . . . States should examine . . . existing online programs before allowing expansion."[19]

Key leaders of the charter sector were forthright in lamenting these sorry findings. Nina Rees, head of the National Alliance for Public Charter Schools (NAPCS), commented that "the breadth of this underperformance convinces us that states may need to change the parameters within which full-time virtual charter public schools can operate."[20] Greg Richmond of the National Association of Charter School Authorizers (NACSA) declared that "there is a place for virtual schooling in our nation, but there is no place for results like these."[21]

Online learning surely offers a potentially valuable mechanism for educating some K–12 students. And the CREDO analysis points out that some online schools are doing this tolerably well. On the other hand, the overwhelming negativity of these results is cause for alarm. A key question in need of attention is the role of profit-seeking by those running the schools. Surely, their authorizers need to consider applications more judiciously and to monitor school performance more vigilantly. Policy makers, too, need to look critically at statutes allowing for the freewheeling creation of these schools. It's their job to ensure school quality. Yet they should take care not to discard the baby, too. Online learning isn't going to vanish from K–12 education any more than from higher education. How to organize, deliver, and oversee it to benefit the most students is the challenge ahead.

OHIO AND MASSACHUSETTS: QUALITY CONTROLS AND TRADE-OFFS

A 2014 CREDO study found that the typical Ohio charter pupil learned less in a year than did a typical district peer. This difference equated to approximately fourteen fewer days in reading and forty-three fewer in math, though the gaps varied considerably across the four cities studied (Cincinnati, Cleveland, Columbus, and Dayton). In Ohio, 19 percent of charters performed significantly better than their district peers in reading, while 28 percent did so in math. On the other hand, 18 percent of Ohio charters performed significantly worse in reading, as did 24 percent in math. That means the largest proportion of Ohio charters did not differ appreciably from traditional district schools.[22]

These glum results weren't very different from CREDO's 2009 report on Ohio charters, indicating that Buckeye charters made scant progress during this five-year period. In seeking an explanation, the analysts noted that "authorizers in the state of Ohio vary in their ability to provide monitoring and oversight . . . with schools monitored by small authorizers hav[ing] the lowest academic gains."[23]

Until recently, Ohio was notorious for allowing all manner of nonprofit groups (as well as districts and the Ohio Department of Education) to authorize schools. Anyone wanting to start a school could "shop" among this profusion of potential sponsors. Combine this with slack limits on how many schools could be authorized, and the inevitable result was a fiesta of almost unlimited chartering by too many authorizers. With relief, we note that after much delay and many battles, 2015 brought a major overhaul of the state's charter law, changes designed to curb questionable practices and, in time, yield schools with stronger outcomes. (For a more detailed account, see chapter 10.)

In Massachusetts, by contrast, a 2013 CREDO study found that a typical Bay State charter pupil gained thirty-six more days per year in reading and sixty-five days in math than did a typical district counterpart.[24] Forty-four percent of the state's charters tallied significantly greater gains in reading compared with district schools, while 56 percent did so in math.[25]

The study included a special analysis of Boston, home to about 13 percent of the state's charter pupils. These results display the largest gains—and gaps—that CREDO has found anywhere. A typical Boston charter student had more than twelve months of added learning in reading and thirteen months in math. This equated to 83 percent of charter students with significantly greater learning gains than those of their district peers, while no Boston charter showed lesser gains.[26]

Why have Massachusetts and Ohio occupied opposite ends of the effectiveness continuum? The Bay State has a single sponsor for its full-fledged (Commonwealth) charter schools—the state board of education—which enjoys a well-earned reputation for persnickety authorizing. Combine this with a stringent statutory cap on the number of students who can enroll in Commonwealth charters, and one can plausibly expect school quality to surpass Ohio's. Yet painful trade-offs are also evident. The Bay State's charter cap has severely constricted the growth of quality schools and produced epic waiting lists for those that exist. In Ohio, by contrast, at least until the 2015 reforms kick in, almost any nonprofit has been able to become an authorizer, some authorizers have been promiscuous in approving charter applications, and many charter schools have empty seats.

DISTRICT OF COLUMBIA: PURPOSEFUL PERFORMANCE MANAGEMENT

The District of Columbia's 1996 charter law created an independent authorizer called the DC Public Charter School Board (DCPCSB). Now the only sponsor in town, the board is widely respected for careful attention to school quality. Today, the DC law is among the strongest in the land, according to NAPCS.[27] Charters enrolled about 44 percent of all public school students in the nation's capital in 2015, with over 37,800 of them studying on 112 campuses.[28]

In 2008, DCPCSB set out to create a performance management system with multiple gauges of its schools' success.[29] It issues annual updates on each school's progress across five domains, mostly related to pupil achievement and mainly based on the District's "state" test scores, but also including pupil attendance, graduation rates, and high school students' performance on Advanced Placement exams and the like.[30] These ratings assist the board with decisions about individual schools' futures, including whether to renew or terminate their charters and whether to require a weak school to change its governance, leadership, or outside operator.

Schools are rated in three tiers. Tier 1 schools excel academically, and tier 3 schools perform below expectations. (Tier 2, predictably, is in between.) In 2014, there were twenty-two DC charters in tier 1, thirty-seven in tier 2, and four in tier 3.[31]

Tier 1 schools are located all over town, and their racial and income demographics reflect the District as a whole. Eight of the top ten schools serve students who are more than 75 percent low-income. Fifty-seven percent of DC charter pupils scored proficient or better on the "state" test in 2014, marking the eighth consecutive year that the proportion of proficient charter pupils had risen. According to the 2013 CREDO study, the average one-year impact on academic growth of a student attending a DC charter was an impressive 72 additional days of learning in reading and 101 days of learning in math when compared with similar students in district schools.[32]

We cannot prove that these impressive gains were caused by the DCPCSB's performance-management system—many other education reforms and policy changes were under way at the same time—but we're reasonably confident that it contributed.

From the impressive results achieved by KIPP schools to the bleak performance of the online version, the charter sector of American public education exhibits great variability at the quarter-century mark. The sector has also generated a plethora of school models and governance arrangements. Indeed, experience has taught us that hanging a charter sign over a schoolhouse door (or its cyberspace equivalent) actually says very little about it, beyond signaling that those running it have an opportunity to do things differently from—and potentially better than—the norm in traditional schools serving their communities and children. Some charter leaders have seized this opportunity to do great things. Others have tried and failed. Still others haven't tried very hard.

Above and beyond the performance of schools, it's important to ask what the chartering strategy itself has wrought. As Ted Kolderie observes, the latter may bring benefits to K–12 education even when a given school produces meager test-score gains.[33] In the next chapter, we examine seven strategy-linked developments that seem to us notable and generally valuable, albeit less than perfect.

5

What Chartering
Hath Wrought:
Notable Developments

IN THIS CHAPTER, we look at seven broadly positive features of the present charter landscape while also acknowledging their drawbacks. A few of these accomplishments tie directly to student outcomes; others relate more to the delivery system itself. Several were anticipated by charter pioneers in the early 1990s, although no one could have imagined all the ensuing wrinkles. Other developments could not have been foreseen, because they emerged from the shifting priorities of funders, entrepreneurs, and authorizers; changes in state and federal policy; technological progress; and the predilections and strengths (and weaknesses) of would-be school operators.

FOCUSING ON AT-RISK KIDS

As explained earlier, US charter schools primarily serve poor and minority children. Several forces drive this concentration. Families with few options for quality schools are more apt to seek out charters when given the opportunity. About half of state laws declare that a specific purpose of chartering is to boost options for targeted students, especially those at risk. And some states have statutorily restricted charters to urban areas (and, sometimes, to low-achieving districts or pupils).

Thus it's not surprising that charters have emerged principally as a niche delivery system aimed at urban, minority kids. This focus has been good for those kids, as the achievement data suggest. It has also been a positive force in calling attention to the needs and potential of these children in the K–12 system as a whole. At the same time, the emphasis on at-risk kids has limited the potential of charters to serve more and different students.

Charters' concentration on inner-city children has also led some to claim that these schools are resegregating public education. Analysts affiliated with the Civil Rights Project of the University of California, Los Angeles, assert that "charter schools are more racially isolated than traditional public schools in virtually every state and large metropolitan area in the nation."[1]

Examining the same data, however, University of Arkansas analysts reached very different conclusions:

> The data actually reveal small differences in the level of overall segregation between the charter school sector and the traditional public-school sectors. Indeed, we find the majority of students in the central cities of metropolitan areas, in both charter and traditional public schools, attend school in intensely segregated settings. . . . [T]he fact that poor and minority students flee segregated traditional public schools for similarly segregated charters does not imply that charter school policy is imposing segregation upon these students. Rather, the racial patterns we observe in charter schools are the result of the choices students and families make as they seek more attractive schooling options.[2]

Arguments over segregation and racial isolation will continue, as always. For now, we simply note that charters mostly serve children who need a boost.

DEMONSTRATING DEMAND

As we showed earlier, charters have come to play a major role in the education ecosystems of some cities. In 2014–2015, 14 districts saw 30 percent or more of their students enrolled in charter schools; 45 districts had at least 20 percent; and more than 160 had at least

10 percent. If the 151,000 charter pupils in Los Angeles were a separate district, it would rank among the twenty largest in the land.[3]

School waiting lists indicate that many more families would utilize the charter option if they could, illumining the extent of latent dissatisfaction with traditional public school offerings. Bellwether Education Partners estimates that more than one million individual children were on such lists in 2013.[4] In the fall of 2014, Boston had about 25,700 children on such lists—nearly three times as many as were enrolled in that city's twenty-seven true charters.[5] And in New York City, the Success Academy network reports that for the 2015–2016 school year, it had 25,000 applicants for three thousand places. The tribulations that can result were poignantly portrayed in *Waiting for Superman,* a 2010 documentary in which children and parents agonize as names are drawn during an admission lottery that determines who gets in and who gets wait-listed.[6] Plenty more want in than there's space for.

FOSTERING INNOVATION

The promise that charters would innovate within public education, devising and piloting strategies and models—R&D style—that the traditional system could then adopt, was indisputably part of chartering's original appeal to educators, policymakers, and philanthropists. And some innovation has indeed happened, mostly for the good, although the charter sector has been somewhat better at innovating than the district sector has been at picking up and scaling these charter-crafted advances.

The word *innovation* is overused and ill defined, and nowhere more than in K–12 education. Harvard Business School professor Clayton Christensen has made a useful distinction between *disruptive innovation*—a truly novel change that creates a new market and value network by displacing something that previously existed—and incremental change in an extant product or service that boosts productivity and performance within an existing market.[7]

Chartering has turned out to be some of both. Like most innovations that ultimately proved disruptive, it started small and held scant interest for districts, which is why most charters are start-ups, not conversions of extant schools. But charters have gotten much more notice as they siphon market share from more districts. The charter sector has also sometimes done better at such things as blended learning, personalized instruction, inner-city education, and the empowerment of principals. Moreover, charters have essentially eclipsed the district arrangement in one major city and are headed that way in several more. And a handful of forward-looking superintendents (e.g., in Denver, Colorado; and Spring Branch, Texas) have embraced some of the flexibility that chartering can afford them, too. The high-touch, high-impact, no-excuses schools are another example of an important innovation that probably could not exist at scale without the chartering mechanism.[8] Nor would we have had as much experimentation— by no means all of it successful—with technology-assisted learning at the primary-secondary level had charters not pioneered this realm.[9]

We would never suggest that every charter school has invented something original, much less something never before glimpsed in the K–12 universe. Indeed, a 2015 report from the pro-charter Mind Trust and Public Impact faulted this sector for how many of its schools resemble—in structure, curriculum, pedagogy, uses of time, and so forth—the district schools to which they're meant to be alternatives. (The Mind Trust went on to convene a Charter School Innovation Summit in 2016 to tackle this problem.)[10] Chartering creates opportunities to innovate but doesn't require that such opportunities be seized. Still, from a child's or family's perspective, a school that does something better than another school—even when there's no fundamental difference in the concept or practice—is a gain that feels innovative. And a decent number of charters and networks have tried, and continue to try, instructional models and strategies that have little precedent, at least in their own communities. Let us underscore that a practice already familiar in one location may be revolutionary in another. Just because something can be observed in the schools of Houston, say, doesn't mean it has yet been tried in Cleveland, Memphis, or even Dallas.

REALIZING THE POWER OF NO EXCUSES

Charter schools have considerable leeway to respond to niche demands and opportunities in the education marketplace; to vary in philosophy, pedagogy, and organization; and to address particular pupil needs, community priorities, and family preferences. Thus we find Montessori charters, Waldorf-style charters, STEM charters, outdoor-education charters, virtual charters, language-immersion charters, and special-education charters. There are also teacher-governed schools, business-operated schools, start-up schools, conversion schools, and more.[11] The variety is impressive. But the most conspicuous and notable model to emerge is the no-excuses charter school, characteristically focused—again—on low-income and mostly minority inner-city residents.

Much has been written about these schools, beginning with an early portrait by Abigail and Stephan Thernstrom in a 2003 book that also helped name them: *No Excuses: Closing the Achievement Gap in Learning*.[12] Such schools are characterized by high behavioral and academic expectations for their pupils, including a clear and rigorously enforced discipline code; more time in class, including longer days and years; a rather traditional academic curriculum geared toward college entry (and stressing college as the premier goal for students from the moment they walk into school); and a strong focus on a robust school culture that incorporates and reinforces the previous elements. They accept no excuses for failure, either by children (provided that they strive and behave) or by teachers and schools.

Education's district sector has always contained examples of schools (and, sometimes, principals and individual teachers) that impressively boost outcomes for poor and minority students.[13] But these tend to be exceptions to the rule. With its ability to innovate, replicate, and leap jurisdictional borders, the chartering strategy has facilitated a more systemic no-excuses approach. This, in turn, has led to chartering's signal accomplishment to date: the track record of such prominent "brands" as KIPP, YES Prep, the Success Academy network, Achievement First, and Uncommon Schools in educating inner-city children who had lacked adequate access to the kinds of schooling that truly put kids on track toward college. Indeed, the best of the no-excuses charters have excelled at helping poor kids escape from faltering schools and tough neighborhoods and tread the path toward the ivy gates. A "proof point," one might say, that it's possible for schools to do this and to do it at scale.

Proof is one thing, acceptance quite another. Successful though it may be, this education model is not universally admired. A 2014 *Washington Post* article evoked the main criticism in its headline: "Why 'No

Excuses' Charter Schools Mold 'Very Submissive' Students—Starting in Kindergarten."[14] This concern about what some see as students' near-robotic behavior grates against the progressive, discovery-oriented approach to learning that dominates American public education. Critics also assert that funders' focus on no-excuses schools promotes the idea that successful charters are only to be found in this singular niche, while denying resources to other promising school models as well as traditional districts.

While no-excuses schools do garner much attention and philanthropic support, a recent study of charters in seventeen cities found roughly equal numbers of no-excuses and more progressive schools. And plenty of other schools fit under neither category. In truth, the charter sector has more players—and teams—than is commonly realized. But the no-excuses model has hit the most home runs. (For more on no-excuses schools, see chapter 11.)

ENERGIZING (AND REDIRECTING) DONORS

For good and, some say, for ill, chartering has unleashed a wave of education-linked philanthropy that has drawn hundreds of millions of dollars into K–12 reform efforts. It's hard to imagine much of this money entering education at all were it not for this flexible and tantalizing instrument. But not all the private funding for charters and related endeavors has been additive; some has been diverted from the district sector and entities associated with it.

Sarah Reckhow and Jeffrey Snyder of Michigan State University have chronicled several dynamic changes in the makeup and giving patterns of the top fifteen US grant-making foundations from 2000 to 2010. These changes were often tied to opportunities to invest in education strategies and models that fell outside the familiar structures.[15]

As Reckhow and Snyder report, a significant number of unfamiliar donors and foundations entered the K–12 arena during that ten-year period. Among them were seven sizable "newer line" foundations—Walton, Dell, Robertson, Broad, Fisher, Daniels, and the Silicon Valley Community Foundation—that displaced more established foundations like Annenberg, Wallace, Joyce, and Lilly from the top tier. (The Gates Foundation, however, was the largest K–12 donor over that entire period and remains so today.)

The funding focus of these newer foundations was different, including much support for "jurisdictional challengers" like charters and organizations such as Teach For America and New Leaders for New Schools, all of which compete with or offer alternatives to long-standing K–12 institutions. Among the top fifteen philanthropies, funding for district schools dropped from about 16 percent of total grant dollars in 2000 to 8 percent in 2010, while funding for charters rose from 3 to 16 percent.[16]

Also visible over this period was greater convergence in grant making, as the new foundations—and some older ones—teamed up to support similar activities and programs, sometimes in the same places. By 2010, five grantees (Charter School Growth Fund, Teach For America, KIPP, DC Public Education Fund, and NewSchools Venture Fund) together received more than $150 million from the top fifteen foundations—a sum that amounted to 18 percent of their total giving. Cities like Washington, Newark, and New Orleans emerged both as centers of reform and as philanthropy magnets.[17]

In short, new funders have entered the field and devoted themselves to outside-the-system strategies like chartering, particularly the creation and replication of no-excuses schools.[18] Predictably, however, the engagement of these deep-pocketed donors (and others such as Mark Zuckerberg) with grantees that challenge the traditional K–12 system has provoked pushback from those left out—and those worried that plutocrats are distorting American public education. Thus we see such caustic article titles as "Got Dough? How Billionaires Rule Our Schools" and "When Billionaires Become Educational Experts."[19] (See chapter 8 for more details on philanthropy.)

MOBILIZING TALENT AND SUPPORT STRUCTURES

Any attempt to grow new schools requires an adequate source of suitable school leaders, instructors, and support personnel. The charter sector has benefited from—and has catalyzed—much enterprise on this front while mobilizing energized young people to join its ambitious adventures. This in turn has intensified the push for alternative routes and mechanisms that can overcome structural obstacles and speed entry.

The freedom of many charters to staff themselves with people who have not been conventionally credentialed, as well as the human resource demands of this fast-growing sector, has encouraged considerable creativity in this sphere. After all, charter-linked innovation need not occur only at the building level. Charters (and others) have gained much from Teach For America (TFA), which has infused contemporary education-reform initiatives with teachers, leaders, and others who might not otherwise have considered this career stop. From 2010 to 2014, one-third of TFA corps members—slightly more than 1,700 annually—were placed in charter schools. Over that same period, TFA nearly doubled the number of its alums teaching within the charter sector (from 5,900 to 11,200) and more than doubled the number who headed charter schools and networks (from almost 1,900 to about 4,300).

TFA is not alone. Also entering this space have been TNTP (formerly The New Teacher Project), Leading Educators, Educators 4 Excellence, 4.0 Schools, Teach Plus, and the National Academy of Advanced Teacher Education. And some charters, frustrated by the slipshod quality, iffy content, long timelines, low stature, and high cost of conventional school-leader and teacher-preparation programs, have launched their own alternatives. Match Education in Boston created the Charles Sposato Graduate School of Education to prepare teachers for "the intensity and rigor" of teaching primarily in no-excuses charters. Its faculty consists entirely of veteran classroom practitioners and school leaders.[20] In 2012, the Massachusetts Board of Higher Education approved Sposato to award master's degrees in effective teaching. New York City's Relay Graduate School of Education was launched in 2007 by Uncommon Schools and has been approved by the New York Regents as the first stand-alone graduate school of education in the Empire State in more than eight decades. Today, Relay's programs include master's degrees for teachers, fellowships for experienced principals, and a partnership with Coursera, which offers online, open-enrollment courses. It now trains more than seventeen hundred teachers and principals annually.[21]

Other examples include California's High Tech High, a charter management organization (CMO) that now operates its own state-recognized Graduate School of Education and Education Leadership. Such endeavors recognize that charter principals typically wield substantial real authority across many more elements of their schools than do most district principals.[22] They also recognize that most charter teachers enjoy considerable freedom in curricula, pedagogy, and instructional materials, but are often expected to work long hours, to be accessible to students during even longer hours, and to shoulder responsibility both for children's cognitive growth and for their development as upstanding, motivated, and well-behaved people. The emergence of such preparation programs for educators is hard to imagine without the lure—and flexibility—of chartering.

Yet charters aren't always the ultimate destinations of those who tread these paths. Lots of terrific people who entered K–12 education via charters now occupy key positions in districts, state agencies, and more. As we write, John King, who cut his education teeth in the charter sector as cofounder of Boston's Roxbury Prep Charter School and then as managing director of Uncommon Schools, has been named to succeed Arne Duncan as US secretary of education.

BUILDING NEW GOVERNANCE STRUCTURES AND SUPPORT ORGANIZATIONS

The charter mechanism is not just as a source of new schools but also a structural reform of public education's governance and delivery systems. Indeed, viewed that way, chartering is as close as K–12 has come to disruptive innovation in a century: it explodes the exclusive franchise and creates an alternative system that affords families access to different, potentially better schools without requiring them to pay for private schooling. This breakthrough was recognized in 2000, when Harvard's Kennedy School awarded the state of Minnesota the school's Innovations in American Government Award, and was honored again in 2006, when Indianapolis won the same award for Mayor Bart Peterson's charter school initiative.[23]

Examples of governance innovation include the virtual districts that we know as CMOs and EMOs. Both run schools in multiple locations, create more schools, brand their schools, produce some uniformities within their brands, sometimes troubleshoot problems in their schools, and generally provide back-office services to their networks.

They've become a key way to expand—scale up—charters within and across states. As a result, they've developed some familiar characteristics of school districts. Although the majority of charters are freestanding, which leaves ample room within this sector for the proverbial start-up, scaling is undeniably best undertaken by a larger entity with organizational, managerial, and financial capacities seldom found in individual schools.

Another charter-linked governance innovation is the *recovery school district*, generally a state-controlled entity that takes over low-performing schools and their facilities—in effect extracting them from their local districts—and reboots them as charter or charter-like schools. A recovery district, too, resembles a virtual district, though within the geographic bounds of a state or city. The most visible examples are Louisiana's Recovery School District (discussed in chapter 12), Tennessee's Achievement School District, and Michigan's Education Achievement Authority (focused on Detroit), but by 2016, at least half a dozen other states had created or were headed toward creating similar entities.[24]

CMOs, EMOs, and recovery districts function somewhat like nongeographic school systems. The concept of a school authorizer (discussed in chapter 7) represents another innovation in public education, the more so when it enables nondistrict entities (e.g., universities and nonprofit organizations) to license public schools to operate, then hold them accountable.

Within traditional districts, too, chartering has paved the way for rethinking central-office and school relationships, and some districts have incorporated chartering into their own improvement efforts. The Center on Reinventing Public Education has a network of more than forty-five districts working on *portfolio management strategies*.[25] Under this arrangement, the central office remains in charge but confers considerably greater autonomy than in the past upon its schools, some of which are typically full-fledged charters authorized by the district itself.

Charters operating outside districts—that is, the great majority of today's sixty-eight hundred charters—have typically found that they need (or at least can benefit from) some of the services traditionally supplied within the district structure. Unless they're very large, individual schools have difficulty doing everything for themselves—and a community's needs are not necessarily well met by a congeries of unconnected schools. Absent the traditional district-based support structure, new entities have proven necessary to assist charters with staff development, leadership training, financial services, facility financing, special education, and more. To meet such needs, hundreds of for-profit and nonprofit organizations have emerged. Groups such as Building Hope, Pacific Charter School Development, and Civic Builders aid charters with facility financing, sometimes using program-related investment funds from foundations. On the R&D front, the charter sector has spawned entities like Tulane University's Education Research Alliance, whose purpose is to understand how the new era of New Orleans school reform has influenced teaching and learning in the Big Easy and what this may mean for the future of school reform.

In chapter 6, we examine some shortcomings of today's charter marketplace, and in chapter 13, we discuss the many forms of support that have emerged (and need to emerge) to enhance its functioning. Although some such enterprises existed in precharter days, the sector's growth has caused them to proliferate, innovate, and often compete with one another. Because charters are also a marketplace for service providers, the schools themselves can often choose among the enterprises that offer assistance. And when extant providers can't meet their needs, the schools can catalyze the creation of new ones.

None of the developments described in this chapter is a finished product. Yet in our eyes, they demonstrate how chartering has shown its capacity to boost the life chances of at-risk kids; to foster innovation in the governance realm and beyond; to catalyze philanthropic donors and redirect their role in K-12 education; and to widen the human capital pipelines and multiply the institutions that support it. All of this has advanced public education as a whole, even while complexifying it via the entry of new actors and alternatives to the traditional K–12 model.

PART III

Today's Charter Dilemmas

6

Pros and Cons of Districts and Markets

AS WE EXPLAINED IN CHAPTER 1, one prominent strand in the origins of chartering was the belief—articulated by serious thinkers on the right such as Friedman, Chubb, and Moe, as well as respected liberals such as Shanker, Sizer, and Kolderie—that the existing public school system—the "one best system"—was not meeting the educational needs of every child. Whatever their other differences, these analysts agreed that poor kids in particular needed alternatives and that a competitive schooling marketplace would yield greater quality, dynamism, and enterprise in the K–12 space. In this chapter, we probe some of the ways that the marketplace as it developed has not worked as well in practice as many of us had hoped (and later in the book, we offer suggestions for making it work better).

First, though, we review the different operating principles and theories of action that separate the district and charter sectors in their pure forms. Understanding these differences is helpful, not least because we end up recommending some hybridizing of the two approaches. Although both sectors function within a common framework of laws, academic standards, financial formulas, and the like, they can be said to belong to congregations with different theologies.

REFORMING THE "ONE BEST SYSTEM"

Except for Hawaii, geographically based local districts are ubiquitous in American public education, and most people take them for granted as *the* delivery system. The first districts arose from the needs of rural residents who lived too far from a town to use its schools but still wanted to educate their children. In 1789, Massachusetts granted legal rights to such communities to oversee their own schools. Twelve years later, Bay State lawmakers conferred on districts the authority to tax to support those schools, a power that previously belonged only to towns. Beginning with Horace Mann's education reform efforts—also in Massachusetts—in the mid-nineteenth century, states themselves shouldered responsibility for, and authority over, the education of the public, but typically delegated the delivery of that education to local school systems, generally with their own elected boards. (Also left to localities was much of the burden of paying for their schools!)

The progressive movement of the late nineteenth and early twentieth centuries led to another evolution: the concentration of operating authority for district schools in a professional superintendent, chosen and empowered by the district board. Industrial bureaucracies became the model for this governance structure with "efficiency, expertise, professionalism, centralization, and nonpolitical control [being] the watchwords of reform," according to Michael Kirst. Paul Hill describes the "accretion" of management authority as districts gradually accumulated layers of legislative mandates, regulations, and judicial decisions, meaning that over time, "school boards' duties became more detailed, explicit and intrusive."[1]

All of these developments have bequeathed to us today's principal education delivery system: public schools organized into geographically defined areas (typically contiguous with town or county borders), managed by professional educators, and answerable to locally elected officials, most often in the form of school boards. The district is charged by the state with meeting the primary and secondary education needs of every child under its jurisdiction. The district board engages a superintendent to lead a central office that acts as the board's administrative arm. Money flows to the district from local, state, and federal sources, much of it with clear directives about its use. Labor relations are generally based on collective bargaining agreements that control many educator activities and school practices. Kolderie has aptly described US public education as "a pattern of territorial exclusive franchises."[2] For the most part, only school boards can create public schools within their territory, usually assigning children to schools according to their home addresses.

Many reform efforts seek to make districts work better. Berkeley professor David Kirp has admiringly chronicled the "homegrown gradualism" by which Union City, New Jersey, has revamped its own school system.[3] Similar stories can be told of hundreds of other communities. At least as widespread are initiatives by state leaders and federal policy makers to push uniform changes—in standards, teacher qualifications, accountability, treatment of at-risk children, preschools, technology, and more—on all districts. Yet districts, as creatures of their states, remain the delivery vehicle, and the "one best system" remains the dominant approach to organizing, fueling, and steering that vehicle.

THE MARKETPLACE ALTERNATIVE

We hope that more such renewal efforts succeed, and we do not expect districts—or the top-down reforming of them—to vanish anytime soon from the American education scene. Yet rigidity, antiquated practices, and flawed assumptions within the traditional delivery system remain, which is what brought many people to chartering and other forms of school choice in the first place. Some districts work well enough to satisfy their constituents and their state policy leaders, but too many don't, particularly districts whose schools brim with disadvantaged children. Even as top-down reformers and local leaders struggle to improve them, we believe these young people need alternatives, and the charter strategy is a plausible way to supply them. Early boosters also expected that charters' freedom to be different would lead to worthy innovations that district schools could adopt or adapt, that the ever-more-variegated educational demands of an increasingly diverse society would be more flexibly met, and that competition would tone up the entire enterprise.

With the benefit of hindsight, we weren't wrong about districts. Twenty-five years of reform have done significant good in places. Some districts—often called *portfolio districts*—have adapted elements of chartering and choice as part of their own strategies to improve operations and boost student outcomes. But far too many poor kids still forfeit their futures in district-operated "dropout factories" or emerge with what the *New York Times* terms "counterfeit diplomas."[4]

Charters, by contrast, operate on the theory of action that a lightly regulated marketplace of diverse and generally autonomous schools will ensure high-quality education for all children who participate in that marketplace, while also empowering families to determine which school is best suited to their unique daughters and sons. That's the theory. But just as we weren't entirely wrong about districts, we weren't entirely right about markets. Indeed, if he were alive today, Milton Friedman would likely share our disappointment (if not our surprise) at the shortcomings of today's charter marketplace. Although nearly seven thousand of these schools of choice exist, the market has inadequately matched supply with demand, winnowed out the shoddy, or delivered sufficient quality to those who need it.

Friedman, to be clear, was no huge fan of charter schools. He saw them as an improvement over the district monopoly but not nearly the equal of a voucher-based education strategy that would set loose all the beneficent forces of market capitalism and individual choice within the K–12 market. In his words:

> Charter schools are at best an unstable halfway house on the road to effective parental choice. They do provide a wider range of alternatives to some parents and in this way introduce some competition on the demand side. But they remain government institutions subject to control by the educational establishment. . . . Despite this analysis, I have not opposed and do not oppose charter schools. The drive for them is a welcome sign of a reaction against our unsatisfactory educational system and I believe in as much experimentation as possible. In Mao's words, let a hundred flowers bloom and let the market do the weeding.[5]

Friedman clung to the vision of a perfectly free market in education that would yield efficiency, productivity, diversity, and quality, as parents demanded better schools for their children at prices the families (with the aid of vouchers when needed) could afford. In his mind, the basic mechanism at work here, as in all forms of school choice, would be multiple providers competing with one another for the patronage of many consumers who possess the freedom and wherewithal to select the educational arrangements that are best for their kids.

WHAT'S NOT WORKING

Friedman saw charters as a step in that direction. They do provide some families with choices—and often with the means to act on their preferences. Where charters have competed with traditional districts, the latter have sometimes responded with changes that produced at least a few more schools attuned to consumer preferences in curriculum and pedagogy. Moreover, charter authorizers have sometimes—though not often enough—assiduously pressed for quality in their schools and closed those that didn't measure up. In still other places, charter caps plus rigorous authorizing practices have yielded an impressive proportion of strong schools (but with the harsh trade-off of limited supply and long waiting lists). The charter marketplace has done a respectable job of responding to families' noneducational priorities, such as safety, convenience, and a welcoming ambience, and where the marketplace has had the freedom and capacity to grow, it has developed a mixed crop of schools that cater to the varied educational tastes of our complex society. As described in earlier chapters, a number of those schools are also doing a first-rate job of instructing their youthful charges and widening their future opportunities.

On the downside, however, across much of the nation, the charter marketplace has done only a mediocre job of matching supply with demand and ensuring solid educational quality. This partial market failure has multiple elements and sources, none of which would likely surprise Friedman. We will highlight three of them.

The Perils of Scarcity

Because the supply of charters is far from meeting the demand in most places, many families consider themselves fortunate to gain entry to any charter school, regardless of its academic performance. They often judge their new school to be an improvement over the one they left in ways that matter to them (again, including safety, convenience, and ambience). They're also apt to like it better simply because they chose it, a form of confirmation bias. In that sense, the charter marketplace is indeed responding to customer priorities, and that's a good thing. So, too, is the cafeteria of educational specialties—from schools that focus on children with dyslexia or autism to those that emphasize the study of Latin or Hebrew—that are now available in some locales to families seeking such options. No argument on that score from us. But academic achievement, character formation, citizenship, and noncognitive skills matter, too, both for the larger society and for the long-term interests of individual children, who are far likelier to get good jobs, be good neighbors, finish college, and enjoy the fruits of upward mobility if they gain the requisite skills and knowledge. There, as we showed in chapter 3, the charter sector's track record is distinctly mixed. And that's partly the result of too few charters in some places (and too many in others).

Distracted Suppliers

Because most charters are strapped for funds and feel overregulated by their states, those who run them often struggle to keep their heads above water (which includes keeping enrollments up) and see little reward in becoming more rigorous or investing in stronger curricula and more experienced instructors. Indeed, more than a few charter schools of our acquaintance have watered down their curricula, relaxed their rigor, or shortened their hours in response to consumer complaints that they were just too demanding or because the cost of maintaining all this rigor was breaking their budgets.[6] Even schools with a queue of prospective attendees cannot always afford the extra staffing and extended hours that both add to their expenses and sometimes irk their clients.

Weak Consumer Information

Even where parents are mindful of school quality and try their best to be discerning, the requisite consumer information in this marketplace is incomplete, hard to access, or difficult to understand. Because public education is a free good, pricing signals don't help customers make informed choices. The primary-secondary education marketplace isn't much like those for bicycles, hotel rooms, or hairdressers. Choosing a school is hugely consequential, yet many factors that matter to parents are truly hard to measure and investigate.

Think of all that you would like to know about a school (no matter the sector) before enrolling a cherished child or grandchild there. What about attendance, discipline, and behavior? Are its finances sound and audits clean? Do students and teachers like it there or flee as soon as possible? How well does the school deal with the learning needs of exceptionally bright, troubled, or disabled pupils? What do the school's climate and culture feel like? What does it truly value, and is it good at those things? Does it have particular specialties—or curricular weak spots? How does it handle pupil transportation? Is there a lot of homework? Too much? Not enough? What sports and extracurricular activities are on offer, and how many kids participate? How does it handle issues of diversity? Are its classrooms quiet and orderly or lively and engaged—or some of both? Does it take values, virtues, and character seriously and, if so, how does this seriousness manifest itself? (A character education class or virtue of the month is by no means the only or best approach. Some great schools opt to model rather than teach character.)

State report cards on school performance are ubiquitous yet lacking. Even when they adequately display academic achievement in tested subjects, they cannot begin to convey all the other relevant information, much of which is hard to quantify and present objectively. Even the most basic data in these reports are frequently presented in user-unfriendly ways, and it may be tough to discern such fundamentals as which schools are geographically accessible, serve the right grade levels, have the appropriate educational philosophy, and so on.[7] Private efforts such as GreatSchools, a prominent online school-review website, are more helpful for those searching for and comparing schools, yet their information on any given school is also limited, as much of it must be supplied by the school itself. But not all schools are entirely candid. Where supply exceeds demand, some will bombard parents with slick marketing claims intended to recruit enough pupils to fill their seats and balance their budgets.

Faced with incomplete, obscure, or unreliable information about schools and weighing the practical factors that influence what's workable for their families, inexperienced parents may simply turn for help to friends, neighbors, and current patrons of the schools that they're considering. That's not a bad thing to do—and vital when other sources are scarce or inscrutable—but it also attests to the imperfections of today's charter marketplace.

————————

In some countries, parents' preoccupation with gaining educational advantages for their daughters and sons creates competitive forces that reward schools with impressive records of achievement.[8] Such competition also infiltrates some sectors of American society, most conspicuously in the largely upper-middle-class race to gain admission to elite colleges and universities.[9] For the United States as a whole, however, we've come to believe, sadly, that at this point in our history, the marketplace alone—understood as individuals choosing the school their child will attend—is not a sufficient mechanism for assuring strong academic achievement and other important educational outcomes.

CHARTERS AS COMPETITION

How much difference has competition from charters made to those responsible for the district sector? Seeking to answer that question, an imaginative study gauged the level of competitive awareness and responses by district officials in a dozen locations where charters' market share varied from 8 percent to nearly 70 percent. The study included more than eight thousand print and media reports between 2007 and 2011, reports that were then cross-checked with district records and websites, including board-meeting minutes, to determine whether the media accounts were true. Here is a summary of the analysts' findings:

> Contrary to the largely symbolic reactions to competition evident when the [charter] movement was just beginning, we find evidence of significant changes in district policy and practice. The most common positive response . . . is district cooperation or collaboration with charter schools . . . [including] partnerships with successful nonprofit CMOs or . . . education management organizations (EMOs), to operate schools; the replication of successful charter school practices; and an increase in active efforts to market district offerings to students and families. . . .

. . . The most common obstructive response . . . was districts seeking to block access to buildings. . . .

The five other categories of obstructive responses observed are: 1) excessively denying charter applications, 2) creating legal obstacles to charter schools, 3) freezing or delaying payments to charter schools, 4) withholding information from charter schools, and 5) using regulations to restrict choice or interfere with competition.

. . . Where school districts once responded with indifference, symbolic gestures, or open hostility, we are starting to see a broadening of responses.[10]

Charters compete with each other—and with private schools—as well as with districts, but to devotees of the "one best system," the mere existence of competition is as foreign as the idea of school choice. Yet as we show in chapter 13, the steps needed to improve the functionality of the charter marketplace share many district-like qualities. Such actions are mostly beyond the capacity of individual schools to do for themselves and therefore require the assistance of outsiders—policy makers, philanthropists, entrepreneurs, non- and for-profit vendors, and operators of multischool networks. At the same time, elements of choice have been creeping into state and federal policies and district operations. We describe in chapter 12 some ways in which a few districts are incorporating charters into their own reform strategies. As examples in that chapter will show, both market-style and standards-based education reforms work better when each approach contains elements of the other.

All of this is to say that rival theologies—or, in the jargon of the field, competing theories of action—are no longer the only way to view the two approaches to delivering public education. We can glimpse some "interfaith" activities and joint worship services, even the stirrings of some fusion beliefs, in addition to the traditionally separate temples. We'll dig deeper on these issues in part IV. In chapters 7 through 10, however, we continue to examine major challenges faced by today's charter sector.

7

Authorizing, Governance, and Leadership

IT'S CLEAR THAT charter schools are governed differently than districts, but it's unclear to many exactly how that works and how well it's functioning. Districts have had eons to refine their operational arrangements and are now fairly set in their ways—that's why innovations such as mayoral control are so rare—even if conventional district governance does not always yield successful schools.

The charter sector, by contrast, is still ironing out kinks in its governance arrangements, which include *authorizers, governing bodies*, and *operators*. A major reason for today's problems is that those present at the creation of the charter enterprise (including ourselves) paid too little attention to how these roles would actually be played. Consequently, many states got off to a bad start. A major reason we wrote this book is to push for needed corrections. But getting them made is no cakewalk.

REFRESHER

Before delving into problems and possible solutions, here's a brief recap of the key roles, offered with the caveat that there are many differences between descriptions on paper and reality on the ground.

- *Authorizer*: Also known as a sponsor, this state-sanctioned entity licenses a school to operate in the first place and is then responsible for monitoring its performance and renewing its charter if that performance is satisfactory.[1] Authorizer failure, combined with policy failure to create a properly accountable authorizing

87

structure, is the biggest reason in most places for weak charter performance.

- *Governing board*: This is the school's governing body or corporate entity—generally an Internal Revenue Service–approved nonprofit with five to ten individuals in trustee-style roles. The governing board applied for and now holds the charter. It also adopts the budget, has fiduciary responsibility for all funds, is accountable for academic results, and is legally responsible if anything goes awry. The board either hires the school leader and staff directly or contracts with an operator.

- *Operator*: The operator—when there is one—is generally responsible for employing staff, selecting curricula, handling the funds, getting the building heated and cleaned, and dealing with individual children, teachers, and families, as well as vendors, the local district, the community, and more. In effect, the operator contracts with the governing board to manage the latter's school.

- *Charter*: This legally enforceable performance contract between authorizer and governing body describes the school's program and its expected results, the rules the school will follow, and the metrics by which it will be evaluated.

Each school ordinarily has its own governing board and charter, although sometimes one board holds multiple charters, one school operates multiple campuses, or a single charter spans multiple schools. (Among the best known is the Chicago International Charter School, where one nonprofit entity with a single charter is responsible for sixteen scattered campuses, encompassing multiple instructional philosophies and serving nearly nine thousand students.)[2]

Many charters, especially the one-off schools that still dominate this sector, run themselves without help from outside operators, although they may purchase back-office and other services from external vendors.[3] In those cases, the governing board typically engages the principal and oversees her as she selects teachers and leads the school. In chains or networks of charters, however, an external operator typically runs all the schools. It may be a nonprofit organization or for-profit firm and may be based in the same city or far away. It may manage a couple of schools or more than a hundred, and its schools most often follow a uniform education model. Although the school's governing board is formally accountable to its authorizer for results, the operator is counted on to produce those results, an expectation that should be carefully spelled out in *its* contract with the governing board.

THE CENTRALITY OF AUTHORIZERS

Authorizers are a diverse lot. The United States contained 1,077 of them in 2014–2015, ranging from 65 in Ohio and more than 100 in Wisconsin to 3 in New York and just 1 apiece in Massachusetts, Arkansas, and the District of Columbia.[4] Although the vast majority of authorizers are local school districts—a situation that often gives rise to problems that we discuss in chapter 10—others range from state agencies to universities to a mayor's office, even (in Minnesota and Ohio) nonprofit organizations that meet certain prerequisites.[5]

Some authorizers do exemplary work. More than 120 of them—including many of the largest, which together oversee more than half of all charter schools—adhere to the sound principles laid down by the National Association of Charter School Authorizers (NACSA), at the heart of which are these three:

- *Operator standards*: Maintain high standards for approving charter applications and for overseeing schools. This encompasses safeguarding the rights of students to equal access to the school of their choice and to fair treatment in receiving needed services. It may also include closing schools that fail to meet standards and targets described in law and contract.
- *Protect school autonomy*: Preserve a charter school's core school autonomies as these relate to independent boards, personnel, budgeting, and programming, all the while holding the school accountable for results.
- *Preserve the public welfare*: Uphold the public interest by making the interests of students the fundamental value that informs all that the authorizer does, ensuring that its own work is transparent and guided by the highest ethical and professional standards.[6]

Yet the overwhelming majority of authorizers, responsible for nearly half of all charter schools, are not affiliated with NACSA, and some do a mediocre (or worse) job of overseeing the schools in their portfolios. Some are driven by incentives that may be rational for them yet perverse from the standpoint of quality chartering. This is most evident in the impulse to maximize their own revenues by taking on more and bigger schools, selling extra services to the schools they sponsor, and failing to curb mediocrity, lest the money the authorizer derives from pupil numbers should decline.[7]

Plenty of authorizers also lack judgment, courage, or expertise. Especially when it's responsible for just one or two charter schools, as is common when districts serve in this capacity, an authorizer is unlikely to employ specialized staff for this function and may not even know what best practices in this realm look like. Habituated to running all its schools directly, a district authorizer may not understand how to handle the delicate charter balance between autonomy and accountability. If it isn't excessively casual about shoddy school performance, it may err in the opposite direction and slip into overregulating and micromanaging the schools in its portfolio—a temptation that also lures nondistrict authorizers bent on minimizing risk and avoiding error.[8]

These problems illustrate the challenge of the regulated marketplace. If competition alone does not yield adequate instructional quality, child-oriented priorities, and sound business practices in the charter sector, and if more regulation by government causes at least as many problems for charters as it solves, then top-notch authorizers become essential. They must strike a balance that is neither the old-fashioned uniformity of a bureaucratic monopoly nor a laissez-faire regime in which anyone can do whatever they wish in regard to the education of children. Freedom, openness, and opportunity bring many good things that public education has lacked. But these qualities also create gaps and temptations that allow mischief. This, in turn, invites regulations that can go too far and sap the potential of chartering. Calibrating this balance and fine-tuning it when necessary is the core duty of authorizers, yet they don't have total control, for they and the schools in their portfolios are also subject to myriad state and local laws and regulations. These ground rules from government also call for attention if balance is to be achieved. But authorizers, too, need to be held accountable, which is another issue that few states have fully worked out.

WHO WATCHES THE WATCHERS?

How and to whom is the authorizer itself accountable? Where local districts and state agencies are cast in this role, they're theoretically accountable to the voters for how well they play it. That's not entirely persuasive, however, because public bodies can be captured by stakeholder factions and buffeted by politics. They, too, should be accountable in other ways: transparent in their decision making, evaluated by outside parties, and more. But the challenge deepens when authorizers are essentially independent entities (including universities and nonprofits) rather than government units. In those cases, the authorizer functions as an agent of the state and sometimes must be approved by the state to serve in this capacity. That does not, however, mean the state is diligent about monitoring authorizers' probity and effectiveness. Often, it has limited capacity to do this, and it, too, is battered by politics and other pressures, including pressure from authorizers and their political allies not to fuss too much.

Eighteen years after passing the nation's first charter law, Minnesota officials realized that their state had too many authorizers, that some were doing shoddy work, and that more oversight was needed. This led to a statutory change in 2009, to a culling of North Star State authorizers, stepped up monitoring by the state education department, and a higher ranking in the National Alliance for Public Charter Schools (NAPCS) appraisal of charter laws.[9] On the ground in Ohio, we at Fordham were learning the same lesson, but there, too, it took years to persuade lawmakers that the state must actively monitor the performance of charter sponsors acting on its behalf. A reform measure finally cleared the legislative hurdles in 2015 after overcoming intense opposition from wary authorizers, the schools that had benefited from lax oversight, and the campaign contributions of some prosperous charter operators (see chapter 10 for more details). In other states with iffy accountability for authorizers, private organizations have begun to rank or grade them. For example, Education

Trust–Midwest, together with several other Michigan-based groups, produced a 2015 report card on fourteen authorizers in the Wolverine State. Only six earned A's.[10]

TOO FEW OPTIONS FOR AUTHORIZERS

Good authorizing can make a material difference in school performance. As noted earlier, a study by analysts associated with the National Bureau of Economic Research showed the importance of authorizers' work (among other factors) in closing and opening schools—labor that led to gains in Texas charter quality from 2001 to 2011.[11] Yet nearly all authorizers, good and bad, are plagued by a shortage of workable solutions to sundry difficulties that their schools may encounter.

Recall the fundamental bargain: a school succeeds and is renewed, or it fails and is closed (or non-renewed at the end of its charter term). These stark, binary, life-or-death options are not wrong in theory. In practice, however, such choices are too limiting. What if a school is simply mediocre? Poorly administered? Inefficient? Effective with some students but not others? Strong in some grades or subjects but weak in others? Must it be shut down? Or given a free pass to continue in its disappointing ways? What are the alternatives to closing an ineffectual charter school and turning its pupils onto the street? Is it the authorizer's duty—and does it have the expertise—to play school doctor and try to rectify the situation? Should it provide some services or functions itself, or possibly sell them to the school? Does it have the courage—and legal authority—to restart a charter by finding a different operator, principal, or governing board for the faltering school while keeping the same students in that building? But if it does intervene to set matters right, how does it avoid turning into the heavy-handed central office of an old-fashioned district? How does an authorizer finesse the conflict of interest that can arise when—driven by its earnest understanding of the children's best interest—it compromises its own capacity to judge a school's results objectively? (The school team could reasonably ask its authorizer, "How can you ding us for weak results when they were produced by following your own recommendations?") America's charter laws and regulations today fail to provide a sufficient arsenal of responses to questions like these.

Authorizers, for the most part, must simply point their thumbs up or down.

When shutting a school, or not renewing it, does turn out to be the best (or unavoidable) option, other tough questions arise. What, for example, is the sponsor's duty with regard to the future education of the children who have been attending the school? Must the sponsor find an alternative for them? A *better* alternative? Who owns the closed school's assets, pays its debts, and handles the residue of its contracts with staff and vendors? What if the state auditor hasn't finished digging through its murky financial records?

As we noted in chapter 2, thousands of charter schools have failed or been closed over the years.[12] Moreover, despite the expectation that academic results determine a school's longevity, in reality most closings don't happen because of educational shortcomings. Instead, the schools shut down as a consequence of financial miscalculations, misbehavior, faulty governance, flawed leadership, lack of student demand, or pure bad luck (e.g., a key person moves away or gets ill). In these situations, sometimes the authorizer pulls the plug, sometimes auditors or law enforcers determine its demise, and sometimes the school simply implodes or quietly declines into bankruptcy and nothingness. Still, closures for reasons of academic performance are increasing with time, which suggests both that authorizers are getting fussier about academics and, maybe, that they're taking greater pains with who gets charters in the first place.[13]

In short, today's authorizer challenges began twenty-five years ago with little awareness of the intricacies that this role would involve. Over that period, much has been learned and codified both in law and through groups like NACSA. But the authorizer's key role in quality control remains unsettled in most states. As of January 2016, NAPCS lists only three jurisdictions (Alabama, the District of Columbia, and Hawaii) that include all the elements that the organization's model law deems necessary for authorizer and program accountability, and just one jurisdiction (Louisiana) incorporates all the recommended processes for ensuring a transparent charter application, review, and decision-making process.[14] The bottom line is that much still remains to be done on this front, most of it by way of strengthening state policy and adding both to authorizers' options and to their own oversight.

GOVERNING BOARDS

Many charters begin when a group of parents, teachers, or community leaders comes together to write an application that, if successful, enables them to form their own school (or possibly convert a district school), select its leaders, and get under way. In those cases, the initial group usually morphs into the school's governing board.

In other instances, a strong school founder—an individual or firm with a passion to launch or replicate a school—recruits its board, which may end up more beholden to the leader's (or outside operator's) desires than to student needs and the public interest. Board capacity and competence are challenges, too, as schools need all manner of know-how, including strategy, finance, real estate, pedagogy, human resources, employment law, community relations, and the subtleties of stakeholder engagement. In traditional public education, deploying such expertise is the district's responsibility (which isn't to say it's always done well). Such an array of talent is a lot harder to assemble within a five- or seven-member board for a stand-alone school that has a tiny leadership team and serves a few hundred kids.

The District of Columbia's 62 charter boards contain more than 690 individuals, about 11 each. California has 1,260 charter schools with some 560 governing bodies. At just 5 members each, the California boards would need almost 3,000 individuals to serve on them.[15] At 10 each, they'd need nearly 6,000. Multiply the total number of charters today by five to ten board members to get national estimates. This daunting task has led to the emergence of new organizations like Charter Board Partners in the District of Columbia, whose mission is to recruit and train individuals for governing boards in the nation's capital, and BoardOnTrack, which operates nationally and already provides training to nearly 3,000 board members. This is also a further reason for the emergence and growth of charter networks—virtual districts, in many ways—that can handle sundry duties and muster many kinds of expertise on behalf of the schools they run.

OPERATORS

Many of America's highest-performing and most respected charters participate in networks and are operated by management organizations that are at least partly separate from the schools themselves. There's much to be said for this arrangement, which can bring economies of scale, sophisticated back-office services, distinguished boards, and multitalented leadership teams. Such networks can also offer competent troubleshooting, well-planned HR pipelines, coherent curricula, and the capacity to raise private funds and press for favorable public policies. In addition to providing stability in times of transitions, this structure can deliver consistent instructional programming that may span the students' entire K–12 sequence and beyond, and the benefits of name branding that signals some uniformity from school to school across municipal and state boundaries.

Not every operator, however, delivers consistent quality. Some run few or no top-notch schools, while others have mixed track records. That's true of several nonprofit CMOs, but the most troublesome operator issues have arisen with profit-seeking firms that contract with schools to oversee their entire operation. (To our knowledge, only in Arizona can a for-profit entity receive a charter directly from the state and function as the school's governing body.) Such firms have occasionally spearheaded the entire creation of the school, forming their own nonprofit shells to hold the contracts, then stocking those governing bodies with handpicked teams of generally compliant individuals. This deck stacking makes it highly unlikely that a school's governing board will warn, penalize, or dismiss the operator, no matter how poorly the school performs, and places the entire accountability burden on others, such as the authorizer or state. Profit hunger also comes into play on the operator's part, driven by owners, shareholders, or investors, which can lead to cutting corners on staff and other pricey resources that serve students, as well as diluting academic standards so as to attract and retain more pupils and the public dollars that accompany them to school.

Entrepreneurialism and private investment have brought much energy, inventiveness, and resources into education reform. We've got nothing against profit (which has been present in public education since the first school bought its first pencil from a commercial firm). But we've also observed a sizable number of for-profit operators that operate low-performing schools yet fiercely fight—in courtrooms and legislative corridors when necessary—all efforts by the governing boards, authorizers, and public authorities to terminate the relationship. Clearly, someone with authority must also look after the best interests of a school's pupils—and the state's taxpayers.

SCHOOL LEADERSHIP

When it comes to school leaders, save for a few tightly run networks in which they function more like unit managers, most charter principals have wide-ranging authority and weighty responsibility. They resemble independent-school heads more than conventional public school principals, as they have the power to make staffing, budget, and curriculum decisions and must deal with boards, parents, community leaders, and local politics, not just internal school operations. In most states, charter principals need not hold conventional administrator certificates or credentials from colleges of education, even when their teachers must hold standard licenses. Leading—and often founding—charter schools has turned out to be a grand opportunity for visionary education reformers, Teach For America alums, inspired entrepreneurs, good-hearted community leaders, and—alas—some sorely inadequate (and sometimes greedily corrupt) individuals.

The freedom to hire almost anyone as principal cuts both ways. It creates the opportunity for charters to recruit outstanding leaders who would probably never seek conventional certification as school administrators. Consider, for example, Donald Hense, who made his career in civil rights organizations and university leadership before founding the District of Columbia's highly regarded Friendship Public Charter School, which over fifteen years has grown into eleven campuses serving disadvantaged neighborhoods of the nation's capital.[16] Yet that same freedom meant that former football player William Peterson, with no relevant experience of any kind, could found and lead a half dozen Ohio charters (one of them gallingly misnamed the Colin Powell Leadership Academy) until he and his brother pleaded guilty to fraud and theft of public dollars in connection with their exceptionally low-performing schools.[17]

Considering that no industry consisting of nearly seven thousand start-ups is going to have great leaders at the helm of every single unit, the charter sector has generally fared well on the leadership front. Indeed, some of the most highly respected charter networks (KIPP,

Building Excellent Schools, High Tech High, etc.) center their entire growth strategy on the identification and preparation of top-notch principals. Diligent authorizers also have considerable say in this realm, as one of their duties is to vet a proposed school's leadership and governance arrangement and the bona fides of the individuals associated with it. Greater challenges are associated with burnout and succession issues, particularly in one-off schools, many of which are founded by highly motivated individuals who put their all into making the schools succeed but cannot keep doing that forever.

Legally, the responsibility for finding a new leader—and, really, for everything else—is vested in the school's governing body. Since most charter boards, like other nonprofit boards, are self-perpetuating, the initial group is usually responsible for any replacements and additions to itself. This means that, as in other spheres, there's a risk of in-group coziness and obliviousness to key constituencies, markets, relationships, sound business practices, and potentially superior education strategies. There is also, inevitably, the risk of board member collusion with an avaricious school operator or crooked school head, as well as the simpler risk of clueless board members not knowing enough about dubious practices within the school to halt them.

By no means do we suggest that thousands of charter boards are failing to do right by their schools and pupils. Most, in our experience, comprise earnest, honest, selfless people who range from prominent civic and business leaders to fired-up inner-city residents bent on getting more kids a fairer shake. But sound character and noble intentions do not equate to multifaceted expertise and diligent oversight. As the charter sector continues to grow, moreover, the demand for individuals to serve on its school boards will someday rival the ninety thousand members of traditional district boards. On the one hand, charters represent a remarkable example of civil society in action: a twenty-first-century illustration of what Tocqueville admired in America and an education equivalent of Burke's "little platoons" that are so important to a viable, free society. On the other hand, because we're dealing with the future of children and sizable amounts of taxpayer dollars, we need to keep risk within bounds and not just assume that any old group of people can be counted on to run a viable public school. Ultimately, school leadership, too, must be monitored by scrupulous authorizers that rigorously vet the competence and track records, as well as the character, of those to whom they're entrusting a charter.

GOVERNANCE DILEMMAS

The often-fraught intersection of authorizer, operator, governing board, and school leader illustrates but by no means exhausts the structural and governance quandaries that chartering has surfaced. Consider this question: Is a charter school best viewed and governed as a district in its own right—the equivalent of a local education agency—or as part of a traditional district? What happens, and who pays, when a school draws students from other districts, even other states? And what to make of—and how to govern—charter networks that function like virtual districts in their own right but sprawl across municipal borders and sometimes state lines? (Some EMOs and CMOs now also operate schools in other countries.)[18]

Nothing in America's history of locally based public schooling, with its layering of three or more levels of government (and funding and regulations from all of them), aligns very well with the charter phenomenon. Of course, it was—we believe—shortcomings and blind spots in the traditional arrangement that gave rise to chartering in the first place, so we ought not be surprised that the arrival of a new model for public education has led to uncertainties and unresolved questions as well as friction with the old one.

The policy theorists, political leaders, and advocates who gave birth to chartering plainly failed to think such questions all the way through. With the benefit of hindsight, however, we can also see that this wasn't just heedlessness. Honest, thorough answers to such queries must inevitably disrupt the traditional arrangements (as indeed they have done) while alarming those with stakes in those arrangements or in the philosophies and policies that undergird them. Tactically, because advocates believed that charters were needed to improve public education for at-risk children, it was prudent to let sleeping dogs continue to slumber and not surface too many such challenges in advance. Instead, they would let matters take their course and devise ad hoc answers in specific situations. Such improvisation, however, is not the wisest course going forward.

Proponents of chartering now need to revisit some fundamentals regarding governance, both tightening excessively loose arrangements, particularly regarding the obligations and accountability of authorizers, while at the same time encouraging further innovation in this realm. Why should state laws require every school to have its own governing board? What about more options for authorizers faced with mediocre schools? How about paying for authorizing in ways that do not create conflicts of interest for tough-minded sponsors—but simultaneously barring authorizers from selling ancillary services to the schools in their portfolios? What about statewide financing arrangements for charters that draw pupils from multiple districts—and multistate authorizers to oversee multistate CMOs and EMOs? This list can and should be extended. The point—a frequent one in these pages—is that the future of chartering should not be a linear extension of the past. That we left some problems unsolved (or didn't know they would become problems) in 1991 is no reason not to strive to set matters right in 2016.

8

Funding, Philanthropy, and the Profit Motive

BUDGETS ARE OFTEN tight in charter, district, and private schools alike. Administrators from Hawaii to Maine too often find themselves hacking into programs and activities that many children and parents regard as important—arts education, gifted and talented classes, athletics, and more—in order to give teachers the raises they are owed and to preserve the academic core of the curriculum. Early charter advocates, however, may be said to have cut their schools' budgets preemptively and, in retrospect, naively. Among the compromises they made in order to get charter laws passed and schools launched was acceptance of funding arrangements that yielded less for their classrooms than was being spent in nearby district schools attended by similar children. Assisted by a rearview mirror, we can see that those compromises in most places amounted to a damaging misjudgment, however necessary it may have seemed at the time. Faced almost everywhere with influential opponents skeptical of chartering and loath to forgo any district revenues or teacher jobs, and earnest in their own belief that charters could do more with less as long as the schools had the requisite freedom, advocates settled almost everywhere for fiscal formulas that would prove very lean indeed.

They also settled in most places for weak, vague, or nonexistent help with the cost of school facilities. That wouldn't be a big issue for conversion charters, which generally remain in the same buildings, like a snail in its own shell. But start-from-scratch schools, unless entirely virtual, need some usable space—space that fire marshals and building inspectors approve—in which children and teachers can gather. For that, however, school founders often had to scrounge. Philanthropy lent some of them a hand, occasionally a big hand, and this proved crucial in the spread of chartering and the replication of some successful models. But philanthropy, as usual, brought strings of its own.

Another early and welcome but ultimately mixed blessing on the fiscal front was the infusion of private capital and entrepreneurial zeal into chartering. This, too, made possible innovations and expansions that likely would not have occurred without it, as well as much dynamism and influential connections. But it also brought charges of privatizing and profiteering—allegations that would prove politically damaging and were sometimes justified. This chapter examines the related issues of charter funding, facilities, philanthropic involvement, and the profit motive.

PER-PUPIL REVENUES

Charter and district schools draw their revenues from the same four main sources. Three are public: federal, state, and local governments. The fourth is private, comprising philanthropic grants, private contributions, earned income, and investor dollars. In combination, moneys from these sources constitute a school's operating budget. (Capital and facilities funding are generally treated separately.) In policy discussions, this total is routinely divided by a school's enrollment and restated as per-pupil revenue. That number ordinarily rises and falls with several variables, including which state and district the school is in, the grades that it serves, and its students' special needs. For present purposes, what matters is that per-pupil funding also varies by school type—that is, charter or district.

A simple per-pupil average is, of course, a wild simplification of some of the most complicated realities to be found anywhere in public finance. Treating the sum of multiple funding streams as a single figure is misleading, too, as each stream comes from sources that dictate the uses of their dollars. Charters can, up to a point, commingle funding streams. But mostly they, too, must spend their dollars on the activities, programs, services, and other categories for which they were provided.[1] Most states furnish their charters with a fixed per-pupil sum of operating dollars, which may be augmented for special-needs and low-income pupils as well as various other categorical programs.

Federal dollars come almost entirely from such programs, which are mostly earmarked for the education of specific categories of children, particularly those who are poor, disabled, or English language learners, and for lunch subsidies, professional development for teachers, and other targeted activities. Whether and how these categorical dollars reach charters can vary enormously from school to school and place to place—and generally entail much paperwork, so much so that small one-off charters sometimes forgo the money because they can't realistically navigate the bureaucratics of getting and keeping track of it.

The biggest fiscal challenge faced by charters is that they seldom share in the funds that local districts raise to supplement their state and federal dollars. Those moneys come from municipal or county taxes, which are often property-based and levy-generated. Nationally, the local share of public school funding is about 45 percent, but in many places, it's much larger. (In Montgomery County, Maryland, where two of us live, local funding constitutes two-thirds of the school system's budget.) Under most state laws, however, charter schools cannot access such locally generated dollars, even when they're located within district boundaries and enroll children who would otherwise attend district-operated schools. And in places where charters have some access to local dollars, the per-student portion is almost always less than district schools receive.[2]

This disparity between what charter and district schools derive from local sources causes the greatest shortfall in charter operating funds. A 2014 University of Arkansas study found that the typical charter gets 28 percent less per pupil in weighted total funding than nearby district schools get.[3] Averaged across the nation, that's a $3,800 per-pupil gap, amounting to nearly $1.6 million in missing revenue for an average-size charter, equivalent to the salaries and benefits of at least twenty teachers. Moreover, the disparity appears to be widening: similar studies in 2004 and 2007 found gaps of 22 and 19 percent.[4]

Table 8.1 displays the shortfall for five states and Washington, DC, illustrating the size of these gaps and their variance from place to place. The study from which these data come looked at thirty-one jurisdictions. In nineteen of these, the weighted disparity was at least

TABLE 8.1   Per-pupil revenue (PPR) for district and charter schools,
             selected states, 2011

State	District weighted PPR*	Charter PPR	Weighted funding disparity*	Percentage variance
Louisiana	$26,735	$11,134	−$15,600	−58.4%
Washington, DC	$32,822	$20,086	−$12,736	−38.8%
Ohio	$11,764	$8,580	−$3,184	−27.1%
Minnesota	$14,843	$11,429	−$3,414	−23.0%
Arizona	$9,532	$7,783	−$1,749	−18.4%
Tennessee	$10,621	$10,635	$15	0.1%

Source: Meagan Batdorff et al., "Charter School Funding: Inequity Expands," School Choice Demonstration Project, Department of Education Reform, University of Arkansas, April 2014, www.uaedreform.org/wp-content/uploads/charter-funding-inequity-expands.pdf.

* Weighting assumes that "districts have the same urban/metro vs. suburban/rural proportion of enrollment as charter schools." PPR and funding are weighted because charters are more likely to be urban, and urban schooling costs more than suburban and rural schooling. Meagan Batdorff et al., "Charter School Funding: Inequity Expands," School Choice Demonstration Project, Department of Education Reform, University of Arkansas, April 2014, www.uaedreform.org /wp-content/uploads/charter-funding-inequity-expands.pdf.

25 percent.[5] In just three was it less than 15 percent. Only Tennessee gave its charters *more* money—a paltry fifteen dollars more per pupil each year.

Money does not cause schools to be great, but an impoverished school—in any sector—has difficulty meeting every child's education needs. A few years ago, for example, students in a Miami charter high school went weeks without textbooks. Seventh graders in another Miami-Dade charter (now shuttered) went to class in a tool shed.[6] Yes, those are extreme examples, and funding is also a problem for many district schools, far too many of which house students in "portables" and teach from tattered, obsolete textbooks. But overall budgets are even tighter in charters, which generally respond by employing fewer adults per child than traditional schools. The freedom of most charters from collective-bargaining constraints means they have greater flexibility on the HR front than do most district schools, and some charters have made impressive moves toward blended learning and other potentially cost-saving delivery arrangements. Yet classes can get only so large and the curriculum only so narrow before the school ceases to be an attractive option for children and parents. It needs to attract teachers, too, but along with bigger classes, charters typically pay their instructors and other staff less than district schools (and sometimes less than private schools), which puts them at a competitive disadvantage in the always-tight marketplace for outstanding classroom practitioners (see appendix table A.2). Although many charters match district salaries for beginning teachers, few of the schools can keep up with the rising pay scales for classroom veterans, who are the most likely to have families and therefore also the most likely to exit the charter sector for other schools or lines of work where they can make a better living.[7]

FACILITIES

Facility costs pose even greater challenges for many charters. Districts typically have separate capital budgets, often involving state dollars, sometimes "tobacco settlement" dollars, and frequently bond-issue dollars. This money is meant to construct, improve, and replace school buildings and often covers new equipment—furniture, technology, ADA-compliance modifications, etc.—for those buildings.[8] For charters, however, separate capital funding from public sources is rare and, when available at all, generally skimpy.[9] In 2015, one third of the forty-three jurisdictions with charter laws made no provision at all to assist these schools with facilities. Just seven gave them access to the facility-financing programs that serve district schools. Fifteen provided some per-pupil facility allowances for charters, but only in Arizona, Georgia, Minnesota, and the District of Columbia did the amount exceed $1,000 per pupil. And of those jurisdictions with facility grant or loan programs on the statute books, barely half were actually funding them.[10]

Although learning can occur with a teacher on one end of the proverbial log and a pupil on the other, parents understandably care about the condition of the place where they leave their kids all day, and teachers care about the condition of their workplace. ("Do I have my own classroom, or am I moving around all day?" "Is there a place where I can relax and eat lunch—and one where I can meet with students for tutoring or advising?" "Is there safe nearby parking?") The nature of the facility also affects the education program. Charters aren't always housed in buildings meant to serve as schools. Some are in church basements, community centers, even storefronts. Often that means teachers and students must clear out when those facilities revert to their other functions.

The absence of adequate capital funding means that charter schools must often cover the cost of their facilities from within their already-strapped operating budgets. Typically, they lease or borrow a facility rather than owning it. But if your classrooms must be returned to the Boys and Girls Club at 3:00 p.m., it's impossible to run an extended-day program. If the building isn't air-conditioned (or the budget won't cover the electric bill), it's hard to run an extended-year program in much of the country. Few such buildings have conventional schoolhouse features like libraries, kitchens, gyms, and computer labs.[11] According to a ten-state survey by the Charter School Facilities Initiative in 2013, most charters lacked kitchens sufficient to prepare meals in accord with federal standards. In three of the ten states, half the charters operated without access to a gymnasium.[12]

Private dollars assist some charters with facility costs. The for-profit Turner-Agassi Charter School Facilities Fund, for example, helps with predevelopment, design, construction, and purchase options, as well as site selection and acquisition.[13] It has already assisted schools in at least ten states with more than $225 million in development costs.[14] The nonprofit Local Initiatives Support Corporation has, since 1997, given "more than $265 million in loans, tax credit allocations, guarantees and grants to finance charter school facilities in low-income neighborhoods."[15] In other places, local donors spring for charter facilities. For example, the KIPP schools in Columbus, Ohio, sit on a lovely $30 million 124-acre campus—a former golf course—that opened in 2014 with the help of a major capital campaign led by Abigail Wexner, the vice chair of the Columbus KIPP board (and one of the community's wealthiest residents). At its unveiling, the school's executive director announced that Battelle Memorial Institute was donating an additional $3 million to build an adjacent science center.[16]

Few charters are as fortunate. There isn't enough philanthropic money to go around, and what's available isn't spread evenly. Instead, the obvious solution to charter facility challenges is to move into disused school buildings that belong to the district, to share underused district structures, or to acquire former Catholic schools. Many charter laws provide for such arrangements, and a March 2015 report by the National Charter School Resource Center found that charter access to such facilities has been improving.[17] Yet many districts resist sharing their buildings with upstart schools that they view as nuisances or rivals. And where district schools are full or enrollments are rising, there's little space to share. This poses a particular problem for charters in places with high-priced real estate, such as Los Angeles and New York City. One solution—much used in the latter—has been to co-locate charters along with district-operated schools in city-owned buildings.[18] But co-location is the source of endless conflict, both at a political level and within a building where two or more schools may jostle for use of the gym, the lunchroom, even the down staircase.

PHILANTHROPY

Private money, which makes up less than 1 percent of all public school revenues, is far more unpredictable than government dollars.[19] Both charter and district schools actively pursue such funding, however, and the charter sector and other jurisdictional challengers in K–12 education have fared pretty well, at least in some communities—and sometimes at the expense of districts and their programs. Some of these benefactions can be large. Besides the Columbus KIPP example noted above, KIPP DC received a $4.2 million gift in 2015, the largest in the network's history. (Yet KIPP DC schools took in almost $100 million in total revenue that year, the lion's share of it from public sources.)[20]

Even as some charters have succeeded at private fund-raising, others reap little or nothing from philanthropic sources.[21] In the District of Columbia, for example, between 2012 and 2014, eight of the city's many charters accounted for 75 percent of all charitable dollars received by the entire sector—and three of them brought in half. This asymmetry is partly caused by capital campaigns that attract very large gifts to a few fortunate or enterprising schools. So while philanthropic dollars are surely welcome when they arrive, they're a shaky source of support for school operations and facilities.

Still, some critics contend that philanthropy plays an outsized role in supporting charters and regard this money as pushing public education ever closer to privatization.[22] They also note, with some justice, that more money for charter schools has meant less for district schools and district-supported programs and organizations.[23] Yet this playing field, if tipped at all, slopes slightly in the opposite direction. Analysts at the University of Arkansas—a research team whose enthusiasm for charters and other forms of school choice rivals their solid scholarly credentials—found that "traditional public schools received slightly more funds from nonpublic and charitable sources, per-pupil, in 2010-11 than did public charter schools." The difference amounted to $571 going to district schools versus $552 to charters.[24] The larger point is that both figures represent drops in the schools' respective revenue buckets.

A different and more vexing issue regarding charter-related philanthropy is how the evolution of this education sector has intersected with the evolution of philanthropy itself, from individual donors and foundations responding to requests from diverse directions to a more proactive strategy whereby philanthropists—often working in league—deploy money in pursuit of their own predetermined ends. Such "strategic" or "venture" philanthropy has led major donors to try to mold the charter sector by deciding which populations should be served by what kinds of schools located in which communities, then focusing their largesse on grantees that advance their agendas. The typical recipients of such support are urban schools for poor and minority youngsters, schools with a traditional academic focus, and a no-excuses approach to teaching and learning. A related issue concerns philanthropy "partnering" with government agencies that seek to leverage private dollars to further their own agendas. This was a feature of some Obama education programs that required recipients to match federal monies with philanthropic dollars, which wound up being spent on projects selected by government.[25]

There's been huge philanthropic emphasis on growing the charter sectors in cities like New Orleans, Los Angeles, San Antonio, Newark, Washington, and New York. Donors have also teamed up to develop *expediters* such as the Charter School Growth Fund and the NewSchools Venture Fund (which in turn focus on certain places and kinds of schools, again most often the no-excuses kind). And much private giving has concentrated on scaling favored school networks (e.g., KIPP, Achievement First, and Aspire) that have proven especially innovative or effective—or enjoyed great press.[26] The KIPP network, as described earlier, has grown from 2 schools in 1994 to 183 today and plans to expand to serve over one hundred thousand youngsters at a time.[27] Little of this would be possible without philanthropy.

Even as we laud the private generosity that has brought many fine charters into being to serve tens of thousands of needy children, we must also ask whether philanthropy's role in shaping this sector over the past two decades has excessively narrowed its scope and constrained its possibilities. When the bulk of available donor dollars has gone into missions determined by the donors themselves, there's not much left with which to explore other potentially valuable roles for chartering or to serve populations of children with other needs that charters might address. And that's without even getting to the question of whether philanthropy's interest in charters and affiliated groups has kept district schools and district-linked programs from doing all they could for other needy children.

THE PROFIT MOTIVE

Nearly 15 percent of today's charter schools operate under the aegis of profit-seeking organizations such as National Heritage Academies, Imagine Schools, Charter Schools USA, K12, and the Leona Group.[28] These entities, beholden to investors and shareholders who legitimately seek a return, employ business models quite different from the nonprofit version.

Although actual charters for schools must, nearly everywhere, be held by nonprofit entities, in most states the schools' governing boards may engage for-profit firms to operate them.[29] How often this happens varies by state (table 8.2). We see that EMO schools are widespread in Michigan and Florida, for example, but not in Texas, Wisconsin, or Minnesota.[30]

There's nothing new or—in our eyes—reprehensible about investor profits arising from private firms' participation in various elements of public education, any more than a paving contractor that profits from work it does for the highway department. And such investment brings substantial benefits. As Frederick Hess has explained, "In sector after sector, solving new problems—or more effectively addressing stubborn ones—has been the province of new entrants."[31] Indeed, the pursuit of profit has long played a valuable role in US public education. Most schools—district as well as charter—have long obtained their

TABLE 8.2   School management in states with the most charters, 2014

State	All charter schools	One-off schools	EMO schools	CMO schools
California	918	660	21	237
Texas	559	229	2	328
Arizona	509	284	100	125
Florida	460	298	147	15
Ohio	340	171	101	68
Michigan	241	74	149	18
Wisconsin	206	202	4	0
New York	170	102	19	49
Colorado	167	142	15	10
Minnesota	149	147	1	1

Source: Data provided by the National Alliance for Public Charter Schools, January 8, 2016.

Note: EMO = education management organization (for-profit); CMO = charter management organization (nonprofit).

textbooks from companies like Pearson, McGraw-Hill, and Houghton Mifflin Harcourt.[32] The current K–12 school publishing business is estimated to yield such firms about $5.5 billion in revenue per year, or about $110 per student.[33] Private firms supply schools with their furniture, their technology, even the erasers for their whiteboards.

Many districts also contract with such companies for services that are easier, better, or cheaper to outsource than to provide directly. These include bus transportation, building security, hot meals, and, sometimes, direct services for individual children in need of speech therapy, psychological counseling, or other treatments. Other districts hire private consultants to advise on budgets, administrative structures, and leadership strategies. Online learning systems run by for-profit firms are widespread. And the creation, administration, and scoring of standardized tests and related measures are ordinarily entrusted to such firms.[34]

Within the charter sector, entrepreneurs and investors have infused much energy, vision, and managerial expertise, as well as many millions of capital dollars. Some firms have prospered by supplying auxiliary services to charters rather than running entire schools, and these services have often been efficient and valuable.[35] Rosetta Stone, for example, sells language-learning services to schools as part of its Global Enterprise & Education unit, which brought in $84.7 million in 2014.[36] And that's just one company among many. To assist its members, the California Charter Schools Association lists vendors of services in more than thirty-five categories.[37]

There is, of course, a difference between vendors that provide a service to a public education enterprise and private firms that take on the whole project, in this case, running entire schools. Only in the charter sector do we find the latter, and for some firms, this has indeed proven profitable, though seldom hugely so. For example, in the fiscal year ending in June 2015, the firm K12, which operates virtual schools in thirty-two states and the District of Columbia, earned a net income of $9.3 million (down from almost twice as much the prior year).[38]

There's nothing inherently wrong with profiting from running a school as long as it's a good one. But schools that utilize outside entities for some or all of their work must still deliver satisfactory student outcomes. In chapter 4, we reviewed the weak academic results of many virtual charters, most of which are run by profit-seeking firms. But this problem goes beyond online schools: in 2009–2010, for example, 51 percent of charters operating under EMOs made adequate yearly progress (AYP) as defined by No Child Left Behind, compared with 66 percent of schools managed by nonprofit CMOs and 59 percent of freestanding charters that made AYP that year.[39]

Something is plainly awry when schools or their service providers enrich their owners while producing shoddy pupil outcomes. One inevitably suspects that a profit-seeking school with low-performing students is shorting its educational mission in order to make money, while one may suppose that a nonprofit school with similarly weak results is simply incompetent. Both sets of assumptions undoubtedly oversimplify complex reasons for success and failure—but in some instances they're probably valid.

One lesson we have learned from twenty-five years of chartering is that while this sector welcomes the capital, enterprise, and dynamism that accompany the profit motive, it didn't take seriously enough the downside risk of profiteering. Nor did early enthusiasts consider that the pursuit of such gain might lead some enterprises to engage in practices that tarnish the brand itself. In Ohio, for example, the Imagine Columbus Primary Academy charter school was managed by Virginia-based Imagine Schools, Inc. In May 2015, six of the school's board members resigned "amid ongoing concerns about a high-cost building lease [that consumed more than half of the school's $1.3 million yearly budget], teacher turnover and adequate services for students."[40] The $58,000 monthly lease was with a subsidiary of Imagine Schools called Schoolhouse Finance, which had purchased the building in 2005 for $1.5 million. After spending $2.6 million on capital improvements, Schoolhouse Finance sold it to a real estate trust for $5.2 million—enjoying a $1.1 million profit—and then leased the building back from the trust and charged rent to Columbus Primary.[41] An earlier 2011 investigation in Missouri uncovered "complicated real estate deals through which the six Imagine schools operating in St. Louis with public dollars 'are generating millions of dollars' for Imagine and a Kansas City–based real estate investment company," and reported that the city's Imagine schools had performed worse than "practically any other school in the city."[42]

In other cases, individuals associated with management firms have been accused of using school dollars improperly. In Pennsylvania, five people were charged "in connection with schemes to defraud three charter schools of more than $6.7 million."[43] And a 2015 case in the District of Columbia found that a management company led by Kent Amos had received more than $14 million from the Dorothy I. Height Community Academy Public Charter Schools (which Amos had founded) since 2004.[44] Amos himself received about $1.15 million in income in 2012 from the management company and $1.38 million in 2013.[45] (He agreed to pay $3 million "to settle a lawsuit that alleged he used the company to divert taxpayer funds from the school for his personal gain.")[46]

Such instances of malfeasance are exceptional, and plenty of examples of greed can also be found in the nonprofit and public sectors. Such behavior is obviously unacceptable wherever it occurs. But rotten apples in the for-profit sector of K–12 education pose the greatest risk of spoiling the entire barrel.[47] In our view, just as teachers who add great academic value to their pupils should get bonuses, school operators that run quality schools yielding solid student results deserve whatever profit they can legitimately derive from their effort. Nobody, however, should get rich by producing shoddy goods, and the regulated marketplace of public education needs transparency and oversight procedures that minimize such incidents.[48]

THE EFFICIENCY CONUNDRUM

Were early charter proponents right to think that their schools could do more for less? As noted earlier, people eager to pass laws and get moving agreed to compromises that meant less money per pupil and little or no help with facilities. One impulse behind these concessions was the earnest belief—or hope—that charters would prove to be more efficient than traditional district schools as long as they had the requisite freedom.

Up to a point, that is surely true—or can be, when competently led schools are free to deploy their resources most efficaciously. As described in chapter 3, charters are often faulted because their average pupil achievement is no better than that of district schools. Yet charters accomplish this with 28 percent less money, plain proof of greater efficiency when it's simply defined as student learning divided by school revenues. Indeed, using such methods, University of Arkansas analysts found charters to be 40 percent more cost-effective than district schools in math and 41 percent more efficient in reading.[49]

That's not the whole story, however. Certain charters are exceptionally effective but accomplish this with the help of extra resources. Some no-excuses schools, for example, employ intensive learning models like longer school days and years that call for (and often obtain) more funding than the average charter school. The SEED schools, which include five nights per week of boarding facilities for exceptionally disadvantaged middle and high school pupils, cost at least $30,000 per student per year.[50]

Other schools that accomplish as much as, or more than, district schools, despite having less revenue might do *even more* if they had equivalent funding. And if that money were coupled with greater autonomy, the charter schools would be better able to experiment with novel educational models, imaginative uses of technology, and individualized progress of children through innovative, rigorous curricula.

Today, it's clear that charter schooling this past quarter century has been built on financial expectations and assumptions that need revisiting. In practice, this sector has concentrated on disadvantaged, minority youngsters—kids with costly educational needs, no matter where they attend school. While philanthropic dollars are a welcome if partial gap-closer, that's no excuse for denying charters—especially high-performing charters—the same public dollars that flow into other public schools serving similar children.[51] Accompanied by additional policy changes—such as curbs on abusive behavior by greedy entrepreneurs—the charter sector could do even more to produce solid results for children and to pioneer valuable innovations across the K–12 landscape.

Of course, the public education pie is only so large. But its long-term tendency has been to grow: average per-pupil revenue more than tripled in constant-dollar terms between 1965 and 2010.[52] If charters are expected—as they should be—to do a solid job of educating the children who choose to attend them, they deserve equitable funding, workable facilities, and certainly their fair share of future revenue growth.

9

Balancing Freedom and Regulation

THE *CHARTER BARGAIN*, as we have noted, is the exchange of operational freedom for schools in return for accountability tied to their results. As the then governor of Tennessee, Lamar Alexander, offered back in 1986, "governors are ready for some old-fashioned horse-trading. We'll regulate less if schools and school districts will produce better results."[1] Charters embody such a swap, which, as we've shown, also partakes of the tight-versus-loose approach to organizational management and the "steer, don't row" approach to reinventing government. States would prescribe the desired educational outcomes while freeing schools to produce those outcomes in the ways the schools themselves think best.

This, however, is far easier said than done. Three large realities contaminate any pure version of the charter bargain.

- *Necessary regulations*: Some rules are needed to ensure the safety and equitable treatment of children, the quality of their education, and the legitimate use of public dollars. But which regulations are truly vital and which are not? Where to draw the line between enough and too much? That's the perennial Goldilocks question—and one that elicits strongly conflicting views and different answers in different circumstances. We've already described cases of insufficient oversight (especially in the realm of authorizing), but we will also offer examples of gratuitous overregulation.

- *Long-lasting romance with inputs*: Few aspects of contemporary American life are more tightly regulated on the input and process side than public schooling. When we layer federal, state, and local statutes; standard practices (e.g., human resource and procurement procedures); the strings attached to categorical dollars; and multipage contracts with multiple unions, we find schools mandated and standardized in myriad ways. Although some districts have made earnest efforts to deregulate their schools and empower their principals, and although it's been a half century since James Coleman showed the wisdom of shifting accountability to outcomes, a systematic push to liberate and diversify any part of public education runs afoul of the thoroughly habituated culture of this enterprise.
- *Entrenched interests*: Innumerable interests within and around the K–12 cosmos benefit (or think they do) from regulation and standardization. These can be counted upon to oppose moves to undo, loosen, or waive provisions that protect their jobs, their contracts, their programs, their prerogatives, and the rights, safeguards, or privileges of their children. Moreover, because educational institutions contend for students, revenue, facilities, staff, status, and more, any initiative to ease the regulatory burden on some can be counted upon to elicit hostility from others that see themselves as having to compete on a tilted playing field.

To repeat, some requirements are fundamental to children's welfare—criminal background checks for school staff and fire safety inspections of facilities, for instance—and many are intended (successfully or not) to assure the thoroughness and quality of children's education. For example, laws in nearly every state require students to take a US history course during high school.

Yet many other mandates and regulations that bear on schools have more to do with the convenience of employees and the idiosyncrasies of politicians. Consider, for example, section 3313.801 of the Ohio Revised Code:

> If a copy of the official motto of the United States of America "In God We Trust" or the official motto of Ohio "With God, All Things Are Possible" is donated to any school district, or if money is donated to the district specifically for the purpose of

purchasing such material, the board of education of the school district shall accept the donation and display the motto in an appropriate manner in a classroom, auditorium, or cafeteria of a school building in the district, provided all of the following conditions are satisfied:

(1) The motto is printed on durable, poster-quality paper or displayed in a frame.
(2) The dimensions of the paper or frame are at least eight and one-half inches by eleven inches.
(3) The copy contains no words other than the motto and language identifying the motto as the motto of the United States of America or Ohio.
(4) The copy contains no images other than appropriate representations of the flag of the United States of America or Ohio.[2]

Hundreds of such regulations constrain district-operated schools—a problem much in need of solution—and all of those rules apply to charters, too, unless state law provides for them to be waived, either across the board for all charters or by allowing individual schools to seek specific exemptions. (Where the law permits negotiated waivers and exemptions, it's generally up to authorizers to decide which ones to grant to which schools.) Many of these rules and mandates serve to standardize and micromanage key elements that any private school or truly independent public school would routinely decide for itself: staff employment and HR issues, budgeting, curriculum, instructional practices. But to what extent should charter schools be truly independent?

Individual states, districts, and other authorizers have resolved this in myriad ways, with some cutting their charter schools considerably more slack than others.[3] One variable is whether the state treats charters as local education agencies in their own right, that is, the equivalent of school districts, or regards them as constituent parts of regular districts. In 2013, about 40 percent of charters were of the latter variety, while the majority were independent entities akin to districts themselves.[4] But each version carries its own long-established regulatory obligations for charters unless these are eased by statute or authorizer.

HOLES IN THE CHARTER BARGAIN

On the whole, these new schools never enjoyed the degree of autonomy that the charter bargain was intended (at least in the eyes of its designers) to confer on them. As of 2014, for example, of the forty-three jurisdictions with charter laws, twenty-one capped the number of charter schools within their borders. Just twenty-seven provided what federal analysts termed "automatic exemptions from many state and district laws and regulations." Nineteen jurisdictions kept charters under district collective-bargaining contracts, and a full thirty-six required most or all charters to select most teachers from the ranks of individuals with state teaching certificates. In other words, just six states (Arizona, Arkansas, Georgia, Louisiana, Oklahoma, and Texas) and the District of Columbia actually permit charters to hire anyone they think would be effective in the classroom without regard to whether they've passed through the credentialing hoops for district schools.[5] This type of restriction is especially vexing—and hard to justify—in light of considerable research indicating that state certification per se has little to do with classroom effectiveness.[6] Removing such unproductive credentialing burdens from district schools would also benefit public education. But for charter schools—which are meant to be uniquely self-governing—such regulatory burden is altogether inappropriate, as long as background checks and other child-oriented safety precautions remain in force.

Nor are charters and those who seek to operate them treated fairly *within* many states. The Massachusetts cap, for instance, limits charter enrollment to 18 percent of public school pupils in any district, a constraint that applies in the Bay State's *lowest*-performing districts, where charters might do children the greatest good. Ohio allows brick-and-mortar start-up charters to operate in only about 10 percent of its districts.[7] Illinois has separate caps for Chicago, its suburbs, and downstate. In Maryland, charters are entirely creatures of their local districts, which means that only the few counties that want them have any—and they're subject to districtwide bargaining contracts and teacher-assignment practices. Their staff members are district employees, not employees of the charter school itself.[8]

Almost all charters are included in state assessment and accountability regimes and thus expected to follow state academic standards.[9] In practice, this means that their curricular core, particularly in English and math, is apt to resemble that of district schools—a further constraint on charters' ability to be different. The standards and accountability obligation is not objectionable on its face, but it does constrain educators who favor a different curriculum sequence, perhaps teaching in fourth or sixth grade something that state standards specify for fifth (and that also appears on the mandatory fifth-grade test).[10]

As for money, because charters are subject to the restrictions of federal and state categorical programs, some schools shun red-tape-heavy programs such as subsidized lunches. Though these schools should certainly get audited and be able to show that their public dollars are used for legitimate purposes, flexibility as to how those dollars can be deployed is doubly important to a resource-strapped school that seeks to distinguish itself from district schools. Moreover, fear of audit can have a chilling effect, not to mention the hassle and expense. The Fordham Institute's Ohio authorizing team offered this example of how this might affect a law-abiding school: A charter school that uses federal Title 2-A dollars to cover the costs of recruiting a guidance counselor may be told by the auditor that this outlay did not qualify, because the federal program is intended to pay for recruiting and hiring only teachers and principals. But what if the school has greater need of a counselor to round out a professional team that fulfills the intent of the program (and may even have noted this in its original plan for use of Title 2-A dollars)? The school treasurer may be able to satisfy the auditor and get the expenditure reclassified as qualifying. But what does this say about the charter school's autonomy? And is this the best use of the treasurer's time?

Along with controls imposed directly by several levels of government, authorizers often further tighten the regulatory screws—a practice that seems slightly ironic considering the loose regulatory oversight of authorizers themselves in much of the country. Some authorizer-imposed rules are proper, as these entities are typically responsible for ensuring that schools in their portfolios comply with applicable laws. In other words, the authorizer is usually the government's lead enforcer (though definitely not the only one). Yet authorizers often go beyond their compliance obligations, as shown in a 2015 study by the American Enterprise Institute, which found that

many of them—striving conscientiously to vet applicants for charters—demanded greater standardization than is healthy for a movement that prizes diverse and autonomous schools.[11] Let us underscore
once again the paradox of freewheeling authorizers, rarely accountable for their own practices, imposing excessive uniformities on the
schools they oversee.

CONTRASTING APPROACHES:
BOSTON AND MILWAUKEE

A close look at charter performance in Boston and Milwaukee illustrates the value of school autonomy—and the variability of laws and
authorizer practices. Boston is well regarded in the charter world for
its high-achieving charter sector. The success is partly the product of
meticulous authorizing of Commonwealth charters by the state board
of education, plus tight caps that encourage careful selection of operators, as well as impressive work by some remarkable school founders, leaders, and teachers, many of them thrilled to live and work in
the Bay State.[12] An interesting 2010 study compared the performance
of Boston's Commonwealth charters with the city's *Pilot Schools*, a locally developed, quasi-charter genre that confers some independence
on participating schools (all of them conversions) but not nearly as
much as Commonwealth charters enjoy. A notable difference is that
Pilot School teachers must belong to the Boston Teachers Union, and
many elements of their work and school programs are determined by
that union's contract with the Boston Public Schools. This restriction
limits, for example, the length of their school days and years and imposes costly districtwide pay scales that restrict how many teachers a
school can afford within its budget.

The study showed far stronger achievement gains by similar students in Boston's Commonwealth charters than in the city's Pilot
Schools. This success could, of course, be caused by many factors—the
authors cite, for example, the no-excuses culture of most Commonwealth charters in Boston—but the study also flags the constricted
autonomy of the Pilot Schools as a possible cause of their lesser
performance.[13]

Milwaukee also has two types of charter or charter-like schools:
non-instrumentality charters are independent of the Milwaukee Public

School District and free from its collective bargaining agreements, while *instrumentality charters* are part of the district and subject to its contracts and various other regulations. A study by Hiren Nisar of the Wisconsin Center for Education Research looked at student achievement in both types of school. He found that attending charter schools in general did not boost the achievement of Milwaukee children any more than did attending conventional district schools, but she noted that "as the level of autonomy from the district increases, charter schools are more effective at improving student achievement." He went on to conclude that "the details of charter school policy matter."[14] We agree.

RIGHTS IN CONFLICT

The regulatory realm that's most fraught, even among charter advocates and other education reformers, involves the admission, retention, and disciplining of students, including those with special needs. Closely linked is the touchy topic of whether charter schools should be able to delimit their student populations. On this issue, educators hold strong and often diametrically opposed views as to what's good for children and how best to secure their civil and educational rights. The issue also draws us into something of a legal thicket.

One approach focuses on access, due process, and fairness in matters such as admission and retention. Keepers of this view are extremely sensitive to anything resembling discrimination against individual children on any grounds and are wary of schools that focus on specific populations to the exclusion of others. They also generally emphasize level playing fields such that district schools are not forced to educate the most challenging students while charters "cream" those who are more able, more docile, or perhaps better parented.

The other approach focuses on creating and protecting schools that produce successful learning outcomes for their enrollees—most of whom are needy—through the freedom to shape the schools' own environments and norms as well as their curricula and pedagogy. Adherents of this view generally reject the claim that every school must be willing and able to address the needs of every child, and they're serious about schools developing and safeguarding their own distinctive cultures.

There's no obvious compromise between these worldviews. Both are anchored in sincere conviction about what's best for children and for public education.

It's incontrovertible that charters are public schools and nearly every charter law signals that they're supposed to accept all who wish to enroll and to use lotteries when demand exceeds capacity.[15] Yet nothing in this realm is as straightforward as it first appears. Geographic limits on who can attend individual charter schools are fairly common. So are enrollment preferences for children in one or another category, ranging from disadvantaged children to children of the school's founders to children of active-duty military personnel.[16] And that's just the beginning. What about siblings of children already enrolled in the school? The progeny of teachers who work there? Children previously enrolled in low-performing district schools? How about those coming from the district school that was converted to charter status as part of a turnaround strategy? Or former students seeking to reenter after a time away? What about children emerging from an affiliated preschool, primary, or middle school with an aligned curriculum?

When all the preferences set forth in existing state laws are put together, we find that charter schools are not necessarily equally open to every child and that unweighted lotteries are not the only way to apportion spaces when demand exceeds supply. Nor is that the end of it. A number of charters intentionally and legally target special populations. In Ohio, for example, Summit Academy (Cincinnati) serves alternative learners (children with ADHD and autism-spectrum disorders); the Autism Academy of Learning (Toledo) does just what its name suggests; and the Menlo Park Community School (Cleveland) is a charter school for gifted and talented youngsters, as defined under Ohio law. There are many more specialized-population schools—former dropouts are a frequent target market—and not just in Ohio.[17] The Maya Angelou Academy in the District of Columbia, for example, operates within a juvenile detention facility, as do a number of charters bearing the Five Keys label in several California cities.[18]

To be sure, many districts also operate special schools—or schools within schools, pull-out programs, and resource rooms—for children with severe disabilities, as well as alternative schools for those with other needs (often including chronic misbehavior).[19] Yet such schools generally remain exceptions to the "one best system," whereas specialization in the charter sector is so widespread as to approach normal.

In both the district and charter sectors, however, school specialization surfaces complicated questions of which children will attend which schools and how this is decided. Must one have an autism-related disability to attend an autism-specialty school? How does the system determine who is a potential dropout? What if a youngster who has not been incarcerated wants to enroll in a charter designed for those who have recently been released into halfway-house settings? These are important, challenging issues for district and charter schools alike, and they interact, sometimes painfully, with the doctrine that charter schools are open to all comers.

Still other issues arise when a small, freestanding charter simply lacks the staff and budget to meet the diverse needs of a multiply disabled pupil whose parents—wisely or not—want this to be their child's school. What about the girl or boy who does not speak the school's language of instruction? What happens when some kids cannot or will not achieve a school's ambitious academic standards or abide by its strict disciplinary code—particularly important to the no-excuses schools that are the charter sector's greatest success story and that exist entirely to reboot the lives and prospects of disadvantaged children?

How to strike a legally defensible, morally acceptable, fiscally manageable, and educationally sound balance between the rights or interests of one child and those of many others who attend that school? Must the school forgo key distinguishing features and stop functioning as a bona fide alternative to the district schools that would otherwise deal with those children? In that case, what happens to other children who enrolled in this school precisely because it would be different?

Such questions have no easy answers. People have strong feelings. State and federal laws governing such matters, complicated as they are, are often misaligned with the peculiar circumstances of individual children and schools. And the application of these laws depends on many school-specific variables and local conditions.

Lately, there's been a stronger push from civil rights groups, federal enforcement agencies, and some within the charter movement itself to advance equity-minded measures such as new rules for admission, pupil discipline, and *backfilling*—that is, admitting additional students when space becomes available during the school year. Those doing the pushing are mostly organizations and individuals certain that they're looking out for the best interests of needy children. They reason that when a family must move midyear (perhaps because of housing or employment issues), its children should be able to enter a charter school with vacant seats whenever they arrive. But what if the school has worked hard to create a culture of learning and move its pupils through the curriculum at a rate that the newcomer may not be able to maintain? And what if its vacancies are due to suspensions or expulsions of children who cannot or will not keep up, or whose behavior makes it harder—even dangerous—for other children to do so? Should disparate-impact calculations and enforcement threats cause such a school to compromise the features that made it worth attending in the first place?

Even close colleagues find themselves disputing these matters. For example, veteran charter observer and theorist Paul Hill asserts that "a high-output school has to let those kids who won't fulfill their obligations go elsewhere, unless it is willing to abandon requirements that it considers essential to full college preparation. It should be free to fill seats that become vacant with kids who have a good chance of succeeding in the school, but shouldn't be forced to fill vacancies."[20] Yet Robin Lake, Hill's successor at the helm of the Center on Reinventing Public Education, disagrees:

> It is a very slippery slope to suggest that some charters should be required to take students with severe academic deficiencies, and other "elite" schools should not. Who decides which schools do or don't have to take more challenging students? Why restrict the challenge to academics and not behavior or special needs or other differences? I can't support a public school system where some government official decides who gets to attend which school. Worse, if it is left to schools to decide, outright discrimination is assured and we'll certainly end up with some schools that are dumping grounds for kids that everyone has given up on.[21]

From where we sit, they both make compelling arguments.

THE SPECIAL CHALLENGES
OF SPECIAL EDUCATION

One of the most sensitive issues in the charter world, and one that draws at least as much criticism down upon these schools as anything else, is the matter of whether they do right by children with disabilities. This is most often gauged by whether the proportion of special education students (i.e., children with individualized education plans, IEPs) enrolled in charters equals the proportion in district schools.

This is an important topic and not one adequately addressed via superficial comparisons of enrollment numbers. Federal law mandates that children with disabilities have the right to a "free appropriate public education" in the "least restrictive environment" that is appropriate for them. Moreover, states have the constitutional and statutory responsibility to ensure that children within their borders are educated. Although many regulations spell out how this should be done, the actual provision of education to children, including those with disabilities, is generally entrusted to districts, which in turn make a variety of arrangements that range from full inclusion of such youngsters in ordinary classrooms to entirely separate, specialized public schools, to district-financed placement of individual children in private schools and other settings. Parents of disabled children have the right to participate in determining how their daughters and sons will be educated. In the end, though, it's the state's responsibility, and that's true for states with or without charter schools.

Charters, however, are something of an awkward fit within a legal framework and educational philosophy that confer the right to individualized education on some children while withholding it from others. Numerous charters seek to personalize the education of every student and to avoid labels and distinctions among them—and lots of parents, including many with youngsters with disabilities, want this for their children. (Hence the push within special education for more mainstreaming.) We've come to believe that *all* children in America deserve an appropriate education tailored to their needs and that *every* parent should have the right to determine how and where this will be done. Perhaps the greatest opportunity facing US education in the years ahead is to customize the schooling experience of every child and enable all students to move through the primary-secondary sequence with the help they need—and at their own speed.[22] One can think of this as a less bureaucratic version of universal special education, and we applaud the schools—charter and other—that are doing their best to make that happen. Even more promising, several states are also taking this approach seriously.[23]

We've also come to believe—and have written elsewhere—that special education as practiced in the United States (primarily under a law that dates to 1975) needs a major overhaul.[24] Meanwhile, of course, states must ensure that their education systems meet children's needs under current law. This does not, however, mean that every school in the state must be able to meet the needs of any child. Rather, the total public education system must satisfactorily do that. In the district sector, it's long been common for schools to specialize in particular disabilities, for separate schools to accommodate the most severely disabled, and for private-school outplacements (paid for by the district) to deal with children whom public institutions cannot serve adequately.[25] And the charter sector itself already contains more than a hundred schools that specialize in educating children with disabilities.

Individual schools ought not be forced to try to be all things to all children. Each can have norms, academic standards and procedures that optimize the greatest good for the greatest number of its pupils, although such rules may not include the usual proscribed categories of discrimination.[26] In the end, the state and its designees must determine how, in a given locality, every child will have access to high-quality educational opportunities properly tailored to his or her circumstances. If and when charter or other specialty schools come to predominate in a locality, the state or its designee must still ensure that there's an acceptable place for every child and that a default arrangement looks after the youngster who may otherwise fall through the cracks of a choice-based system.

As we noted earlier, charter schools nationally enroll a somewhat smaller proportion of children with IEPs than do district schools. The most recent data from the federal Office for Civil Rights (OCR) indicate that this gap is not very wide: 10.4 percent in charters nationally in 2011–2012, compared with 12.6 percent in district schools. As with almost everything in special education (and charter schooling), however, national averages mask enormous state-to-state variation.

As table 9.1 shows, of the forty states for which data were available that year, five had differences of less than 1 percentage point between special education enrollment rates in district and charter schools, while the charter sector in four states actually had rates more than 3 percentage points higher than their district counterparts.[27]

On the plus side, charter schools appear to have done a better job than district schools at mainstreaming their pupils with disabilities—a key goal of many special education policy makers, reformers,

TABLE 9.1   Percentage of students with disabilities, by type of public school, 2011–2012

State	District	Charter	Difference	State	District	Charter	Difference
AK	14.95	10.30	4.65	MN	15.06	14.20	0.86
AR	11.08	8.21	2.87	MO	13.56	9.13	4.43
AZ	11.99	10.19	1.81	NC	12.37	10.82	1.54
CA	10.26	8.17	2.08	NH	15.76	15.88	–0.12
CO	10.37	6.46	3.90	NJ	15.40	9.15	6.25
CT	11.94	8.26	3.68	NM	13.99	12.28	1.71
DC	14.67	13.76	0.90	NV	11.11	9.41	1.70
DE	15.51	11.65	3.86	NY	14.63	12.09	2.54
FL	12.79	9.51	3.27	OH	14.28	17.50	–3.23
GA	10.73	9.71	1.02	OK	14.95	8.57	6.38
HI	11.60	10.07	1.53	OR	13.46	9.42	4.04
IA	12.84	16.82	–3.99	PA	15.23	15.11	0.11
ID	9.38	7.21	2.17	RI	15.32	13.17	2.15
IL	13.48	12.01	1.47	SC	12.99	10.19	2.80
IN	14.86	12.90	1.96	TN	13.88	11.09	2.79
KS	13.47	8.03	5.44	TX	9.01	7.41	1.59
LA	10.75	8.95	1.79	UT	12.69	11.38	1.31
MA	16.71	14.03	2.68	VA	13.06	18.54	–5.48
MD	11.14	14.23	–3.10	WI	14.07	13.21	0.86
MI	13.45	9.56	3.89	WY	14.45	12.50	1.95
Nation	**12.55**	**10.42**	**2.13**				

Source: Lauren Morando Rhim, Jesse Gumz, and Kelly Henderson, "Key Trends in Special Education in Charter Schools: A Secondary Analysis of the Civil Rights Data Collection 2011-2012," National Center for Special Education in Charter Schools, 2015, http://static1.squarespace.com/static/52feb326e4b069fc72abb0c8/t/567b0a3640667a31534e9152/1450904118101/crdc_full.pdf, 38.

and parents, as well as many charter leaders. According to a recent report from the National Center for Special Education in Charter Schools, 84 percent of charter students who received "special education or related services" were in "general education" (i.e., regular classrooms) at least 80 percent of the school day in 2011–2012, compared with 67 percent in district schools.[28] This higher percentage may be because charters are more likely to enroll children with milder disabilities, that is, kids with IEPs that emphasize mainstreaming. We can find no data on those distinctions. The report describes, however, 115 charter schools that "focused primarily or entirely on students with disabilities," of which 49 "specialized in a single disability category (e.g., Autism or Deaf-blindness)."[29] The federal data that inform the report also suggest that on the hot-button issue of school suspensions, while charters had a slightly higher rate than district schools (7.4 versus 6.9 percent in 2011–2012), the difference "appears to be driven by the higher rate of suspensions among students without disabilities. . . . [T]he two groups of schools suspend students with disabilities at rates around 13.4%."[30]

To summarize, states and their designees must devise a fair, moral, and legal way for all children in a community—including those who may be suspended or expelled by a particular school—to gain access to acceptable education options that suit their needs and circumstances. We don't believe every school in town—be it traditional or charter—must serve every child. But we're mindful of the two sectors' basic difference in approach. In a perceptive analysis of special education issues in charter schools, Loyola law professor Robert A. Garda, Jr. called the disconnect between charters and special education law a "culture clash . . . based on conflicting education reforms and agency oversight principles." Charters, he explains, "are an integral and growing part of the education reform movement, but they will struggle to appropriately serve disabled students until changes are made in the law that reduce the direct and profound clash between charter culture and special education culture."[31] There's no denying the awkward fit between America's heavily regulated approach to special education and our pluralistic, relatively autonomous, and somewhat messy charter sector.[32] The latter confers freedom on schools and choices on parents, while the former gives parents some control and often some choices but does so within a framework that tightly constrains the actions of school systems.

Special Education in Denver and New Orleans Charters

Denver and New Orleans, both cities with large charter market shares (see chapter 12), illumine some of the ways that charter-heavy communities can serve students with special needs. In Denver (17 percent market share), the district has formed a compact with its charters, a key element of which is special education.[33] Under this arrangement, charters agreed to host centers for high-need special ed students, with children placed according to their IEPs. As all charters in Denver are authorized by the district, the district pays for everything, from staff to administration to transportation. In 2015, Denver's fifty-four charters contained fifteen such centers.

New Orleans is today's foremost example of a city where charters have become the dominant educational provider. After several false starts, the Recovery School District (RSD) that authorizes nearly all of the city's charters has entered into an agreement with the vestigial Orleans Parish School Board and some nonprofit partners. The aim is "to ensure [that] students with disabilities have equitable access to schools that meet their needs and schools have the budget flexibility needed to fully support these students."[34]

Schools around the Crescent City now receive their operating dollars via a student-need-based formula so that the most challenged children—including special education pupils—are funded according to the services that they require rather than a disability category. A citywide exceptional-needs insurance pool covers students whose costs exceed twenty-two thousand dollars per year. Schools must apply to the RSD for these funds, which permit the ReNEW Schools charter network to serve sixteen students with severe emotional and behavioral issues in a self-contained K–8 program.[35] A separate cooperative for special education provides professional development services and other support to schools. While not every school is expected to serve the same number or type of special-needs students, the RSD monitors whether these new financial inducements and services set the right incentives to create suitable programs for all needy students. Ultimately, the RSD is responsible for the proper placement of every child. And there's certainly evidence of progress: In 2001, just 5 percent of New Orleans students with special needs earned high school diplomas. By 2014–2015, 60 percent did so, 17 percent better than the state average.[36]

LEVEL PLAYING FIELDS?

The combined force of statutes, regulations, and the practices of authorizers, auditors, enforcers, and others has kept most charters on a tighter leash than the charter bargain contemplated. Consequently, they've had to act more like district schools than like independent schools, even when this sameness may not benefit the pupils. A 2011 study of charter autonomy by the Thomas B. Fordham Institute termed the current practice of chartering a "half-broken promise" and declared that "the typical charter school in America today lacks the autonomy it needs to succeed—a degree of freedom that we equate with a grade no better than a C+—once federal, state and authorizer impositions are considered. For some schools, the picture is brighter but for many it's much grimmer, with far too many charters in the F range."[37]

Political pressures to keep it that way are strong. When a charter gets exempted from some mandate or procedure that district schools must follow, district leaders respond that the playing field is tilted because they must do things that charters are spared. Thus spoke the head of the Buffalo teachers union in May 2014, as New York legislators wrestled with possible expansion of the Empire State's charter program: "The state should require that the charter schools have a population that is reflective of the regular public schools. We're not against charter schools. What we want to do is have a level playing field, so that they have the same type of students that we have [and] they have to meet the same certification requirements."[38]

Partly in response to such concerns, but also because of mistakes made by individual schools, the trend in recent years has been to tighten rather than loosen the screws on charters. Seeking to satisfy the inevitable cry that "this must never happen again," a single school's blunder can bring more restrictions down on all of them. Ohio governor John Kasich's words to a Chamber of Commerce audience in December 2014 typify this position: "We are going to fix the lack of regulation on charter schools. There is no excuse for people coming in here and taking advantage of anything. So we will be putting some tough rules into our budget."[39] Kasich is a Republican, pro–school choice and pro-charter. But he was responding to reports—including one commissioned by the Thomas B. Fordham Institute, where two of us work—that some Buckeye charter schools and their authorizers had misbehaved in various ways and had ill served their students. The Ohio charter sector had indeed experienced failures of both policy and practice, and Kasich was correct to press for reforms. But would the resulting regulations, designed to make it harder to run bad schools, also make it harder to run good ones?

A better way to balance the field is to give district schools more of the freedoms that charters crave and sometimes get. But except for a handful of portfolio districts, this solution is lamentably rare. Still, the National Alliance for Public Charter Schools (NAPCS) opened an interesting window on what this solution might accomplish. In 2015, NAPCS conducted a study of three CMOs that states or districts—encouraged and underwritten by federal school improvement grants—had enlisted to turn around low-performing schools. This strategy has not been widely used, as many states and districts are loath to take on the politics of "charterizing" any of their schools while many charter operators are loath to tackle the onerous challenge of school transformation. Thus NAPCS could find just seventy-nine instances out of some two thousand schools receiving grant dollars. Still, the CMOs that undertook these transformation efforts reported which autonomies proved most helpful in this work:

- *Staffing*: Freedom in hiring, staff assignments, incentives, professional development, and removal of staff;
- *Use of Time*: Freedom to determine the length of the school day or year and how to allocate student and staff time;
- *Programming*: Freedom to determine the academic program and wraparound services;
- *Finances*: Freedom to allocate district, state, and federal dollars to priority areas that benefit students; and
- *Access to Facilities*: Freedom to own, maintain, and renovate a building, or have the building renovated and maintained by the district according to the operator's standards.[40]

Elsewhere, NAPCS has highlighted key domains of school independence that inform its model charter law:

- *Fiscal and legal autonomy*: Schools should have clear statutory authority to receive and disburse funds, incur debt, and pledge, assign, or encumber assets as collateral and to enter into contracts and leases, sue and be sued in their own names, and acquire real property. And school governing boards should exist as legal entities that are created specifically to govern their charter schools.

- *Automatic exemptions from many state and district laws and regulations*: This includes all laws except those covering health, safety, civil rights, student accountability, employee criminal history checks, open meetings, freedom of information, and generally accepted accounting principles. Charters should also be exempt from state teacher certification requirements.

- *Automatic collective bargaining exemption*: Charter schools authorized by entities other than local district boards are exempt from participation in any outside collective bargaining agreements while those authorized by local boards are exempt from participation in any district collective bargaining agreements.[41]

That's another fine list that can serve as excellent guidance for district and charter schools alike, yet many of those freedoms are denied to most of today's charters. This raises a necessary question: to what extent could the challenges to charter autonomy have been anticipated at the outset? In hindsight, while nobody expected school autonomy to be absolute, charter pioneers could have pushed harder to get what they considered essential freedoms nailed into the law and not left this issue up in the air. They would have faced plenty of pushback and inevitably would have had to compromise, but early compromise seems preferable to the ongoing struggle to secure their schools' essential freedoms. The pioneers certainly should have pushed harder against the kinds of regulations that serve adult interests and political egos more than children's education needs.

Especially through the movement's swelling corps of authorizers, associations, and support organizations, the advocates could have done—and today should still do—a better job of getting the charter sector to police its own ranks for quality and integrity. It should have been more selective about who could open schools in the first place.

BALANCING FREEDOM AND REGULATION 133

It should have better monitored the schools' practices, fiscal management, governance, and academic results. Under such a proactive approach, this sector might have narrowed—and might yet narrow—the opportunities for politicians and charter opponents to demand new rules for all. It would have been closer to self-regulating, as a proper profession or trade group should be. How much better it would have been, again with the benefit of hindsight, to have kept bad apples out of the barrel—or discarded them when they rotted—than to invite regulations that could squeeze the juice from all.

10

Political Tussles with Friend and Foe

OUR PREOCCUPATION THROUGHOUT THIS BOOK—and in education reform generally—is not the well-being of schools, whether district or charter (or other), but the opportunities that America affords to children who need better ones. Regrettably but inevitably, however, the politics of education as they concern both district reform and charter schooling have too often been dominated over the past quarter century by adult and institutional interests. So let us be clear: we believe that charter schools, done right, are important additions to American public education that can bring significant opportunities to children who need them. We believe, as well, that charters are *part* of public education and should coexist on peaceable and mutually beneficial terms with district-operated and other kinds of schools. If the goal is educational excellence for children, we should be agnostic as to what sorts of institutions can best deliver it.

In terms of broad public engagement, charter-related politics are a far cry from, say, gun control, health care, or taxes. Because few Americans have any direct experience with or knowledge about charter schools, the whole topic stays below most people's radars. As a result, the arguments that envelop it take place primarily among policy elites and interested parties. That's a problem for charter advocates—and probably an advantage for their opponents, most notably teachers unions. As Paul Hill and Ashley Jochim point out, "compared to groups that depend on the schools for their incomes, elites have weaker incentives to endure harsh conflict or make a stand against long odds. . . . [I]n the long run, elite support is not a sufficient basis for a winning coalition. Elites can be early supporters and valuable opinion leaders, but reformers also need to draw parents, neighborhood leaders, professionals, and faith leaders to their side."[1]

Such wider support is beginning to be mustered in a few places, as we note below. But most charter-related political activity still happens inside the arena. There, school operators and advocates understandably push back against what they see as excessive and inappropriate regulation and struggle to fend off more of it. They campaign for fairer funding. They press for the scrapping of restrictions on school numbers, locations, and enrollments. And they nudge states to enact new charter laws and strengthen existing ones. Critics respond that the charter sector needs to clean up its act, do a better job of educating kids, shut down its bad actors, ensure that the money it already has is well spent, acknowledge the flaws in its marketplace, and recognize that education is a public good as well as a private one.

As we've shown in previous chapters, both sets of contentions have some merit. But also playing in this arena are plenty of adults motivated by their own interests. There are people who want no interference with their underperforming charter schools and, indeed, want to expand them. Other people don't approve of or resent charter schools overall, seeing their own schools and jobs threatened by charters' rising attendance—and the funds that go with it—and therefore doing their utmost to make these intruders go away. This is the nature of politics, of course, and in the charter arena it has produced something of an arms race. Charter partisans make ever more forceful efforts to defend and advance their interests through advocacy and political action. Their opponents also try hard to fence charters in, burden them with more rules, add to their costs, deny their legitimacy, and get them declared illegal or unconstitutional. Fortunately, in a few places, charters and districts have reached limited forms of détente, making earnest attempts to bridge their differences—even unite their interests—on behalf of kids in their communities.

BIPARTISAN BUT STILL CONTENTIOUS

Among top political leaders and others who devote themselves to large public-policy challenges and reform opportunities, chartering has

enjoyed considerable support since day one. As noted earlier, this reform had bipartisan origins in nearly every state that embarked upon
it. At the national level, every president from George H. W. Bush to
Barack Obama has been a charter fan. Viewed ideologically, however,
charters are no perfect fit for either side of our schismatic politics.
Conservatives fret that they're neither vouchers nor home schools;
they're still public schools under government's thumb. And partly because many GOP legislators represent suburban and rural districts
that want no part of such schools, they've been largely confined to
cities and troubled districts. For their part, plenty of Democrats are
closely allied with teachers unions, which—pace Albert Shanker—have
almost always opposed charters (and other school-choice strategies),
particularly when these occur outside their collective-bargaining
umbrellas.[2] More than a few liberals, bullish as they are about other
forms of diversity and the right to choose, oppose the segmenta-
tion of public education, fret about its privatization, and lament the
re-segregation that they see following in the wake of school choice.
None of this is made easier by the widening divides that characterize American public policies more generally. Charters are frequently
caught in the same polarized pincers.

The traditional public school establishment still doesn't want
much to do with charters, either. With notable but rare exceptions,
district boards and superintendents are wary of collaborating with
them, would rather not authorize them, and press lawmakers to
limit them. As charters' market share has grown anyway, these upstart, tuition-free schools are also viewed as competitors by many
long-established (and tuition-dependent) private schools, even as
daggers at the breast of urban Catholic schools.

Charter proponents can be stubborn, too. They often appear unwilling to cooperate with districts even while demanding help from
them, oblivious to the difficulties created for traditional public and
private schools that lose students, self-righteous in their certainty
that charters represent the future, and disparaging toward those
who disagree.

All these disputes were relatively muted while the charter sector remained small and marginal and especially as long as it targeted children that other schools were not succeeding with. Charter
leaders' understandable desire to minimize conflict, combined with

state laws' and authorizers' emphasis on inner-city children and poor neighborhoods, helps explain the focus on these groups and communities. Philanthropy, too, pushed charters in similar directions. Yes, idealistic charter founders mostly wanted to serve the neediest kids, but even people out to profit from the venture would soon observe that it was easier to open schools and attract pupils in places where there was innate parental demand for something different. As a result, most charters found themselves flooded with disadvantaged and often low-achieving kids, which added to the challenge of proving the schools' educational effectiveness.

As the charter sector grew to serve millions rather than thousands of students, it naturally posed more direct competition to established schools.[3] The inevitable result, as described in the previous chapter, has been friction over the extent to which charters may continue to proliferate (and the places where they're allowed to do this), the funding they receive, the rules by which they operate, and whether this competition takes place on a level playing field. At the same time, some well-meaning civic leaders, philanthropists, and education reformers still view charters as a sideshow that deflects energy, attention, and resources away from the preponderance of needy children who remain in district-operated schools. Others prefer to view charters as a sort of R&D center for the larger system rather than a substantial alternative to it. As we have shown, the blind-men's-elephant aspect of chartering means there's ample precedent for such divergent views of the sector's role and future. But this diversity is also another wellspring of discord.

Meanwhile, charter discussions are intense within the growing education-reform sector itself, ripe with a full spectrum of opinion over the mission and value of these schools and quarrels about them that often serve as proxies in battles over fundamental philosophy and strategy. Among the large and enduring disagreements among reformers: how much to rely on the marketplace for quality control versus government-driven standards-and-accountability regimes; the extent to which "structural" reforms like chartering can solve education problems without equal attention to curriculum and pedagogy; whether school choice should be universal or focused on poor kids and low achievers; and the role of charters in advancing (or possibly retarding) other compelling reform initiatives such as racial or socio-economic integration, the proper schooling of children with disabilities, and the advancement of character education, civic unity, and cultural pluralism.

Not every education reformer is a huge fan of chartering, although most of them function as advocates for more and better charters. Yet *more* and *better* do not mean the same thing; quantity-quality trade-offs remain contentious among charter partisans. Withal, a host of organizations now strives in myriad ways to build support for charters, reaching out to constituencies and stakeholders that span the general public, policy makers, the media, and families with children in these schools. Many such entities have also plunged directly into the political maelstrom, seeking through multiple means to put in office people who are bullish on charters, and to defeat candidates who are not.

At the national level, several groups—most prominently the National Alliance for Public Charter Schools (NAPCS)—strive to advance the charter movement as a whole while also looking after its interests in federal policy and funding and collaborating with state affiliates to do this in their own jurisdictions. Better authorizing has its foremost promoter in the National Association of Charter School Authorizers (NACSA). And a number of other nationally focused advocacy groups, think tanks, and major funders, while not focused exclusively on charters, place the vitality and quality of this sector high among their reform priorities.[4]

STATE AND LOCAL BATTLES

Still and all, most charter-related action takes place at the state and local levels, and the bulk of charter-related advocacy—and opposition—therefore occurs there. States with robust charter movements typically have their own assemblages of these schools, such as the California Charter Schools Association, Colorado League of Charter Schools, and Minnesota Association of Charter Schools. At least as important in policy-making circles are state-based education-reform groups that include charters within their missions, groups like Tennessee SCORE, Education Trust–Midwest (headquartered in Detroit), the Massachusetts Business Alliance for Education, and the Connecticut Coalition for Achievement Now (ConnCAN). Most of these organizations have come together in the Policy Innovation in Education Network, which now has members in thirty-one states and the District of Columbia. Stand for Children, another reform group with charters on its agenda, has affiliates in nine states, and 50CAN (a spin-off from ConnCAN) is up to seven states and growing.

Within some states, sizable charter operators, both nonprofit and for-profit, also wield substantial clout in political and policy circles. Examples include Success Academy Charter Schools (New York), led by the formidable Eva Moskowitz; Aspire Public Schools (California and Tennessee), with strong backing from the Bill and Melinda Gates Foundation, Netflix founder Reed Hastings, uber-broker Charles Schwab, and the multifoundation Charter School Growth Fund; White Hat Management (Ohio), long led by major GOP contributor David Brennan; and National Heritage Academies, which launched in Michigan and now operates in nine states. Large multistate networks such as KIPP, K12, and Charter Schools USA manage to influence decision making in many places, typically with the help of government-relations staffers, paid lobbyists, and heavy-hitting donors, high-profile board members, and sympathetic politicians.

Some of these groups—especially the state charter associations—rely substantially for revenue on dues and fees from their own members—an arrangement that creates awkward situations when those members fracture over policy and funding issues. Many other groups are nonprofits that live on tax-deductible contributions. But a growing number have been joined by entities openly devoted to lobbying and politics: 501(c)(4) organizations and political action committees, which are free to spend limitlessly on lobbying for specific legislation, getting friendly candidates elected, advancing ballot initiatives, and more. Some of these overtly political groups were affiliated with the nationwide StudentsFirst movement, founded by former DC schools chancellor Michelle Rhee. Democrats for Education Reform has fourteen state affiliates. Also active in many jurisdictions, though usually behind the scenes, are groups associated with, or partly funded by, the American Federation for Children Action Fund. Even further behind the scenes are a number of wealthy individual contributors to pro-charter and school-choice efforts, including members of the DeVos (Amway) and Walton (Walmart) families, former New York mayor Michael Bloomberg, and numerous hedge fund billionaires and other rich folks (such as Los Angeles tycoon Eli Broad and the Denver-based family of the late Don Fisher, founder of The Gap and affiliated companies). Add the many related activities underwritten by the Bill and Melinda Gates Foundation, and it's no surprise that this roster of heavy hitters has led critics such as Diane Ravitch to dub the charter sector "the billionaire boys' club."[5] (Chapters 5 and 8 also discuss the philanthropic sector's role in chartering.)

FROM GRASS TOPS TO GRASS ROOTS

More is at work here than money-fueled lobbying and influence peddling among elites. Unlike, say, academic standards and accountability, which are education reforms that will probably never boast grassroots constituencies, the charter movement can—as Success Academy's Eva Moskowitz has demonstrated in recent confrontations with New York mayor Bill de Blasio—muster thousands of parents and students to promote and defend itself. Here is the *New York Times* account of Moskowitz's effort, just before New York City's 2013 mayoral election, to put the winner on notice that he'd best not trifle with the city's charter schools: "A month before Election Day, she shut her schools for a morning and gathered Success Academy families for a march. She marshaled other charter networks whose leaders worried that de Blasio would try to cap their numbers and charge rent at city-owned school buildings. Moskowitz and her army of 17,000 strode across the Brooklyn Bridge with placards imploring 'Let My Children Learn.'"[6]

The Moskowitz and de Blasio tussles continue. Working with Families for Excellent Schools, Success Academies has transported busloads of parents and students to Albany at critical times to prod state leaders to override and outflank the mayor on charter issues. Joined by other charters, they again rallied thousands of parents in September 2015 to keep the pressure on hizzoner in the name of equal opportunity.[7] Two weeks later, thousands of charter teachers took to Big Apple streets wearing blue shirts that read "I teach to end inequality."[8]

Moskowitz's success in drawing support from teachers and parents who are invested in her schools—what Andrew Kelly of the American Enterprise Institute dubs "the new parent power"—is unusual, but it's not the only instance of chartering's capacity to get beyond elites, politicians, and full-time education reformers.[9] The California Charter Schools Association—one of the few state charter groups that has steadily pushed for quality along with growth—has become adept at mustering parents in Sacramento and other major cities, notably Los Angeles.[10] Massachusetts has become another battlefront over efforts to raise the state's numerical limits on charter schools and their enrollments. There we see a coherent three-part strategy, beginning with a legislative move to amend the Bay State's charter law. In case lawmakers balk, a ballot initiative is in the works, as is a legal move involving a prominent Boston firm that has filed a class-action suit to lift the charter cap, arguing that it unconstitutionally denies children access to an adequate education.[11] As part of all three efforts, Families for Excellent Schools is organizing parents and other charter supporters to participate in an advocacy campaign.

Almost everywhere one looks, this lesson is visible: once charters gain a reasonably sturdy toehold in a state or community and significant numbers of children enroll in them, they have at least the potential to mobilize popular support in ways that policy makers and politicians must reckon with. The need to build a wider base was a big reason that advocates sought to grow the charter sector quickly in the early days, opening as many schools as they could in as many places as possible, even if that meant compromising on quality. It's clear that as thousands of children—especially poor children of color—begin to benefit from a program, curbing or eliminating that program becomes ever less feasible for those who don't like it. Let us therefore suggest that, across much of the country, the charter sector is well enough established that its existence is not in great jeopardy, and advocates should now focus their energies on the quest for quality, innovation, and legitimacy.

OUTSIDE BATTLES

As we've noted, those who run and work in district schools are often ill disposed toward charters, especially the start-up kind. Charters compete with them for students, talent, and resources, and this competition intensifies in places with flat or declining demographics. Although charters typically receive fewer public dollars per pupil than do schools operated by districts, any enrollment loss means less money for the "sending" schools, and district leaders complain that students typically depart for charters in ones and twos from multiple grades and classrooms, making it hard to reduce their budget or staffing in an orderly way.[12]

Tax dollars aren't all that's at stake. Charters also inconvenience the district in various ways, particularly if it is obligated to oversee them (as sponsor), to provide their disabled pupils with special education, to transport their students to school, or to incorporate them in extracurricular activities, school fairs, and athletics. Fluctuating charter enrollments may also destabilize district planning and budgeting. And to the extent that philanthropy shifts its largesse from districts to charters, the former find it harder to attract those coveted incremental dollars with which to do things that public funding cannot cover.

Reputations are on the line, too. Highly successful charters can eclipse district performance by showing that they do better (with less money), at least for certain pupil populations. Charters may also soak up the limelight by drawing media coverage, the interest of community leaders, and the glad hands of politicians.

From the standpoint of teachers unions, charters indisputably threaten their membership rolls and revenues as well as their claim to represent all the teachers in town and the clout that accompanies such dominion. Although unions have managed to bring some charter teachers under their collective-bargaining umbrellas and continue trying to recruit more, the great majority of staff in the charter sector remain free agents.[13] Besides such direct challenges to their organizational interests, charters—and the battle to stop or contain them—make it harder for union leaders to assert that serving children is their top priority, once they're seen striving to block students from exiting bad schools in favor of better ones.

It would be a mistake, though, to suppose that establishment interests are charters' only opponents. As discussed earlier, some civil rights advocates view charters as engines of segregation or re-segregation. More than a few suburban politicians regard them as a fine reform for inner-city children but nothing they or their constituents want coming into their own serene communities.

And people associated with private schooling—and with efforts to widen access to it via vouchers, tax credits, and such—nervously view charters as rivals for enrollments, funding, and attention.[14] There is some justice in their concern, considering that the growth in charter enrollments in recent years parallels the shrinkage in Catholic parochial-school enrollments as well as the flatness of district numbers. In 2012, a scholar at Albany Law School examined the "near-collapse" of Catholic school enrollments in New York State over the previous decade and reported that charters accounted for more than a third of that decline. He estimated "the fiscal cost of Catholic school students transferring to charter schools at $390 million" and observed that "one Catholic school has closed for every charter school that has opened." Worse would follow, he cautioned, if lawmakers eased the state's cap on charter schools—which they did in 2010 and again in 2015.[15]

All the forces that feel threatened or disquieted by charters can be expected to mobilize when advocates seek to widen the sector's footprint, boost its funding, ease its regulation, and burnish its reputation. That's the nature of politics in education. But conflict is not the only possible avenue. A handful of school systems have turned out to be responsible charter authorizers, and some—New York, Denver, Baltimore, Cleveland, and Philadelphia, for example—have intentionally and thoughtfully incorporated charters into their broader efforts to upgrade public education. A few Catholic and other religious schools have "converted" to charter status, thus continuing to serve many of the same children and sometimes retaining optional religious-education programs outside the core school day.[16] In 2010, the Gates Foundation invested nearly $25 million in an effort to create "collaboration compacts" between charter operators and school districts in sixteen cities. But that hopeful project is off to a relatively slow start and by 2016 had bestowed sizable sums on fewer than half of those communities. A report from the Center on Reinventing Public Education highlighted the Gates project's successes while also cautioning that "progress has been episodic."[17] And a recent study by the Thomas B. Fordham Institute, examining the prospects for détente in district–charter relationships, found grounds for only cautious optimism. In the five cities analyzed by the authors, collaboration between the charter sector and the district was "limited and often fragile," and "nobody should expect either sector to cede much territory to the other anytime soon."[18]

INTRAMURAL SQUABBLING

In addition to the compromises with school quality that occurred in some places where charters sprang up like wild flowers, the charter sector faces other challenges to quality and reputation. It's not easy to show great results for thousands of poor kids attending mediocre schools, of which this sector has too many. Yet it takes a resolute authorizer, backed by quality-centric statutes, to close a school attended by hundreds of needy children, most of whose parents are probably content with it despite its lackluster test scores—a problem that districts also encounter when they try to close their own low-performing schools. Consigning those children to schools that might be overcrowded and perhaps even worse than the charter in terms of safety, achievement, and other key indicators poses not just a moral dilemma and education conundrum but also a bona fide political challenge. What's more, by this point in the evolution of the charter sector, existing schools have jelled into interest groups of their own. These cling to their niches as energetically as do other branches of the education establishment—and are vulnerable to similar kinds of complacency, turf retention, and the elevation of adult interests over children's. The profit motive, where present, adds a further wrinkle. This sector can boast hundreds of terrific schools, but the mediocre ones also enlist influential friends to secure their own continuation and thereby frustrate efforts by reformers, authorizers, and state officials to revamp or shut them.

Accordingly, today's reformers, ourselves included, who want both more *and* better school options for children, must joust on several fronts: not just combating those who oppose charters in general and are bent on reining them in, but also those who defend vested but unsavory interests within the charter sector and push back against moves that may cost them students, freedom, or return on investment. We also quarrel with fellow reformers who fret—not without reason—that efforts to boost charter quality will lead to heavier regulation, less autonomy, diminished school diversity, and the replacement of one kind of bureaucracy with another—what some analysts term *institutional isomorphism*, namely, the tendency of public enterprises to come to resemble one another over time, however much they were initially meant to be different.

These quarrels within the charter and education reform movements can sometimes be as heated as those between charter partisans and outside critics. Although long waiting lists show that demand for charter seats exceeds the available supply in many places, some communities are already saturated, meaning that their charters compete with each other, as well as with district and private schools, for pupils. Nor are all charters created equal. Whether due to reputation, location, facilities, connections, academic focus, or grades served, the same city may have some oversubscribed schools with yard-long waiting lists while others have plenty of vacancies and struggle to enroll more kids.

Besides competition for students, the interests and priorities of charter schools often throw them into conflict with each other. Philanthropic dollars and community attention are never distributed evenly. Some schools occupy spacious, purpose-built facilities, the construction of which was subsidized by major donors, while others operate in cramped church basements, dingy old parochial school buildings, district hand-me-downs, and storefronts, giving them very different attitudes toward facilities funding. Some depend on district buses to get their pupils to school and home, while others have arranged their own transportation or enroll children who live within walking distance. High-touch schools with long hours and attended by disadvantaged kids may have different needs for money—and various collateral services—than do virtual schools, suburban charters, or schools that specialize in STEM subjects or the arts.

Moves by reformers, authorizers, or political leaders to boost charter quality also elicit different responses from existing schools, depending on how well they're performing—and their views of the best strategies and metrics to ensure quality. Low-performing schools also crave students, resources, and legitimacy, and their supporters understandably resist efforts to paint them in a bad light, much less to threaten their existence. Firms that earn their living by operating or selling services to schools naturally want to sustain their revenues. So do authorizers that derive their income via a formula keyed to student enrollments within their portfolios. Too often, such competing appetites override any qualms about the conflicts of interest inherent in these situations. Reformers worship a pantheon of different quality gods, too. Some favor government regulation, some trust the marketplace, and others insist that test scores are wholly inadequate measures of school quality, maybe worse than none at all. And as previously noted, while parents naturally say they want their kids to attend good schools, most American parents also tend to believe that whatever school their child attends is pretty good—the more so if they chose it themselves—and will combat all efforts to shut it down, even to overhaul it, no matter what the "experts" say about its objective performance.

OHIO CHARTER POLITICS

Ohio offers an interesting port hole on how these tempests play out in the stormy political environments of a given state. It was an early entrant in the charter sector and, by 2015, was home to 373 charters, which enrolled about 7 percent of all public school pupils.[19] Some are outstanding educational institutions, among the highest-performing in the state, particularly for urban students.[20] Unfortunately, Ohio has also been home to scores of low-performing charters. In 2013–2014, more than thirty-one thousand pupils attended charter schools that received state ratings of D or F for their performance on both student achievement and growth metrics. Another fifteen thousand attended dropout recovery charters, which are exempt from state-conferred letter grades but have historically underperformed.

In most Ohio cities, charter achievement has been no better than that of district schools, and often worse. With more than sixty authorizers, including some that were indiscriminate in awarding charters to almost anyone who asked, the Buckeye State gained a reputation as the Wild West of chartering—a designation once belonging to the Grand Canyon State—and "charter school" (officially called "community school" in Ohio) had become something of a term of opprobrium. Among the worst offenders when gauged by student achievement were a handful of giant statewide virtual schools, the biggest of which are run by for-profit firms; a network of dropout recovery schools consisting mostly of computer terminals; and a group of elementary schools operated by White Hat Management, which was owned by David Brennan. A major political donor and veteran insider in the corridors of power in Columbus, Brennan has won well-deserved accolades for his role in bringing school choice to Ohio. But many schools run by

White Hat (most of which were recently acquired by a firm called Pansophic Learning) were inferior, sometimes so much so that their governing boards sought to "divorce" this management firm—moves that the company stoutly fought.[21]

That's the backdrop to a decade-long effort to reform Ohio's messy and permissive charter laws and weak-kneed oversight by the state department of education. (That's also the backdrop to Governor John Kasich's aforementioned plea for more regulation of this sector.) But the low-performing charters, both virtual and brick-and-mortar, and their compliant authorizers had influential friends in the legislature. Because many of these legislators received sizable campaign contributions from charter operators, any overhaul of the charter sector and its statutory underpinnings was a very steep hill to climb. With Kasich and senate education chair Peggy Lehner (both Republicans) as major allies, dogged reformers finally reached the summit in 2015. But it wasn't easy. One boulder started rolling down upon them in July, when virtual charters sought to alter the state's school accountability system by adjusting its metrics in ways that would benefit their own schools in particular and thereby make them less subject to closure on grounds of low performance. The *Columbus Dispatch* reported:

> [There was] a behind-the-scenes push by the statewide online school Electronic Classroom of Tomorrow (ECOT) to change the accountability system for charter schools from the current value-added model to a California-based system.
>
> William Lager, the founder of ECOT, was the second-largest individual contributor to legislative Republicans last election cycle, giving nearly $400,000 in direct contributions. That does not include any money he may have given to nonprofit political organizations set up by House and Senate leaders.
>
> Sources say ECOT lobbyists have been very active behind the scenes on House Bill 2. That includes the Batchelder Group, which also represents White Hat Management, a major for-profit charter-school operator run by David Brennan, another major GOP contributor.[22]

What the newspaper didn't mention here (but had earlier) is that the "senior advisor" to the Batchelder Group is none other than the former Ohio house speaker William G. Batchelder, who had successfully blocked charter reform until term limits pushed him out of office in 2014.[23]

In any event, while the mediocre schools and authorizers, abetted by their lobbyists and wealthy operators, managed to soften the final reform measure in several places and plenty of implementation challenges await, the bill that Kasich signed on November 1, 2015, represented a big step toward quality, albeit one that includes markedly more regulation of the charter sector.[24] During the intervening years, however, tens of thousands of young Ohioans lacked the educational benefit they could have received if their charter schools had been better.

WHAT LIES AHEAD?

As chartering grows its market share, some veteran observers worry that the politics surrounding it are growing more fractious rather than calmer. Journalist Richard Whitmire, for example, sees the widening polarization of American politics creating a possible chasm into which charters could fall: "Superintendents are getting a lot savvier about stopping charters, the teachers unions have made charters their top target, and the Democratic Party, which helped launch charters, appears to be turning against them as the party moves leftward. . . . Plus, there are myriad of ways [sic] the charter school movement itself may expose its own Achilles' heel: Allowing hundreds of substandard charter schools to stay in business, giving critics easy targets."[25]

In another piece, Whitmire argued that charter supporters are beginning to see the political advantage of emulating Colorado and Utah and creating more schools that serve middle-class families. He pointed to charters like BASIS, Great Hearts, the Denver School of Science and Technology, and the District of Columbia's E. L. Haynes Charter School.[26] New Yorkers can witness the fast march of Eva Moskowitz's Success Academies across the city's boroughs and their diverse socioeconomic strata.[27] Teachers College professor Priscilla Wohlstetter noted that a growing number of charters are integrating their student populations "not only as a matter of social justice and constitutional compliance, but also on the grounds that socioeconomic diversity and academic excellence go hand-in-hand."[28] Recently, fourteen intentionally diverse charters across eight states joined in a coalition to share resources and encourage more such schools.[29] Rhode Island's Mayoral Academies (charters that operate under the aegis of the mayors in—so far—five Ocean State communities) also focus on this type of mixed pupil population. As Whitmire noted, "what's happening here raises a compelling question: could an influx of middle-class parents into charter schools emerge as a political game changer? It's too early to answer that question, but it's the right time to ask it."[30]

Chartering's wider footprint might nudge districts, unions, and other traditional foes to adjust to the presence of these intruders in their midst, in which case the politics would quiet down. Or it could have the opposite effect. Any negotiation for peaceful coexistence between charters and districts, however, will no doubt start with each side placing significant demands on the table. District leaders and their allies will insist on greater leverage over the locations, size, missions, and scope of charters and the terms by which their employees are prepared, licensed, and compensated. And the charter sector will demand more favorable treatment for its schools on the fiscal and regulatory fronts, as well as access to (or subsidies for) facilities and other goods and services within the purview of districts. By 2016, it remained to be seen what kinds of pacts can be achieved in how many communities.

PART IV

Toward the Future

11

More and Better Charters for the Kids Who Need Them Most

AS WE CONSIDER the future of charter schooling within American public education, three questions loom. First and most obviously, how do we extend and advance the mission that this sector has proven best at, namely, extricating disadvantaged children from bleak prospects and placing them on a path to college and upward mobility—and what's the downside (if any) of such a focus? Second, what additional education renewal missions is chartering already showing some capacity to tackle, and what would it take to amplify its contributions? And third, how must leaders and friends of this sector, as well as policy makers, philanthropists, and reformers, alter their priorities, strategies, and practices to address the challenges that chartering now faces while better equipping it to fulfill its potential?

As we've seen, chartering has emerged as a durable yet bumptious element of American public education, with sufficient scale to begin to make a difference. It continues to draw keen interest, substantial support, energized participants, and hopeful, sometimes desperate consumers. It has established a respectable track record in the best of its schools, albeit a record dimmed by the presence of too many weak ones. But this movement has developed no real clarity about what the future should look like. Its participants have been consumed with the headaches of getting started, tackling old problems while being rattled by new ones, fending off critics while cultivating allies, and obtaining more resources while evaluating the payoff from what they've already got. Sometimes, too, charter proponents quarrel among themselves about what exactly this project is all about and how to secure their own niches within it. In these final chapters, we focus on the future, beginning with an extrapolation of past accomplishments and then widening the aperture to take in a bigger picture.

It takes no real thought to predict that chartering tomorrow is apt to resemble chartering today. But let us resist that lazy assumption and instead look at the pluses and minuses of continuing on this sector's present course. What does more of the same look like, and what is needed to produce it? Are there reasons not to continue in this direction?

Aside from educating children with significant disabilities, the toughest challenge facing American K–12 education—and the challenge least successfully met by many urban (and more than a few suburban and rural) school systems—is taking children from poor, dysfunctional, and discriminatory circumstances and rebooting their prospects for success in the twenty-first century. Many deficits and other obstacles accompany millions of such students, but too few schools have had the leverage and resources to surmount these challenges for nearly enough kids. Too few educators have believed that it's even possible to do much more of this with the tools at hand.

Rekindling these children's prospects means subjecting them to a rich and well-taught curriculum and supplying role models who embody educational and career possibilities beyond their previous experiences and expectations. These young people must also be well counseled, relentlessly encouraged on multiple fronts, and socialized into the norms of the American dream. Their schools need to meet their ancillary needs, address their individual problems, and launch them on a path that leads to college, career, and upward mobility.

Such responsibilities are a huge challenge for any school—especially considering what a small slice of children's lives schools occupy—yet the tallest tree in the charter forest to date has been the development and replication of some schools that do these things pretty well. In places with functioning charter sectors, these schools' effects are strongest for children in poverty, black and Hispanic youngsters, and English language learners.[1] The charter schools that have proven most successful at helping these kids to gain a fresh lease on life are usually variations on the no-excuses theme.

THE NO-EXCUSES APPROACH

This model has been advanced and enhanced by many boosters, starting with philanthropists that focus on poverty, mobility, and universal college attendance. Public policies aimed at educational gap-closing and creating better options for needy children have also worked at improving and promoting this strategy. A growing school reform movement, most of whose participants have drunk deeply from the well of equal opportunity, promotes the model, as do companion projects such as Teach For America, TNTP, Educators for Excellence, Teach Plus, and others that have supplied smart, motivated instructors and school leaders who have sipped the same waters.

A rational, defensible future strategy for the charter sector is to do more and better at this important work. It's a mission already embraced with gusto and discipline not only by such sizable, high-profile, multilocation networks as KIPP, Achievement First, and Success Academies, but also by dozens of one-off charters that add value for children in their own communities. Examples include the Milwaukee Collegiate Academy, the Dayton Early College Academy, and Herron High School in Indianapolis.

Not all such schools cling tightly to the orthodox no-excuses model, though all incorporate elements of it, and the term remains convenient shorthand by which to characterize this strategy. Some dub themselves classical academies. Others embrace Montessori-style pedagogy. Just as mixed are the schools' origins: groups of parents, teams of teachers, expansion-minded CMOs, local education reformers, community leaders, change-minded politicians, and more. Their structures vary, too. Some schools begin with kindergarten or pre-K and run all the way through twelfth grade, while others are elementary, middle, or high school only. And although many no-excuses schools are attended almost entirely by black or Hispanic children, others draw a more diverse student population from across the city, sometimes from multiple school districts within a metro area.

Nor are all no-excuses schools outstanding educational institutions at this time. On the GreatSchools ten-point rating scale, based

mainly on state test scores, we find plenty of fours and fives in addition
to nines and tens. While schools with achievement in the middling
range may still be giving their pupils a crucial academic boost—kids
who start low can make impressive growth without yet reaching the
"proficient" bar—results like these make clear that there's plenty of
room for improvement in school performance.

For all their variety, these schools generally have in common a
fairly traditional curriculum, a preoccupation with college (prefera-
bly selective four-year colleges) as the primary destination for all their
students, an urban setting, and pupil demographics that are predominantly low-income and minority. If the schools hew to the full
no-excuses model, they also manifest these six characteristics, which
we adapt from an excellent description by former no-excuses teacher
Max Bean:

- *High behavioral and academic expectations for all students*: These expectations are applied without exception, hence the designation
  no excuses. No-excuses schools provide plenty of extra support—
  both emotional and academic—to any student who needs it, but
  they strive never to lower expectations. No matter how troubling a
  student's home life may be, no matter what difficulties his or her
  neighborhood or family may present, the student is still expected
  to work hard and follow the school's code of behavior. This attitude arises from an idealistic and, in fact, radical assumption
  at the heart of the no-excuses movement: that every student, no
  matter what his or her background, is capable of high academic
  achievement and success in life.
- *A strict behavioral and disciplinary code*: This approach leaves little room for ambiguity or inconsistency. Rules and punishments
  are laid out in Talmudic detail, usually in a document that is required—and tested—reading for all students and faculty at the
  beginning of the year. Often, parents are required to sign a statement affirming that they have read this code and agree with it.
- *More time on academics*: This often includes an extended school
  day and year, minimal recess, and Saturday and after-school tutoring. Math and literacy are commonly infused into every subject, even art, theater, and physical education.

- *A college preparatory curriculum for all students*: Even when the school espouses a different specialty or focus (e.g., law and justice at the District of Columbia's Thurgood Marshall Academy, STEM subjects at Milwaukee's Carmen Schools of Science and Technology), equipping every pupil with the skills and knowledge needed for college is the foremost educational objective and undergirds the entire curriculum.
- *A strong focus on building school culture and community values*: No-excuses schools invest much time and energy in teaching kids how to behave in a classroom and how to be respectful to teachers and peers. They work hard to inculcate school pride and instill in their students a belief in the school's core values and in the importance and possibility of the children's own college education.
- *Strategies to hire and motivate great teachers*: These tactics include higher salaries, bonuses tied to performance, and rigorous teacher assessment based on student achievement and observations. Much effort goes into teacher training and professional development.[2]

Properly applied, the no-excuses model has yielded solid results for many kids. A meta-analysis of pertinent studies came to this conclusion in 2015:

> Attending a No Excuses charter school for approximately one year increases student achievement by 0.25 and 0.16 standard deviations in math and literacy, respectively, net of the typical annual growth that students experience. . . . [A]ttending a No Excuses charter school for one year closes approximately 25% of the Black-White math achievement gap and approximately 20% of the Black-White literacy achievement gap. A straightforward extrapolation of these results suggests that attending a No Excuses charter school for four to five years could eliminate the achievement gap.[3]

The no-excuses model can indeed succeed when gauged—as in the studies reviewed here—by test scores. But as we have noted, the model has also been faulted for emphasizing "robotic" behavioral and pedagogical practices, failing to pay sufficient attention to educational desiderata that don't show up on test scores (e.g., character, creativity, and deep understanding), and not preparing young people adequately for the kinds of independence and self-management they will need to thrive in college and beyond.[4] As dismissed by a former no-excuses teacher in New York (who subsequently moved to a "much more progressive public charter school in Brooklyn in order to get back in touch with my pedagogical values"), "the lessons that students indubitably learn [in no-excuses schools] . . . are that rigidity and compliance are predictors of success, and that imagination and interpersonal skills are of nominal use. They also likely learn that school is boring, that it has little relevance to their lives, or in the case of my last school, it is a place where white ladies try to control Black and Latino children."[5]

Nor does the no-excuses model suit everyone. Besides educators who deplore its regimentation, some children (and families) cannot abide its strict discipline, handle its rigorous academic demands, and tolerate its long hours—and others, let's be honest, have needs that these schools are ill-prepared to handle. (This is why they sometimes get accused of "creaming.")

NO-EXCUSES EVOLVES

In addition to pondering such criticisms and asking whether they justify altering the no-excuses model without discarding the baby along with the bathwater, these schools have been pushed in recent years by three developments that have led a number of them to adjust their original approach. First was a 2011 report, both heartening and disturbing, on the college success rates of graduates of KIPP schools, arguably the paradigmatic practitioners of the no-excuses model.[6] Robert Pondiscio summarized the study's findings:

> Thirty-three percent of the earliest cohorts of KIPP middle-school students were found to have graduated college within six years, four times the average rate of students from underserved communities and slightly higher than the figure (31 percent) for *all* U.S. students. It was a clear and unambiguous accomplishment. Yet two out of three former KIPP students were failing to reach the bar, however audacious, that KIPP itself had established as "the essential stepping stone to rewarding work, a steady income,

self-sufficiency and success." The affirming image of smiling, cap-and-gown-bedecked ghetto kids graduating high school and heading off to college and bright horizons beyond lost a bit of its luster.[7]

Second was the growing realization—underscored by the KIPP study, the experiences of other schools and networks, and feedback from former students—that charters serving disadvantaged children need to be more than a phase within the K–12 sequence. For many years, KIPP itself consisted only of middle schools. But schools that are serious about getting disadvantaged kids to and through college need to start younger and continue longer. Too many youngsters are already far behind academically when they reach fifth or sixth grade, much less high school, and turning them loose after, say, eighth grade meant that many would founder. So KIPP reached down wherever it could to start with preschool and reached up through high school. Of KIPP's 183 schools in 2015, 71 were elementary schools and 22 were high schools, and the network's future is one of educational continuity for students from start to finish. After weighing the implications of the college-completion study, the network also launched KIPP Through College, which supports KIPPsters once they pass through the ivy gates. This program offers newly minted college students mentoring, advising, networking, moral support, help with financing, and other services designed to help them persevere and succeed—support seldom satisfactorily supplied by the college itself or by other adults in the students' lives.

KIPP is far from alone. Upward and downward expansionism is visible in a number of other schools and networks. Freedom Prep Charter Schools in Memphis opened in 2009 with ninety-six sixth-graders and expected by 2016 to enroll twelve hundred students from pre-K through twelfth grade. In northeast Los Angeles, the Partnerships to Uplift Communities charter initiative began with a single middle school in 1999 and has grown into a network of more than a dozen, including elementary, middle, high, and "early college" high schools. Such moves toward comprehensiveness can be viewed as consistent with the enveloping paternalism that characterizes no-excuses schools as well as with the realization that small, separate schools typically fare better within larger networks. But these shifts also signal a change in the mission of those schools, from an intervention meant to steer children onto a different path within the traditional system into something more like a complete, self-contained, alternative system of education.[8]

By no means could the third recent development be termed an extension of the no-excuses model: the 2010 arrival of the Common Core academic standards for English and math and their embrace by all but a few states, along with plans to align their future assessments with the standards' expectations. These are quite different from the learning templates that most schools had been following and the tests for which they had been readying their students. The Common Core emphasizes deeper understanding of core concepts, close reading and analysis of ever-more-challenging texts, and the ability to apply one's knowledge and skills to complex as well as routine intellectual challenges. The Foundation for Excellence in Education characterizes the new standards this way:

> While the old standards focused on simply expecting students to recite facts learned through reading textbook passages, the new standards expect students to read books and textbook passages that are more challenging than what was previously read in each grade level—including reading more original writings whenever possible.... Students are then asked to show a deeper understanding of this material than has previously been required of them, demonstrating greater critical thinking and analytic skills.[9]

Such shifts in expectations for student learning meant that schools needed to revise their curricula and pedagogy. Insofar as no-excuses schools had stressed basic skills, rote learning, and preparation for old-style assessments, they now had to change their approach inside and beyond the classroom. Here is how Doug McCurry, superintendent of Achievement First's well-regarded no-excuses charter network in New York and Connecticut, frames his schools' new instructional mandate:

> Ensure that we make students do the work (ample independent time to think and solve, read and find evidence), make kids find the best evidence in the text (gone are the halcyon days of "text to self-connections" substituting for student thinking), make

kids dive deeper into text (we may spend thirty minutes on three dense paragraphs to push deep comprehension), make kids explain their answers (in ELA [English language arts], justify from the text, in math explain and show their answer), make kids write often and fix their writing based on feedback (academic writing is the gateway college skill—and the Common Core measures student responses by the quality of written expression), and make kids learn content in every class (especially in history and science but also throughout the day, we should be cognizant of content aims as well as skill/thinking aims). Notice that I use "make kids" a lot here, for I believe that it's our job to insist on high standards and push kids to do and think. You could also rewrite the entire paragraph with "inspire kids" or "support kids in." . . . We must inspire, support, cajole, pester, make, ensure . . . whatever the verb, our kids must do it![10]

That's definitely not the classroom strategy customarily—if not always accurately—associated with no-excuses schools, and it shows why we ought not view this model as static or unyielding. But its goal hasn't changed. As Aspire Public Schools (a thirty-one-charter network in California and Tennessee) still insists:

> Education transforms lives. We know that to be true. That simple fact is the reason we work tirelessly to make college for certain a reality for every Aspire student. Our goal is ambitious, and our focus is fierce. At our core, we believe that every student deserves that opportunity, and it's our job to equip them with the skills to succeed when they get there. Where is there? Berkeley, Cal State, Fisk, San Francisco State, Howard, UC San Diego, Johns Hopkins, Columbia, USC—you name it, they'll be ready.[11]

BUILDING ON SUCCESS

Transforming the lives of disadvantaged children by relentlessly preparing them for success in college and beyond—that's a pretty good summary of the no-excuses mission. But the schools embracing it may adapt their programs and strategies to accommodate both their own experiences and the changing realities around them. Doing more of this and doing it better is a worthy role for the charter sector going forward. In the United States, there are many places with lots of disadvantaged children, but not yet any no-excuses schools. These kids need better options, too.

Such a future for chartering carries indisputable societal benefit as well as moral and political appeal. It's not terribly threatening to many established education interests (with the prominent exception of urban teachers unions), because it concentrates on youngsters that the traditional system has not done well by—and everybody knows that. It taps into the most generous and selfless instincts of idealistic educators. Insofar as the charter sector has developed an organizational and support infrastructure, this is the mission to which it's best aligned. And because it has a track record of success and proven strategies for replicating that success, the odds of further success are pretty strong. What's more, this version of chartering is relatively easy to raise money for.

As the mission statement of the multi-million-dollar Charter School Growth Fund (CSGF) declares, "We back entrepreneurial leaders who put underserved students on the path to college success."[12] Supported by nearly two dozen foundations, CSGF has assisted more than fifty charter networks to grow into more than five hundred schools enrolling 250,000 students. Another prominent booster organization, the NewSchools Venture Fund, has directed more than $150 million toward creating and expanding more than three hundred charters serving some 167,000 kids. And one funder—the Walton Family Foundation—has provided direct financial startup support to some seventeen hundred charter schools. Not all are no-excuses schools, but many are—and most are urban schools devoted to improving the educational prospects of poor and minority youngsters.

Hewing to that course in the future—creating more solid charters that embrace the mission and seek to boost even greater numbers of disadvantaged kids up the ladder toward college—truly resembles a no-brainer. But this strategy is not without shortcomings. On the next pages, let's look at these.

ON THE OTHER HAND . . .

Scaling no-excuses schools is hard. It demands a sufficient supply of gifted principals and uncommonly dedicated teachers. It usually calls for supplemental funding from philanthropy and collateral help from a variety of organizations that provide student support and family services. And that's not all. We see ten reasons why the expansion of no-excuses schools perhaps ought not be the central preoccupation of chartering in years to come.

First and most obviously, a single-minded concentration on scaling this model neglects other populations with educational needs that might be addressed via chartering. By sticking to a well-worn path, the charter movement may also discourage further innovation and limit the terrain within which schools even try to experiment.

Second, the no-excuses model does not work well for every needy child or family. It requires strong commitment and a willingness to conform to strict norms and does in fact lead to self-selection and a form of creaming, whether voluntary or school-driven. Nor is its paternalistic, "culture-transplant" approach palatable in every disadvantaged community.

Third, even when the no-excuses model scores high on conventional metrics of educational achievement, the pure version of it may not serve the long-term interests of its pupils. In the words of a critical sociology graduate student who spent eighteen months doing fieldwork in a no-excuses school and interviewing teachers, administrators, and students, "these schools' highly prescriptive disciplinary practices, while arguably contributing to their academic success, have unintended consequences for students. As students learn to monitor themselves, hold back their opinions, and defer to authority, they are not encouraged to navigate the more flexible expectations of college and the workplace."[13]

Fourth, the political constituency built by this focus is relatively narrow. No-excuses schools in a few cities—most vividly Eva Moskowitz's Success Academies in New York—have shown their ability to rally thousands of minority children and parents to press officials to allow their schools to operate and loan them facilities in which to do so and to embarrass union leaders and others who would rein them in. In the big picture of American politics and policy, however, this does not constitute broad-based support for anything akin to a fundamental overhaul of public education or even for charters themselves. And the no-excuses model may itself be vulnerable to large shifts in the political winds, such as any ebbing of interest in disadvantaged populations.

Fifth, this is the territory in which charters compete most directly with urban Catholic schools, many of which have been effective over the years (and at lower cost) with the very populations that no-excuses schools attract. Driving more Catholic schools out of business would be a tragedy, not to mention an added burden on taxpayers.

Sixth, the no-excuses model is expensive, and the more thoroughly it's practiced and the deeper it dips into disadvantaged populations, the costlier it gets. The residential SEED School of Washington, DC, costs more than $40,000 per student per year. And as noted earlier, long-term success with many disadvantaged youngsters entails almost a cradle-to-grave (well, cradle through college) strategy that is beyond the scope of conventional K–12 policies, institutional arrangements, and financing formulas.

Seventh, although college is the goal—which means serious, focused work with kids at least through high school—the no-excuses model has experienced considerable fall-off during the high school years because its single-minded academic focus loses appeal for teenagers who crave sports and other extracurriculars not supplied by their schools. Parents who value such activities for their children may also lose enthusiasm for no-excuses schools that offer relatively few such extras.

Eighth, continued focus on this model cannot avoid several sensitive race-related issues. Children served by no-excuses schools are unlikely to find themselves in classrooms where they can mix with children from different backgrounds. Allegations of re-segregation will persist. And schools serving minority kids are endlessly entangled with the question of whether teachers and principals must "look like" the children and families they are serving—and whether the school is truly rooted in its community or is an intruder placed there by well-meaning outsiders.

Ninth, because this model works best where poor kids are densely concentrated and live relatively close by, not least because of the school's long hours and years, up to this point in its evolution the no-excuses brand of chartering has neglected plenty of needy children in inner-ring suburbs (Prince George's County, Maryland, for example), small cities (like Springfield, Ohio), and rural areas. That doesn't mean it must continue to neglect them in the future, but, when families are dispersed across a wider territory, schools that demand so

CHARTERS FOR THE KIDS WHO NEED THEM MOST   165

much of students and parents find it markedly harder to retain them. And as a school moves farther from a lively metropolis, it has a markedly harder time attracting and retaining the kinds of energized (and usually young and often single) staffers that it must have to succeed.

Tenth and finally, because of its intensity, this educational model can often consume and burn out talent.[14]

We can't imagine a future in which chartering spurns the no-excuses model or turns its back on poor and minority kids. Nor should it. This ought to remain a sturdy pillar of the charter sector and continue not only to be replicated and scaled to serve more kids, but also to be perfected and, insofar as possible, transplanted into district schools. The question is whether American education would be better off if this sector had more pillars. We're convinced that it would, indeed that it's already erecting some that could bear more weight and should rise higher.

12

The Larger Promise
of Chartering

CHARTER PIONEERS PICTURED this reform accomplishing many feats and solving numerous problems:

- withdrawing the district's "exclusive franchise" to operate public schools, thus allowing others—both educators and nonprofessionals—to create different kinds of schools, including specialty schools for children keen on STEM subjects, art, music, and more
- enabling teachers to launch schools freed from many bureaucratic uniformities
- truly empowering principals to lead their schools
- enabling parents and community groups to establish schools that the district was unwilling or unable to do
- widening options so needy children would have alternatives to schools that served them poorly
- building innovation labs where educators could try new approaches that might feed into the traditional system
- creating "brand name" schools via networks spanning far-flung communities and states, thus affording some educational consistency to mobile families
- piloting new, nongeographic structures for delivering (and governing) public education
- competing with traditional districts, thereby prodding them to step up their game

Yes, there was a blind-men's-elephant aspect to this mélange of dreams and ambitions. But inherent in these possibilities were strong hints of the many ways that public education in America might benefit from doing things differently. To its credit, today's charter sector contains examples of almost everything its founders envisioned. But many of them just happened because of circumstance—in the most dramatic case, a destructive hurricane—rather than because leaders and backers of the movement saw them as vital components of a comprehensive strategy. Identifying those additional developments and why they're worth encouraging is the job of this chapter.

MANY FLAVORS FOR MANY APPETITES

Way back in 2000, when we published *Charter Schools in Action*, Berkeley professor Bruce Fuller brought out an insightful volume titled *Inside Charter Schools*, featuring a short catalog of interesting exemplars already visible in this new sector. Fuller's list included dual charters in Lansing, Michigan, that served the city's African American community, one school with a traditional curriculum and student uniforms, the other with a progressive learning-by-doing pedagogy and pupils and teachers clad in traditional African garb. He also wrote about an Oakland, California, junior high "sensitive to bilingualism and other aspects of . . . Latino heritage" and a middle school in Chelmsford, Massachusetts, founded by "dissident suburban parents" to serve "average suburban kids." Another school that Fuller described, the Minnesota New Country School in the small city of Le Sueur, began as a cooperative in which teachers would be owners and leaders rather than workers.[1]

A current catalog of diverse charter schools, many of which do not follow the no-excuses model, would include the Sela Public Charter School in northeast Washington, DC, a Hebrew-English dual-language immersion school that starts with three-year-olds and is attended predominantly by African American children. Across town, the Washington Latin Charter School provides a "classical" education to a demographically mixed group of middle and high school pupils. Fifteen hundred miles away, the highly regarded Denver School of Science and Technology is a charter network—closely integrated with the district (see Denver discussion below)—that expects to operate an eleven-campus cluster for 10,500 students by 2025. Arizona's Great Hearts Academies deliver a character-centric, liberal-arts education to a fast-growing population of mostly middle-class families.[2] In Southern California, the Springs Charter Schools, based in Temecula, combine home schooling with on-site instruction in nineteen "student centers."[3] And in a remote corner of Maine, the Cornville Regional Charter School incorporates agricultural education into the curriculum for 120 students from several rural communities.[4]

These examples demonstrate the versatility of chartering as a means of school creation, and the variegated education niches that such schools can fill. So far, though, these have mostly been side shows, more numerous than media accounts let on and welcomed by their own communities, but often unaided by philanthropy or government policy, ignored by many reformers, and handicapped by constraints built into state charter laws.

Should the cultivation of different flowers in the charter garden become less random and more purposeful? Should such blooms also find their way beyond the usual gardens, perhaps into more inner-ring suburbs, small cities, and rural areas with plenty of educationally disadvantaged children but few or no charter schools? A virtue of chartering is that it allows for schools that are sought—or simply needed—by relatively small populations but that are not necessarily seen as vital by the entire city or county. Once again, Tocqueville's perceptive observations about the new United States apply to education today (note the final word in this excerpt from *Democracy in America*):

> Americans of all ages, all conditions, all minds constantly unite. Not only do they have commercial and industrial associations in which all take part, but they also have a thousand other kinds: religious, moral, grave, futile, very general and very particular, immense and very small; Americans use associations to give fêtes, to found seminaries, to build inns, to raise churches, to distribute books, to send missionaries to the antipodes; in this manner they create hospitals, prisons, schools.[5]

Charters with singular mandates or specialties could—and sometimes already do—take even more diverse and distinctive forms than we sketched above. Many people find it hard to imagine a "truly different" school that might work exceptionally well for their children or for a population of youngsters that need a better option until they can see such a place with their own eyes and escape the blinders we all tended to don when we emerged from the not-very-different schools of our own pasts. Sometimes, extant demand drives the creation of specialized schools, but sometimes it needs a push from funders, policy makers, and sector leaders, if only to demonstrate what's possible. (This is, in hindsight, also the no-excuses story!)

We envision, for example, more schools that concentrate on students' moral fiber, sense of mission, perseverance, civic virtues, and social capital. Besides Great Hearts in a number of Arizona communities, the Eagle College Prep network is operating in St. Louis and Phoenix.[6] But parents in Georgia and Illinois, say, cannot yet view such schools with their own eyes and therefore may not know that their children, too, would thrive in settings like these.[7]

Other examples of specialized charters addressing particular education problems and serving unique population segments include high-quality STEM and career-technical schools that are not exclusively oriented toward four-year colleges. California has fourteen of these, mostly within the High Tech High network.[8] The Native American Community Academy in Albuquerque integrates wellness, cultural identity, and academic preparation for Native American youngsters in grades six through twelve. There's also precedent for charters that serve only boys or only girls, that serve gifted children, and that serve military families as they move around the country and globe. New York City's Brilla College Prep charter school has an optional after-school religious-education program (run by a separate organization) that preserves some of the qualities of the Catholic school that was Brilla's antecedent.[9]

We do not suggest that every imaginable group should have public schools devoted to it, and charters should not be handed out like party favors. But there are many needy populations that charters could educate in ways that are not practical or compelling for districts. For example, Georgia governor Nathan Deal has proposed a statewide network of prison-based charter schools, and lawmakers have earmarked more than $12 million to launch this project.[10] And in Washington, DC, the Carlos Rosario International Public Charter School focuses on the city's adult immigrant population, serving more than twenty-five hundred students annually.[11]

The more specialized the school, the more likely it is to face such hard questions as whether it must accept all comers or whether, by focusing on certain kinds of kids, it promotes separatism at the expense of a common-school experience. We Americans tend to be ambivalent—the familiar *E pluribus unum* tension—about separatism and tracking while we also celebrate diversity, multiculturalism, and ethnic consciousness. We're squeamish about separations imposed by government but tend to accept voluntary gatherings and self-sortings.

Traditional districts typically handle such sorting via top-down decisions to open magnet or other specialized schools that focus on particular themes and that are attended by choice, not assignment. These specialized schools sometimes respond to constituent pressures but are more apt to arise from social-engineering impulses, court orders, and state or federal enticements. Charters are much likelier to emerge from the grass roots, via voluntary groupings of like-minded individuals, usually because the district does not offer the sorts of schools they seek for their daughters and sons. Charters can be education boutiques rather than department stores or malls, and they largely exist to serve families that aren't satisfied with, or whose children are not thriving in, existing schools. Leaders and funders of the charter movement need to encourage more spontaneous groupings and educational specialties, some of which even turn out to be prompted by a desire for greater diversity and less sorting than children encounter in conventional schools.[12] These niche and specialty schools, although seemingly at odds with America's long-standing affection for the common school, are consistent with society's many moves in the direction of diversity and choice. They are compatible with—even essential for—any serious version of more personalized, less factory-like learning, a development that augurs a multiplicity of novel approaches to the delivery of instruction—our next topic.

PEDAGOGICAL INNOVATION
VIA CHARTERING

Schools need not be full-time, brick-and-mortar institutions where instruction occurs in self-contained classrooms presided over by flesh-and-blood teachers. That's scarcely an original insight, and it's one upon which many states and districts have begun to act. Chartering's role here is to push boundaries, to experiment, and to bring this kind of opportunity to places that haven't latched on to it or aren't

likely to without someone prodding, piloting, and supplying proto-
types, proof points, and evidence of demand.

Not every boundary-pushing education strategy involves technology, but the digital revolution has created more ways to teach and
learn than were previously available. For example, the Khan Academy has produced short lectures and modularized lessons on numerous subjects and topics in the form of YouTube videos.[13] These
have been integrated into the curricula of some district and charter schools, including—just in California—the Los Altos school system and the Summit charter network.[14] Given a lengthening menu
of options like these, America is within reach of unprecedented opportunities to make the school experience more engaging, to customize every child's education, to accommodate learning differences, and
to let kids move through the curriculum (and the entire sequence of
formal education) at their own speeds. Although such personalized
learning is neither a new idea nor one that district schools all shun,
it's one that charters, by virtue of being somewhat more nimble, less
regulated, and freer from restrictive contracts, can move more swiftly
to develop and deploy. The charter sector has already seen the greatest gains in virtual and blended schooling, coupled with such other
"radical" ideas as students invited to text their teachers with homework questions in the evening and flipped classrooms, where intro-
ductory lessons happen outside school and class time is used to apply
that learning, work with other students, and get help from teachers.

In chapter 4, we flagged some of the tribulations of virtual charters. But other schools in this sector have successfully pioneered
promising forms of blended learning. Well-known examples, in addition to Summit, are Rocketship Education (thirteen schools in California and elsewhere, and lofty expansion plans) and Carpe Diem
Schools (five schools, and more in the works). Technology isn't all that
makes them tick, however. Journalist Richard Whitmire, author of *On
the Rocketship: How Top Charter Schools Are Pushing the Envelope*, credited
blended learning as "an important ingredient" in the schools' success,
but added, "The biggest surprise was the prominent role that parent
activism played, both at the school level and beyond."[15]

Another close watcher of digital learning, former school superintendent and Gates Foundation executive Tom Vander Ark, observes that what's being developed outside the classroom is at least as

important as what touches students directly: "learning analytics that track student knowledge and recommend next steps. . . . Dynamic scheduling [that] matches students that need help with teachers that have time . . . [and] grading systems that assess and score student responses to assessments and computer assignments at large scale, either automatically or via peer grading."[16] Such arrangements may not be visible to children but carry immense benefit for teachers and school leaders, and not just within the charter sector.

We do not propose to strap small children to machines in hopes that they learn something. Especially for younger students, human interaction—conversation, collaboration, resolving differences, learning how to behave in social settings—is integral to quality education.[17] So is physical activity. Such things can happen, however, in a well-put-together school without the teacher serving as the sole source of instruction, and certainly without the instructor having to function as his or her own back office. What we're really talking about is a rapidly evolving set of education delivery systems, each with many moving parts.

Along with the no-excuses model, blended-learning charters have already attracted substantial help from funders, including the Jaquelin Hume and Gates Foundations and joint ventures such as The Learning Accelerator and the NewSchools Venture Fund Catapult program. Plenty of for-profit firms and investors, mindful of the vast potential market lurking within America's $600 billion annual expenditure for K–12 education, are furiously developing products and systems. Several policy groups and advocacy organizations have made this their beat.[18] And it could turn out to be the realm within chartering that does the greatest good for district schools simply by moving the goal posts farther and showing how more educational touchdowns can still be scored.

Another charter-fostered innovation—more structural than pedagogical, but cherished by the classroom practitioners whose opportunities it widens—is the creation of teacher-led schools. Minnesota's New Country School was an early pioneer, embodying Albert Shanker's vision of chartering as a way to enable teachers to invent and lead schools.[19] He would be disappointed that teacher-led schools did not become the foremost use of chartering, but they have done well on a modest scale. Especially at a time when many teachers lament their shrinking autonomy, it's more important than ever to recognize that chartering makes possible something akin to complete teacher control of what happens in a school.[20] And indeed, teacher-powered schools exist—at least seventy across the United States—and half of them are chartered.[21] More could be.

THINKING BIGGER

Chartering can do more than give birth to individual schools. The movement has already made possible some system-level changes and alternative structures. Most fully developed are the *virtual districts*—CMOs, EMOs, and recovery districts—which show the feasibility and versatility of moving beyond a geographically based delivery system.[22] In some communities, however, charters are reshaping the traditional system itself. We turn to three cities that illustrate such possibilities.

A Mixed Market in Washington, DC

The nation's capital is not the only place where the charter sector has grown large enough to parallel and rival the traditional district, rather than being drawn into it (as in Denver) or replacing it (as in New Orleans)—both discussed below. But Washington is probably the best-functioning example of a mixed market within public education.[23] By 2015–2016, total public school enrollment in the federal city (spanning both charter and district sectors) was 87,443, with nearly 47 percent of students enrolled in charter schools. There were 112 charters and 111 district schools. Scores have risen in both sectors, with charter gains surpassing those of the District of Columbia Public Schools (DCPS).[24]

And rise they surely needed to do. Washington had been infamous for decades for its well-funded but generally mediocre public education system, one with a handful of high-scoring schools in the prosperous far northwest but bleak offerings almost everywhere else. Governed (starting in 1968, when Congress gave the District of Columbia a modicum of home rule) by an elected school board rife with politics and riddled with deficit spending and corruption, DCPS had resisted the turnaround efforts of numerous hardworking superintendents and reform-minded philanthropists.

The situation began to change in 1996, when Congress reasserted itself on several fronts, including the creation of an independent school-chartering body. In chronicler David Osborne's words, "an astonishing variety of schools sprang up." DCPS tried to curb this competition but was stymied by a congressionally mandated "emergency control board," which ran the deficit-burdened city's affairs until 2000—and tended to favor the new charter sector.

By 2007, 27 percent of the city's public school pupils attended charters, but the city was still plagued by low academic performance. In response, newly elected Mayor Adrian Fenty persuaded the city council to give him control of the school system and the authority to appoint its chancellor. He promptly picked take-no-prisoners Michelle Rhee. Many reforms followed, as did the arrival of much philanthropy and talent and the transfer of all charter authority to the DC Public Charter School Board. Scores gradually began to rise in some DCPS-operated schools—and the community began to feel more hopeful about its K–12 opportunities.[25]

The city's education-governance arrangements took final form in 2010, when the mayor gained full authority to appoint both the DCPS chancellor and the DC Public Charter School Board. In effect, the mayor (and city council) now preside over a dual system: both the traditional (but by now very different) school district and a parallel charter sector comprising independently operated schools that are all answerable to a single authorizer.[26]

Today, the sectors both collaborate and compete. On the collaborative side, DCPS and almost all of the charters have joined a unified school-application and enrollment system called My School DC. DCPS has also agreed to take over at least one charter school when its charter was revoked, and a specialized DCPS school is merging with a charter school.[27] Still, conflicts continue over charters' use of vacant DCPS buildings, equitable funding, the location of future schools, and more. A lively debate is also under way within the charter community on exactly how many charter schools Washington should have. One side contends that something akin to the present arrangement is optimal, as competition between two roughly equal sectors is healthy for both and leaves charters free to be different and more autonomous while preserving the traditional district schools as a familiar—and improving—default for those unwilling or unable to navigate the marketplace. The other side views the present situation in the District of Columbia as an awkward, shifting compromise en route to a coherent, charter-centric system like the one in New Orleans.[28]

As for academic outcomes, student achievement has indeed made gains in both sectors, although it's still inadequate in far too many schools. Taken as a group, however, the charters are doing better than DCPS. Osborne offers this structure- and governance-based explanation:

> Charters excel not because their people are somehow better than those in DCPS. They excel because their governance framework—which includes school autonomy, full parental choice, and serious accountability for performance—is superior to the more traditional DCPS approach. It creates an environment in which the extraordinary measures necessary to effectively educate poor, minority children are not only easier to implement, they are virtually required if schools are to survive.
>
> Perhaps the biggest governance difference is that the Charter Board contracts with organizations to operate schools, rather than employing all school staff. This gives it the political freedom to do what is best for the children, even when that conflicts with adult interests. Since 2009, it has closed almost five schools a year, for instance. Some of those school communities have resisted. But when DCPS contemplates closing schools and laying off teachers, the entire system pushes back: employees, their unions, parents, and neighborhood activists. Since all those people vote, the mayor feels the pressure. Indeed, it cost Adrian Fenty his reelection in 2010.[29]

Denver Builds a Portfolio District

Already cited several times in these pages, the portfolio approach for charter schools typically retains the familiar geography of districts and local democratic control via an elected school board or mayor.[30] But it outsources some or all school operations. Other key components of a portfolio district are choices for families; substantial building-level autonomy; some form of pupil-based funding; external sources of school services and support; performance-based accountability; and extensive public engagement.[31] As described by Paul Hill and colleagues, this is a "system of continuous improvement for diverse, autonomous schools governed by performance contracts [where] government would be a performance manager."[32] Today, Denver illustrates this approach better than any other major city.

In 2014–2015, the Denver Public Schools (DPS) had 185 schools, including 54 charters, 36 "innovation" schools, and a collection of magnets, alternatives, and conventional neighborhood schools. With total enrollment around 90,100, almost 57 percent of its students were Hispanic, 22 percent Caucasian, 14 percent African American, and 7 percent "other." About 70 percent qualified for subsidized lunches, 11 percent received special education services, and 38 percent were English-language learners. Charter students constituted 17 percent of the total.

DPS is overseen by an elected seven-member board with authority to hire and fire the superintendent and also to authorize charter schools. Despite the tribulations of many urban districts with elected boards, Denver has seen remarkable leadership stability and a consistent agenda over an extended period, with just two superintendents from 2005 to 2015. Although the school board had some cliff-hanger elections, it maintained at least a four-vote reform majority. Columbia University political scientist Jeff Henig says that through it all, Denver has preserved an even-keeled approach to reform: "politically astute, pragmatic, not ideological, less partisan, less got-to-do-it-now-at-all-costs. And as a result of that, it's avoided some of the backlash we've seen in other places."[33]

The Policy Environment. Denver's reforms owe much to three state policies. The first was Colorado's Public Schools Choice Act (1990), which allowed for open enrollment. That is, families could place their children in schools outside their neighborhoods and in other districts. The second was Colorado's bipartisan charter law (1993).[34] The third, the Innovation Schools Act (2008), provided greater autonomy for district-operated schools.

The combined impact of the first two state policy changes was documented in an April 2007 report in the *Rocky Mountain News*, which said that nearly one-quarter of Denver children did not attend DPS schools, having instead opted for private schools, suburban districts, and charters.[35] The report also noted that "the district is ur-gently working on reform, hoping to attract more students."[36]

Some reforms had been initiated by prior superintendents and boards, but it was Michael Bennet (now Colorado's senior US senator) who took the district helm in 2005 and accelerated these efforts.[37] He and the board seized upon the alarming newspaper report and responded to it. "A Vision for a 21st Century School District" urged the community to unite around a suite of changes that would make Denver "the vanguard for reform in public education," a place where "DPS no longer function[s] as a one-size-fits-all, centralized, industrial-age enterprise making choices that school, principals, teachers, and, most important, parents are in a much better position to make for themselves."[38] This vision drove the DPS portfolio strategy.

In 2008, bipartisan legislators worked with Bennet to craft the third key state law, the Innovation Schools Act. This statute, plus the earlier two, thus formed the policy substructure for much of the education reform that followed in the Mile High City.

Autonomy, Accountability, and Partnerships. In addition to traditional district schools, DPS now has two other types in its portfolio—charters and *innovation schools*. The latter are district managed but can seek waivers from local regulations, state laws, and collective-bargaining agreements. They lack independent governing boards but have seven-member advisory councils. Innovation-school status may only be revoked by the DPS board on grounds of weak academic performance. Groups of schools with similar interests may also seek to become *innovation school zones*.[39]

Since 2010, all DPS schools have been evaluated under a performance framework that allows schools to be compared, regardless of their governance. This system employs multiple measures, including academic growth and proficiency, student engagement, parent satisfaction, and college and career readiness.

The district's portfolio-management team is responsible for overseeing both charter and innovation schools. It also runs the Call for New Quality Schools process, which gauges and publicizes the district's education needs; authorizes schools; provides them with oversight and support; and manages charter renewals. The team is also supposed to spread best practices from charter and innovation schools throughout the district.

As a 2015 Fordham Institute report says, Denver "has increasingly looked to charters as bona fide 'trading partners' and has made supporting and growing high-quality charter schools a central tenet of its reform plans."[40] A district–charter compact has helped to advance this partnership.[41] Some twenty districts around the country have such compacts, but journalist Whitmire pegs Denver's as the nation's premier example.[42] Its elements include a streamlined process for renewing and replicating high-performing charters; joint responsibility for special education (discussed in chapter 9); the common enrollment system; and some shared resources, including charter access to district facilities, joint purchasing, and pupil transportation.

Real but Modest Gains. Led first by Bennet and then by his former deputy, Tom Boasberg, Denver's journey toward portfolio-style operation and related reforms has shown some results. Over the past decade, the number of students scoring at the proficient level or better rose 15 percent, with achievement slightly superior in the charter schools.[43]

Yet Denver's portfolio remains a work in progress. The Fordham study terms its results "modest."[44] Some charters have declined to join the compact.[45] On the other hand, forward movement is visible on some key issues, including the common accountability system, special education, admission to schools, and access to facilities. As for the future, say Paul Hill and his colleagues, we should watch for further progress:

> The core of the portfolio idea . . . is [that] the district seeks continuous improvement by providing the autonomy, data, and the new sources of support, then assessing the performance of all schools, closing the lowest performing schools, and creating new opportunities for students who have been in the least productive schools. This process continues indefinitely, so that the district is progressively less tolerant of unproductive schools. Schools—new and old—that were once considered "good enough" will ultimately experience pressure for continuous improvement.[46]

Denver shows signs of such progress, but the portfolio strategy, when undertaken by a traditional district like DPS, must cope with a fundamental clash between the ingrained management culture of the central office and the market dynamics associated with school autonomy and choice. Can that gap ever be fully bridged and those divergent styles harmonized? In the end, is it more trouble for less gain than creating a parallel system like that in Washington, DC, or a replacement system like that in New Orleans? We're not sure yet.

A Replacement District Arises on the Mississippi's Shores

Louisiana's Recovery School District (RSD) was created by the state legislature in 2003, two years before Hurricane Katrina, when the state's Board of Elementary and Secondary Education was authorized to take over chronically low-performing schools by extricating them from their districts and placing them in the RSD. The new entity could then manage them directly or charter them as it strove to turn them around.[47] It could also override existing contracts, including those related to personnel.

By August 2005, the RSD had converted five failing New Orleans schools into charters. Then came the deadly storm, after which lawmakers widened the RSD's responsibilities, making it the instrument for totally overhauling public education in the Big Easy, a city long known for dismal schools, intransigent unions, and widespread corruption. The transformation, however, did not happen overnight.[48]

The first phase of post-Katrina RSD activity involved converting preexisting district schools into charters and getting enough of them reopened. The second phase consisted of efforts to incubate new schools, work mostly spearheaded by a local nonprofit named New Schools for New Orleans. The third phase, from about 2010 through 2014, involved the growth of charter management organizations, many of them spawned locally. During this period, the share of New Orleans students attending CMO schools rose from 21 percent to 57 percent. High-performing CMOs also led most of the charter restarts—that is, rather than close down a failing charter, the RSD worked with a local CMO to reboot it so that children could remain in the same building.

As of 2014–2015, the RSD's New Orleans operation was entirely charter, overseeing fifty-seven campuses with more than twenty-nine thousand students, some 92 percent of the city's total public school population.[49] The other 8 percent attend schools run by a vestige of the old Orleans Parish School Board (OPSB). Almost all New Orleans pupils are eligible for subsidized lunches, and 12 percent have IEPs. Although originally created to serve students stuck in weak schools and to turn those schools around, the RSD is now the city's main provider of public education. It works with OPSB, the Louisiana Department of Education, nonprofit organizations (e.g., New Schools for New Orleans, Teach For America New Orleans, and teachNOLA), and other community groups (e.g., the New Orleans Urban League and Tulane University) to make sure that all students are served.

In short, the RSD operation in New Orleans has removed almost all of public education from the traditional district and then, via chartering, entrusted it to other entities to operate and provide services to schools. So who now ensures that every child can find a suitable school? How do children avoid discrimination? What about families that aren't good at making choices? Children without families? In addition to its handling of special education (and weighted funding), the RSD has taken several steps to safeguard equity.[50]

School Access and Exit. The unified enrollment system (Enroll-NOLA) is designed to afford children equal access to schools across the city. By 2014, 84 percent of New Orleans students used it. Families complete their applications online or at enrollment centers, and an outreach program led by the New Orleans Urban League canvasses neighborhoods so that children aren't overlooked. School descriptions include letter grades based on the state accountability system. Elementary schools may reserve up to half their seats for neighborhood residents, but high schools have no geographic preferences. Siblings do get preference, however, as do kids who had attended a school that was closed for poor performance. Schools with additional selection requirements—for example, for arts or languages—may keep those requirements. And all RSD schools must provide access to transportation paid for by the school.

At first, the RSD allowed individual schools to set their own criteria for pupil entries and exits, including suspensions, expulsions, and backfilling. Today, it has centralized rules—much like a conventional district—so that no school can unilaterally expel a child. To limit

subtler efforts by schools to persuade wayward or low-achieving pupils to depart, school transfers are restricted to hardship situations,
and all schools backfill when pupil openings arise. Under this revised
approach, suspension rates have dropped, and expulsion rates, for the
first time, have fallen below the state average.[51]

Dollars and Talent. Between 2006 and 2014, the RSD received from
public and philanthropic sources supplemental funds totaling some
$250 million. It's a big number, to be sure, yet it represents less than
6 percent of total spending and has mostly been devoted to charter
expansion and human-capital development. (The Federal Emergency
Management Agency also provided $1.8 billion to rebuild or replace
school facilities.)

At the same time, and again thanks in part to philanthropy, New
Orleans has become a magnet for educator talent and reform energy.
New Schools for New Orleans worked with many local and national
organizations to attract skilled individuals to town. Both the state
and the RSD have also benefited from exceptional leadership, including state superintendents Paul Pastorek and John White and RSD
chief Paul Vallas.[52]

Lingering Issues. The RSD has been active in other key areas that need
attention if the new structural arrangements are to succeed, and some
of this activity again resembles variations on classic district practices.
On the school-accountability front, the RSD now assigns every school
a performance grade on the familiar A through F scale, basing this
primarily on state test scores, incorporating a mix of students' absolute achievement, and their academic growth. A school must receive
a D or better (or demonstrate significant growth) for its charter to be
renewed after its first five-year term. And it must receive a C or better
(or achieve significant growth) to be renewed after its second term.

On the HR front, with RSD schools freed from collective-
bargaining requirements, nearly all New Orleans educators are now
at-will employees. For professional development, schools may join
with independent talent-development groups such as the Relay Graduate School of Education and the local School Leadership Center of
New Orleans. But the history here is still heavy with emotion, as some
seventy-five hundred public school employees were terminated after

Katrina. These wounds linger, aggravated by a decline in the proportion of black teachers, from 71 percent in 2004 to about 50 percent today.

As public education has shifted from the old district structure to today's arrangement, another sore spot has been the loss of traditional local control and the dearth of community engagement in establishing and operating the RSD. Polls indicate frustration among New Orleanians for many reasons. There was the dismissal of many district employees and the demise of collective bargaining. Families faced logistical confusion as a new choice system arrived along with many school openings, closings, relocations, and restarts, not to mention the loss of neighborhood schools. And there was the clumsy initial handling of discipline and expulsions, especially of black children, which many saw as punitive and discriminatory.

As for future control of the schools, the original RSD legislation said that low-performing schools could be returned to the district after five years if they met acceptable academic benchmarks or had significant gains for two consecutive years. A 2010 amendment required that a charter meeting these criteria would decide—by vote of its board—whether to stay under the RSD or return to the OPSB. In 2016, however, a new governor signed a bill that requires all New Orleans charters to return to OPSB oversight, with safguards meant to preserve their autonomy.

Results. Despite lingering birth pains, the overhaul of public education in New Orleans has yielded some notable results. In 2004, 31 percent of the city's students had performed on grade level on state tests. This doubled to 62 percent in 2014, as the statewide percentage rose from 56 to 68. Over the same period, the percentage of New Orleans pupils attending schools ranked in the bottom tenth statewide shrank dramatically from 60 to 13. And the on-time four-year graduation rate soared from 54 percent to 73 percent.

Even so, Louisiana's RSD—and public schooling in New Orleans—also remains a work in progress. It hasn't fully resolved all the tough questions that a new governance structure must confront. Although the issues are universal, their handling within a charter-centric arrangement needs further attention. So many of the familiar mechanisms of public education—academic standards, assessments, accountability systems, teacher preparation and licensure, career pathways, bus schedules, and special education—presuppose uniformity and central-ization. The more the "one best system" gets replaced by structures based on different assumptions, the less satisfactory the old arrangements will prove.

In all three cities profiled in this chapter, the big changes that have occurred with the help of chartering began with a troubled district, exiting families, financial stress, and dismal scores. (New Orleans had the hurricane, too.) This concatenation of woe gave rise to major governance reforms that were made possible—or at least facilitated—by chartering. In all three cases, chartering magnified the capacity of a severely challenged delivery system to do things better, while furthering structural innovation within public education as a whole. In Denver, the changes were mostly part of a strategic plan (although alterations in state policy loomed large in both the problems and the solutions of DPS), while what emerged in Washington, DC, is more like a gradual working out of alternative structures by multiple players, both local and national. Although never a single coherent plan, Washington now looks like a notable example of two systems of schools that cohabit, compete, strengthen, and embolden each other within a mayor-dominated municipal government that's ultimately in charge of both. One might think of it as a different sort of portfolio. There's cooperation where necessary—especially in making the choice system work for families—but there's also plenty of rivalry for students, status, and resources. In New Orleans, the impetus for change (besides Katrina) was bold intervention—and structural creativity—on the state's part, giving rise to a new kind of system that is hard to imagine growing from local roots.

In none of these cities so far is every school a source of quality learning. But more schools in all three places are doing right by their students, and many needy kids are better served by today's restructured systems than back when there was no alternative to the traditional arrangement.

We cannot predict every possible outcome in a community that accepts and deploys chartering as a versatile tool, but doing this creates many opportunities: the chance to invent, reshape, and replace timeworn structures and archaic governance arrangements while giving parents and students the right to choose among varied offerings. It also allows enterprising educators (and community leaders and others) to create schools that embody distinctive visions and address the needs of particular constituencies. The presence of multiple authorizers can help usher more such diverse schools into being. And the charter movement gives great leaders and educational entrepreneurs chances to exercise real authority over schools rather than slog through bureaucratic quagmire.

To push these wider possibilities into the center ring of chartering, however—even to expand and enhance the no-excuses version described earlier in this book—demands changes on multiple fronts. In the next chapter, we outline some important additions and alterations.

13

Toward Better Schools and Stronger Markets

WHETHER ONE FAVORS the "enhanced and improved" no-excuses-centric future depicted in chapter 11 or the expanded view of chartering's potential commended in chapter 12, the reality is that neither will be self-actualizing. Each requires purposeful action on the part of those who want it to happen. Even a simple continuation of today's charter sector will be burdened by its uneven performance record, semifunctional marketplace, and other challenges and shortcomings. It's great to cheer the twenty-fifth anniversary of something so promising, but it's folly to let celebration obscure the need for major-league changes on multiple fronts. This chapter examines the changes most needed to foster strong markets, viable schools and a charter sector that serves its students well.

Some changes amount to recalibrating tricky equilibriums that are key to successful charters. Certain elements of this sector, for example, need greater oversight and accountability (e.g., authorizers and for-profit EMOs), while others—the schools themselves, by and large—need more autonomy and less regulation. Some places need better laws, while others mainly need existing statutes to be enforced. Some glitches, sadly, will be hard to fix because of fundamentally divergent views about how best to educate children, and the structural, cultural, and philosophical conflicts between the standard operating procedures of large bureaucratic systems and the practices of small, independent organizations.

The present situation, therefore, cannot be entirely rectified via a simple list of ready repairs. Even after twenty-five years, and with the partial exception of places like New Orleans, where charters are becoming the main delivery system, these schools remain something of an alien implant in the body of American public education, and an array of immune reactions to them persists. The symptoms can be treated, but continued monitoring and further treatment will remain essential. In this chapter, we place the most important repairs and additions into ten categories.

STATUTORY

As has been clear since Ember Reichgott first introduced her bill in the Minnesota legislature in 1989, state laws both determine whether there will be any charters at all and lay down the ground rules by which they operate. Now that all but a handful of states have such laws on their books, the primary statutory issue facing this sector is not whether the remaining seven states come on board but whether existing charter laws are up to the challenges at hand. As we've seen, states keep revising them—to allow more schools, alter the duties of authorizers, fiddle with funding formulas and facilities help, tighten or loosen the regulatory screws, and more. In short, charter laws and policies are a moving target.

In 2014 alone, for example, reports the National Alliance for Public Charter Schools (NAPCS), ten states moved "to strengthen their authorizing environments," while six "improved their support for public charter school funding and facilities."[1] Still, NAPCS's 2016 appraisal of state laws shows that nine states failed to earn even *half* the points possible in this rating system and just three (Indiana, Alabama, and Minnesota) earned more than three-quarters of what would denote statutory perfection.[2] Even on so fundamental—and relatively benign—a matter as "comprehensive charter school monitoring and data collection processes," only thirteen jurisdictions get high marks. So there's a long way to go—and traveling that distance is the work of state-level policy makers.

The biggest single policy challenge is to end restrictions on the future supply of charter schools in many places, but to do so without forfeiting quality control. No marketplace can function well without a sufficient supply of its products. In the case of charter schools, when tight caps or other external supply restrictions make it hard to gain access to *any* charter, families can't afford to be fussy and suppliers have little incentive to improve their products. But supply expansion also requires adequate capital, which few charter operators have. Because these schools lack taxing authority, cannot issue district-style bonds, and usually have limited borrowing capacity, it's hard to start and house a new charter, even when an authorizer approves its application. The federal government has a long-standing program of grants to assist with the launch of more schools, and some national philanthropies have invested generously in this activity.[3] CMOs with track records of success can seek help from the Charter School Growth Fund to expand their networks.[4] And some cities have seen the emergence of nonprofit groups that coordinate local efforts to augment the supply of charters and assist organizations that support them. These organizations sometimes evolve into incubators that escort new charters through the many start-up minefields.[5] Yet for all of that, start-up dollars remain scarce.

When augmenting school supply, however, charter proponents encounter agonizing trade-offs. As described earlier, caps on charter and pupil numbers, combined with tough-minded authorizing, are part of the reason that schools in a few places have done especially well on achievement metrics. But the restrictions have also led to long waiting lists that frustrate thousands of families. And they've left many needy children without viable alternatives to district-operated schools, which in turn lack pressure to improve, partly because there are too few charters to pose a palpable competitive threat. Nor have parents in these places had a compelling reason to turn into discerning education consumers, because they're grateful for any charter seat their child is fortunate enough to be offered.

Stanford economist Caroline Hoxby has examined the elasticity of the charter market, specifically, whether school supply will expand as long as there is unmet demand. She concludes that this is strongly affected by provisions of state charter laws, especially whether funding is adequate and school autonomy real, particularly in the realms of staffing, budgets, and instruction.[6]

Our goal is not more charters per se. Serving more children well is what matters, and where districts can do that, we say bravo. But those are typically places with little demand for charters in the first place. Charters are meant to function as alternatives for families that need and want them. If the schools are unable to launch and sail, they obviously cannot carry any passengers. All this is intensely political, and a statutory gain as seen from one perspective is generally a set-back when viewed from elsewhere. Still and all, it's essential to keep in mind that lawmakers hold many of the cards in the great game of chartering's future.

REGULATORY

Regulations fly at charters (and authorizers and other key actors) from many directions, including every level of government, local school districts, and innumerable other agencies, as well as foundations and support organizations that attach their own requirements. As we've noted several times in these pages, some regulations are essential and some regulatory realms need tightening, particularly regarding the obligations of, and potential interventions by, authorizers.

As we have also noted, finding a sustainable equilibrium between freedom and regulation is tough. The term *regulated marketplace* is akin to *E pluribus unum*; each contains two seemingly opposite values that must be kept in balance because each is essential in its way, but each can also spin out of control. Americans work at this balance in just about every sector of modern society that allows any market activity at all. (Consider the complex interactions of the US Food and Drug Administration with pharmaceutical firms and food suppliers.) Traditional school districts rely mostly on regulation to ensure quality. Private schools make the most of freedom. Charters fall in between, but with the added wrinkle that they're meant to be accountable primarily for their results, not their inputs, actions, or services—and authorizers rather than traditional bureaucracies are charged with monitoring those results. So it's a delicate, multi-part calibration in need of constant vigilance and fine-tuning.

In chapter 9, we presented NAPCS's short list of crucial school autonomies, including fiscal and legal independence and exemptions from some state and district regulations and from collective bargaining.[7] A more detailed version comes from the Center on Reinventing Public Education.[8] Far too few schools enjoy such freedoms today. But more freedom would be safer (and politically easier) to confer if people could be sure that authorizers were doing their jobs well when it comes to quality control. The National Association of Charter School Authorizers annually surveys the hundred or so largest authorizers (which oversee about 70 percent of all charters) regarding how many of the organization's twelve "essential practices" the authorizers actually employ. The association found gains during 2014, as in most years: "63% of large authorizers reported implementing 11 or 12 *Index* practices—a 50% increase from 2013." Yes, it's self-reporting, and yes, it omits hundreds of smaller authorizers (which collectively oversee a couple of thousand schools), but within its limits, the report shows both that authorizer practices have been improving and that here, too, there's still a considerable distance to travel.[9] School autonomy in return for authorizer vigilance is another crucial balancing act that needs work on both ends.

ACCOUNTABILITY

Both authorizers and schools need to be accountable for their results as well as for fairness, transparency, conscientious handling of taxpayer dollars, and more. But our immediate focus is state (and sometimes district) *accountability systems* of the academic kind, and whether they're properly aligned with charters and chartering. How states handle this going forward has gained even greater salience in light of recent changes in federal law that give them much wider discretion in this realm.

Educational innovations favored by some charter (and district) schools clash with academic standards that are framed by age and grade level. They clash further with accountability regimes based on test scores tied to those standards. Some states have already exempted certain charters (often dropout recovery schools) from the usual metrics and timelines, but greater flexibility will be needed for other kinds of schools to succeed. Most obvious is a school that conscientiously implements personalized learning and moves its students forward according to their mastery of content and skills rather than one grade per calendar year.

Exempting more schools is not our intent. Rather, we seek academic standards, testing regimes, and accountability schemes that do not confine kids exclusively to *proficiency* defined as "meeting grade-level standards" and that refrain from judging schools primarily on how many of their pupils attain that kind of proficiency. (It scarcely needs mentioning that such changes would also be hugely beneficial to reform-minded districts and their pupils.)

FISCAL

Without reasonable operating dollars, no school can afford to deliver a quality product in a pleasant setting. As we have noted, schools with too-tight budgets cut corners in ways that can weaken academic quality. Of course, more money per se doesn't yield better education. But an acute shortage of funds can mean fewer, less experienced, and more transitory teachers; outdated books; and skimpy technology. It can mean a drafty, ugly, cramped facility in which instruction might be outstanding but nobody wants to spend time. When funds are too tight, schools often lack the collateral services that some kids really need (e.g., breakfast, after-school care, extra tutoring, social work, a library). And when a school is financially strapped, its leadership team must work so hard to keep the place afloat that it wears itself out and has little time for planning, curriculum innovation, purposeful attention to character, physical fitness, or any of the myriad other qualities that Americans want their children's schools to foster.

All that is true of both district and charter schools. But in an era of school choice, a key additional consideration comes into play: financing mechanisms should enable children who change schools to "take their money with them," including whatever added dollars are tied to individual circumstances (e.g., disability, disadvantage, and limited English proficiency).[10] In other words, we're not dealing only with the total amounts of public dollars that reach charter schools but also with the mechanisms by which money is apportioned. Today, almost everywhere, those dollars are based on standard K–12 fiscal formulas attached to geographically delimited districts and local (as well as state and federal) taxing and budgeting practices. For many charters, such standard formulas are a fundamental mismatch. Consider, for example, the many situations where a charter pupil attends school outside his or her district of residence.

Several states and cities have begun to move toward portable, student-based funding—sometimes called *backpack funding*—rather than the customary allocation formulas, which often have more to do with teaching positions than actual enrollment and program offerings, much less the educational needs and circumstances of individual children.[11] For this change to work well, however, all the local, state, and federal dollars that apply to a given child's education need to be in the backpack—and that's a goal no jurisdiction has yet reached.

Nothing about this is easy or conflict-free. Education dollars are finite, and the more money that accompanies students into charter schools, the less that remains for traditional districts. Although the sending schools also have fewer children to educate, that doesn't mean they can easily reduce their costs. For now, our point is simply that a marketplace works well only when shoppers can spend their resources at whichever providers they choose.

Separate from the quantity and flow of operating dollars for schools is the matter of facilities funding, where charters almost everywhere have been getting the short end of the fiscal stick. Lisa Grover of NAPCS underscores this problem: "One of the biggest challenges to the continued expansion of public charter schools is the fact that many public charter school laws place the ultimate burden of obtaining and paying for facilities on public charter schools themselves."[12] In places where co-location of charter and district schools is feasible or where there's an ample supply of unused school facilities belonging to the district (or city or state), improved provision for charters does not necessarily entail more direct expense, just the willingness of those in charge of such facilities to make them available to charters. Where that's not realistic, charters need reasonable access to their own capital dollars, whether the money comes from state or local sources, or the capacity to float bonds or otherwise borrow against future revenues in secure and nonexploitative ways.

Up to this point, we've referred only to public dollars, but the priorities and generosity of private philanthropy play a sizable role in the fiscal fate of charter schools and the future direction of the whole sector. Insofar as they continue to concentrate their largesse on the expansion of CMOs that operate no-excuses schools, on related organizations that support such schools and supply staff for them, and on a handful of major cities, philanthropists will surely continue to do good, but they will also limit the scope of chartering. Better, in our view, would be for key private funders to widen their own apertures and be proactive regarding the additional possibilities that a more expansive view of chartering could encompass.

As for the profit seekers in this space, policy makers should not shut off their access, rebuff their dollars, or quench their entrepreneurialism and creativity. What's needed is to ensure, via sound policy, scrupulous authorizing and meticulous audits, that their schools (and the services they sell to schools) yield quality results, and that nobody is running amok with public funds. Everyone needs to profit from this activity, not just the investors!

HUMAN CAPITAL

The human-capital pipelines that support a lively education marketplace differ markedly from those found in traditional systems. So, too, with HR structures and rules, which in the district sector generally operate beyond the purview of individual schools. In the charter sector, where school operators ordinarily have the freedom to staff themselves in flexible and sometimes unconventional ways, a huge issue is how to find and prepare—and deploy and compensate—suitable teachers and school leaders. Developing great principals is a special challenge because their duties and responsibilities generally exceed those of district principals. Yet conventional educational-leadership programs have scant experience in prepping people for CEO-style roles at the building level. That's one reason it's important to free charters from the obligation to hire the products of such programs. But where to find individuals with the skill set, commitment, and temperament to lead a first-class charter school? A whole new set of programs, organizations, and institutions has arisen to help answer that question, including some CMOs that now "grow their own." We sketched a few promising examples of such support structures for charter personnel in chapter 5 but many more are needed if this sector is to flourish.

INFORMATION

Although K-12 education has many constituents—including taxpayers and policy makers—that want and deserve to know how their schools are doing, we focus here on school-shopping parents and other adults directly responsible for children. As we have shown, a bountiful supply of charter seats—caused by open-handed authorizing, adequate funding, and loose (or no) limits on schools—creates ample choices but imposes little market discipline with regard to quality. For kids to end up in schools that serve them well, parents need to be smart consumers.[13]

Better approaches to providing parents with clear, impartial school information are emerging in some cities. In the District of Columbia, the Office of the State Superintendent of Education has teamed up with other organizations to create LearnDC, a one-stop website with information about every district and charter school. It contains test scores, graduation rates, program offerings, enrollment trends, and more. One of the best examples we've seen of collaboration between the charter and district sectors on behalf of children's best interests, LearnDC features extensive information on each school that participates in the shared lottery. It also has staffers who go door to door, canvassing in cooperation with community-based groups, and it sponsors an annual EdFest where families can learn about schools in person.[14]

Another example comes from Houston, where Families Empowered was founded in 2009 by Teach For America alumna Colleen Dippel to help parents understand their options and choose the right school for their child via a number of selection tools. Once families determine which schools they prefer, the program helps them navigate the application process. Families Empowered will readily match children with quality district, charter, or private schools. Each summer, it also runs a bilingual call center to aid parents still searching for schools.

A recent look at parents' experience in eight high-choice cities, conducted by the Center on Reinventing Public Education, yielded interesting responses. There were, of course, some fairly consistent patterns linked to socioeconomic status, race, and a child's need for special education services (with those parents likelier to report marketplace challenges). In Washington, DC, and New Orleans, two cities with relatively mature charter markets and many choices, about four-fifths of parents were likely to rank schools' academic quality as a higher priority than safety and location, compared with 64 percent in Detroit and 69 percent in Cleveland, where the choice environments are quite different. The authors comment: "While these results cannot tell us whether some parents value academics less, it seems likely that safety and locations are more important when some of the available schools are unsafe or when few good schools are available near the home—issues that point to the impossible trade-offs that some parents face when choosing a school."[15]

COMMUNITY ENGAGEMENT AND RACE

Politics are not going away, but the arms race described earlier is expensive, distracting, and seldom in the best interest of children. Because it's caught up in America's larger ideological wars, disarmament will probably not arrive anytime soon at the national level. In particular communities, however, we see both the need and ample opportunity for improved relations between school sectors and with key local constituents, while also facing up to some race-related issues that need attention.

The onset, even the threat, of chartering (and other forms of competition) in a community unleashes groups and institutions—and interests within the "one best system" itself—that press to preserve their own points of view, their own advantages, even their very existence. Such pushback comes with the territory. Yet zealous reformers may be so single-minded in the pursuit of their change agenda that they appear insensitive to the concerns of those who fear change. People whose foremost concern is the education of special-needs children, for example, are understandably apprehensive that school choice may weaken special education. Those focused on minority children worry about issues such as suspension, expulsion, and backfilling. Parents of high-ability students fret that a diminution of central authority will diminish what's available on the gifted-and-talented front. Especially in urban America, big shifts in the delivery system also introduce touchy issues of race and class—education reform is almost never truly color-blind, even if those pushing for change fancy that it is—which in turn may be inflamed by other interests (such as teachers unions) that seek credible, empathy-inducing allies in their resistance fight.

Examples of such systemic shifts and the discontents they give rise to can be seen in New Orleans, Newark, and New York City.[16]

Paul Hill and his colleagues have developed a six-part typology of these conflicts, and he and Ashley Jochim have astutely described the need for carefully cultivated community support if major education reforms are to endure.[17] In her fine 2015 book *The Prize*, longtime *Washington Post* reporter Dale Russakoff vividly documents these conflicts in Newark after Facebook founder Mark Zuckerberg pledged $100 million "to develop a model for saving [education] in all of urban America." As a reviewer of Russakoff's book laments in the *New York Times*, "the . . . main characters in this effort [seem] tone deaf to the demands of the community to be involved in the process."[18] Hill and Jochim add that "Newark built some good new charter schools, and over time it could have used the demand they generated to justify continued expansion of the charter sector. But the absence of a complementary strategy to benefit children still in district schools made many parents and community groups uncomfortable."[19]

The cultivation of local support for quality chartering also means attending to race-related anxieties. Ironically, while the charter sector has concentrated on providing options to poor, minority students, not many leaders of that sector—or of large CMOs and other key elements within it—are themselves members of minority groups. More than a few inner-city residents have felt "disempowered," as if the charter-school reform "was done to us"—to use the language of Howard Fuller, former Milwaukee superintendent and arguably the most revered African American figure in the entire school-choice movement.[20] Nor is this perception eased when interventions, takeovers, and other challenges to local control are undertaken by distant Republican officials while those forfeiting power are closer-to-home Democrats.[21]

Mindful of this problem, some funders and advocacy organizations have begun to support the establishment and replication of more schools led—in the words of the Charter School Growth Fund—by "entrepreneurs with backgrounds that are similar to those of the students and families they serve."[22] The Equitas Academies in Los Angeles, for instance, are Latino-led and serve almost exclusively children with Hispanic backgrounds.[23] Across the continent, Connecticut-based Capital Prep is a three-school network attended primarily by black students and headed by an African American educator named Steve Perry.[24]

Who leads a school can make a difference in a community's receptivity to it, but durable, large-scale acceptance of chartering as an education strategy needs more. We must recognize that in many US cities, the public school system has long been a key source of employment, status, and civic pride for minority residents, especially middle-class blacks, and that when charters appear to undermine that system, these new upstart schools will be resented and opposed by those who depend on it. That's a very practical reason why the charter sector needs to take seriously the recruitment and empowerment of people who look like the children attending its schools—and why reformers, funders, and others pushing for charters as alternatives to district schools need to take pains to cultivate community support for their endeavors. We'd love to point to multiple examples of communities where this has been done well from the outset. Sadly, they are few and far between.[25]

HELP FOR FAMILIES AND STUDENTS

A further set of marketplace improvements involves the mechanisms by which children actually win admission (and then gain physical access) to schools of choice. In cities with mixed markets of public education and dozens of options potentially available to school-shopping families, whether those options are charter or district-operated schools, the marketplace can be exceedingly user-unfriendly. Making children apply separately to each school that might interest them and then line up for each school's lottery means the process is confusing, frustrating, and inefficient, and doubly so when application deadlines and lottery dates differ. Equity challenges also arise here, as it's important to treat all "shoppers" fairly and not discriminate in terms of which children gain admission where. All these issues are doubly important when at-risk kids are involved.

The use of common application-and-lottery systems for determining which kids will attend which schools is a promising solution to this dilemma. Such arrangements give more youngsters a shot at more and potentially better schools. Yet they're hard to create. Multiple stakeholders bring divergent interests to the table, and many complicated questions need to be worked through. For example, can individual schools set priorities for certain types of students—and which priorities are legitimate? Is every school obligated to take anyone who applies (or wins its lottery), even when its educational offerings aren't well matched to their needs?[26] Should children living near a school be favored over kids from across town? What about siblings of current pupils? Or children whose parents work in the school? How will families unhappy with their match be accommodated? What about children who move into town after the school year starts? How are special-needs students matched with schools, taking into account both the dictates of federal and state laws, individual children's situations, and the vexing reality that not every school has the facilities, staff, and other resources to accommodate every need?

Viewed through the other side of this lens, however, is it fair to a child with a disability or behavioral problem (or limited English proficiency, etc.) to limit his or her school options in ways that aren't restricted for other kids? How can the system balance the legitimate interest of schools in developing coherent programs and cultures and concentrating on students likely to flourish in these settings against the equally legitimate interests of children in not being turned away because they don't fit the schools' desired pupil profile?

One can readily see how challenging it is to design and operate such choice facilitators. For those bravely working to construct them, the Center on Reinventing Public Education has flagged four core elements:

- Common dates should be used across all schools for applications and match announcements.
- Families need to complete only one application, listing on it their priorities among the schools that interest them.
- Matches are made using a common process and algorithm agreed on by all and transparent to all.
- When a match is not acceptable, a family can appeal or reenter the matching process.

By 2016, Denver; New Orleans; Washington, DC; and Newark were operating enrollment systems that generally incorporate these features. There are encouraging moves toward creating such systems in Indianapolis, Oakland, Detroit, Memphis, and Cleveland.[27] But until many more communities do likewise, the school-choice marketplace will remain flawed.

As for transportation to the school once a child has been admitted to it, a busing system that gets everyone to any school he or she might select is expensive and complicated—and challenging in different ways in cities that, like New York and Washington, mainly rely on conventional public transportation rather than yellow school buses.[28]

Some schools have longer hours than others or encourage students to arrive early or stay late, leave for fieldwork and internships, or come in on Saturday for extra tutoring. Although some state laws obligate the local district to transport all children to school, including those who attend charter (and, sometimes, private) schools, this requirement can be its own nightmare when school schedules and calendars don't align or when the district can't or perhaps won't accommodate these discrepant schedules. The result is erratic, inconvenient pupil transportation.

Yet choice (whether charter-based or otherwise) amounts to little if kids can't reach the schools they want to attend. Leaving transportation to each school or parent introduces problems of cost, feasibility, and fairness. Designing a universal system, however, one that accommodates the peculiarities of individual schools as well as children's scattered addresses, can be another nightmare. But it's not impossible. Denver's Success Express, for example, operates a fleet of buses, each with both a driver and a paraprofessional on board. The buses circulate through two sections of the city from 6:30 to 9:30 a.m. and from 2:30 to 6:30 p.m., offering free rides to students so that they can be transported between their homes and whichever school they are attending within designated sectors of the Mile High City.[29]

HELP FOR SCHOOLS

Once children enter the schoolhouse door, how well are they served? Successful schools incorporate many elements in addition to direct teacher-student relationships, and a healthy education ecosystem must include means of making these elements possible. When schools, many of them quite small, operate autonomously, they and their pupils benefit if outside organizations can be tapped for sundry services that are difficult or costly for individual schools to handle and that districts generally handle for the schools they operate.

Back-office budget, finance, and payroll services are one category. Curriculum development and teacher professional training are another. Schools also need marketing and community outreach services. They benefit from help with communications, public affairs, and policy advocacy. Then there are more prosaic needs like meal services and occasional—but sometimes urgent—health care, not to mention basic supplies, equipment, building maintenance, and IT. In its own category are special education services, which some children sorely need but which few individual schools can deliver without external experts and other help. The list goes on. Picture a one-off charter as a smallish nonprofit engaged in very complicated work, and it's obvious how much less efficient it will be if it has to provide all these services itself. Wherever charter and district relations are smooth or a well-run CMO or EMO supports the schools in its network, accessing such services may be no great problem. When a school has to procure them all itself, however, suitable suppliers must exist.

LEADERSHIP

Obviously, the charter sector and its friends are not of one mind about the future. There's a wide gap between what Michael Petrilli terms the "choice purists" (people who trust the marketplace) and the "choice nannies" (those who ultimately trust the government).[30] There are optimists confident that a mixed market of districts and charters can productively coexist.[31] There are doubters who believe that fundamental differences in organizational style and culture, together with competition for students and resources, will keep tensions strong and flames burning. And there are clear differences between those who prefer that the two sectors of public education play distinctive roles and those who want more New Orleans–style replacements of districts by charters.

Such differences will continue to roil and ultimately shape the future of chartering. But few education leaders, both within and beyond the charter sector, are focusing on what that future ought to be, beyond some version of "let's do more and better of what we're already doing." People have trouble getting out of their familiar realms of attention—federal policy, better authorizing, greater accountability, enhanced technology, improved pedagogy, and so on—and thinking beyond their own previously crafted strategies. Yet a quartet of converging developments should foster some bigger-picture thinking:

- Charters and chartering (and school choice), at age twenty-five, are here to stay and fairly certain to keep growing. They're not fully mature, but that's a good thing. They are fairly viewed as evolving innovations with room to modify and advance their mission and practices.
- Federal policy is reempowering states to exercise greater control over their own K–12 systems.
- America has, for the first time, a semblance of national academic standards and comparable data that make it possible to discern what's working for whom in which places, even as states differ in their approaches to schooling.
- The many drives toward change currently under way in various realms of K–12 education—from character to technology, from leadership to personalization, from governance to curriculum—create a sense of optimism that the future could indeed be different from the familiar past.

Without suggesting that the big debates and differences within and around the charter sector can be made to go away, we urge its leaders, thinkers, funders, and friends—and those from outside this sector who see that it has a valuable role to play—to devote time and treasure to scoping out both how to solve the problems that linger from yesterday and how to chart a better course for tomorrow.

14

Chartering and Public Education

IN 1995, BARELY FOUR YEARS after the first charter law was passed, David Tyack and Larry Cuban, both then at Stanford, published *Tinkering Toward Utopia: A Century of Public School Reform*. Its first chapter offered this wisdom about earlier efforts to make large changes in K–12 education:

> We call this book *Tinkering Toward Utopia* to highlight the tension between Americans' intense faith in education—almost a secular religion—and the gradualness of changes in educational practice. For over a century, citizens have sought to perfect the future by debating how to improve the young through education. Actual reforms in schools have seldom matched such aspirations, however. Utopian thinking can be dismissed as pie-in-the-sky or valued as visionary; tinkering can be condemned as mere incrementalism or praised as a commonsense remedy for everyday problems. . . .
>
> . . . [H]istory provides a generous time frame for appraising reforms. It is not driven by the short-term needs of election cycles, budgets, foundation grants, media attention, or the reputations of professional reformers. Certain reforms may look successful when judged soon after adoption, but in fact may turn out to be fireflies. . . . Other reforms may seem of questionable benefit in the short run but effective in the long run. When reforms aim at basic institutional changes or the eradication of deep social injustices, the appropriate period for an evaluation may be a generation or more.[1]

Today, we find ourselves twenty-five years—barely a generation—into chartering as an education reform strategy. As pioneer Ted Kolderie wrote, it was conceived as a way "to introduce the dynamics of choice, competition, and innovation into America's public school system, while at the same time ensuring that new schools serve broad public purposes."[2]

A utopian vision? Perhaps. But a worthy one, nonetheless, even if progress toward it has been slower and bumpier than we hoped. Accomplishments to date have been more incremental than revolutionary, yes, but the strategy is surely no firefly.

"Incrementalism" seems tepid, and "tinkering" downright derogatory, yet each term can also be seen as a variation on the principle of continuous improvement, which in today's organizational thinking is viewed as a very good thing. America's charter experiment of the past quarter century is probably better viewed as multiple experiments, altered by experience while they were under way and benefiting from continuous fiddling, the lessons of occasional backslides, and an impressive willingness to persevere, revise and regroup, to venture and even to dare.

As with so many generously hyped reforms, journalists, politicians, and charter watchers—zealots and critics alike—have tended toward binary thinking about chartering. Observers are eager to declare success or failure and loath to look closely and await signs of improvement.

As we've shown throughout the book, chartering has had its full measure of ups and downs, surprises and disappointments. Part of this pathway was predictable: given a dollop of freedom to innovate and run themselves, some schools would surely succeed while others would crash and burn. But other salient developments in the charter realm could scarcely have been foretold: a brutal hurricane on the Gulf coast, for instance, or the advent of mayoral control of schools in New York and Washington. And some matters that turned out to be vital got too little attention at the start, including marketplace frailties, adequate funding, the specifics of autonomy, and the critical role of authorizers. The repairs we listed in chapter 13 are plainly needed, yet the tinkering to date has, on the whole, been fruitful: some trial and error, some misfires, some continuous improvement. Still, no utopia is yet in sight.

People's visions of charter utopia vary. David Osborne imagines the day when every school is a charter. Paul Hill pictures a growing number of ever more successful portfolio districts. The Charter School Growth Fund mostly presses for more high-performing no-excuses schools, although some of its next-generation investments cast a wider net.

As for us, we seek more places trying their own versions of New Orleans–style replacement—and more places trying on the Denver and DC styles, too. Our ardor for such structural overhauls has as much to do with enduring flaws in the governance, efficiency, effectiveness, and capacity of American public education as with affection for charters per se. As we've noted before, chartering is the best example to date of reinventing government applied to public education. And we feel as strongly as we did in 2000 that American public education needs reinventing.

Such change is obviously not going to happen overnight, and many other reform efforts are under way: big alterations in academic standards, accountability, the federal role, teacher preparation, technology, local governance, and more, including multiple forms of school choice. Many smart, experienced individuals remain confident that what David Kirp terms "homegrown gradualism" within the framework of the "one best system" can set matters right, even in troubled urban districts—and the DC and Denver sagas both display elements of that strategy.[3]

Yet both cities now also contain lots of charter schools, which would not have happened had state policy makers not created that possibility, and in the New Orleans case it's hard to imagine that local initiative would have produced anything resembling the fundamental changes wrought by state action and a new governance structure. It's unlikely that many cities—especially sans hurricanes and earthquakes—will systematically reconstruct themselves along the New Orleans model, and few states will force such reconstruction on their communities. Yet versions of recovery districts are already visible in several more places, including troubled Memphis and sorely afflicted Detroit, and additional mixed markets and portfolio districts are likely to emerge.[4]

As such governance experiments and system innovations take place, the charter sector will also continue to expand its chief success to date, namely, the provision of promising school options for poor and minority children. Doing more of this, doing it in more places, and doing it better is consistent with the experience and priorities of most policy makers, philanthropists, and education reformers. It aligns with today's anxieties about social mobility and equity. There remains ample demand and plenty of need around America for more top-notch no-excuses schools as well as plenty of opportunities for retooling many that already exist.[5]

As we look ahead, the charter movement's current lack of unity on goals and priorities is both helpful and worrisome. It's helpful because with disunity come opportunity, flexibility, creativity, and enterprise. The worrisome flip side is that fragmentation in any enterprise invites a loss of focus and clout while inciting more opponents and boosting their opportunities to divide and conquer.

Some leaders of the charter sector will push their colleagues to hunker down, build on success, solve today's problems, and avoid opening risky new frontiers. We disagree. This multifaceted education experiment still enjoys bipartisan backing in many places, a rarity in today's bipolar policy world, and broadening its focus may bring more new supporters than enemies. Charters remain freer than the district sector to innovate and shape their own destiny. The energy, human talent, philanthropic resources, and private investment flowing into this sector remain robust. Demand is strong, both on the part of kids and families wanting to choose and among people and organizations wanting to start and lead schools. We also have solid proof points not just about the ability of charters to educate poor kids, but also—at least as important in this context—about the capacity of chartering to do things differently and sometimes better. That's what American education needs more of. And this strategy for improvement is already being embraced by reform-minded policy makers and innovators in a lengthening list of other countries, including England, New Zealand, Canada, Sweden, Chile, and even poorer nations such as India and South Africa.

We haven't been shy in advancing our view that chartering has ample potential to do good things for children and communities. Yet it would be irresponsible to end without locating this sector more precisely within the larger universe of American public education in the twenty-first century.

The constitution of every state assigns to that state's lawmakers the obligation to educate its young people. The wording varies from place to place, but the intent and spirit are nearly identical. The lofty exhortations of the Massachusetts Constitution of 1780 are a peerless specimen:

> Wisdom and knowledge, as well as virtue, diffused generally among the body of the people, being necessary for the preservation of their rights and liberties; and as these depend on spreading the opportunities and advantages of education in the various parts of the country, and among the different orders of the people, it shall be the duty of legislatures and magistrates, in all future periods of this commonwealth, to cherish the interests of literature and the sciences, and all seminaries of them; especially the university at Cambridge, public schools and grammar schools in the towns; to encourage private societies and public institutions, rewards and immunities, for the promotion of agriculture, arts, sciences, commerce, trades, manufactures, and a natural history of the country; to countenance and inculcate the principles of humanity and general benevolence, public and private charity, industry and frugality, honesty and punctuality in their dealings; sincerity, good humor, and all social affections, and generous sentiments, among the people.[6]

Observe that lawmakers are advised to "cherish . . . *all* seminaries" and to "encourage *private* societies and *public* institutions" (emphasis added) to accomplish the purposes of this article. The writers were really pretty open-minded about how their ambitious mandates were to be carried out.

These seminal documents often contain phrases such as "public schools" and "common schools," which are generally left undefined even as the documents laud the role of education, such as this sentence from the preamble to Washington State's education clauses: "It is the paramount duty of the state to make ample provision for the education of all children residing within its borders, without distinction or preference on account of race, color, caste, or sex."[7]

Judgments can legitimately differ regarding the place of charters within a "common" education system. Washington State's supreme court justices didn't think they fit there, although jurists in other states are fine with them. In a couple of cases—recently including Washington—charter laws have even been modified to reconcile them with state constitutional barriers.

Charters' place within public education is indeed a judgment call, but in our judgment, and that of a growing number of other Americans, they satisfy the essential criteria: schools open to the public, paid for with public dollars, and accountable for their results to duly constituted public authorities. Furthermore, in a country that generally places local control of schools on a pedestal—coexisting, however awkwardly, with state and federal mandates—charters typically get closer to true local control than do sprawling districts with hundreds of schools and millions of people. One-off charters in particular are typically created by residents of a particular community or neighborhood to supply opportunities and address needs that the larger system is not handling well. Networked charters—of both the CMO and the EMO varieties—often have deep local roots, funders, and advocates of their own, even when they look to distant entities for curriculum and management.

That charters are legitimately regarded as part of public education does not end the matter, however. Public education does not always mean good education, and even when it works well for some children, it may be sorely lacking for others. Chartering's capacity to serve more kids well by diversifying school options, widening families' choices, and responding to singular needs and preferences is why this sector should be extended and improved. This is one way the state can fulfill its large obligation to its children. Through charters, the overall public education system can supply alternatives that the district structure hasn't provided, at least not in satisfactory quantity, quality, and accessibility. Although educating the public demands some commonalities of curriculum and standards, schools should not be identical any more than children are, and it's simply wrong to view the charter sector through the lens of uniformity.

Well-to-do families have always enjoyed a quasi-marketplace in K–12 education, because they have substantial sway over where they live and, hence, which schools will teach their children. Many such families have the additional capacity to exempt themselves entirely from the state's offerings and instead make use of private schooling. Many also augment their kids' learning with sundry other materials and opportunities.

The American school-choice movement exists partly to give such fortunate families even more options. It exists partly to respond to niche demands for children with particular needs or interests. And it exists partly to boost educational quality and efficiency through competition. Primarily, however, the choice movement exists to bring the benefits of the marketplace to families that lack the wherewithal to enter it on their own. Those families—typically poor, frequently minority, sometimes disorganized, often residing in troubled communities, and very often with weakly educated adults—are likeliest to find their neighborhood schools lacking in various ways. In many cases, they also find their districts unresponsive to—or unable to afford or just not very good at accommodating—their yearning for better opportunities for their daughters and sons.

Enter school choice, which can take myriad forms. In these pages, we've focused on the charter version. We believe in giving people quality choices; it's immoral to confine children against their will in schools that don't work well for them. But simply providing more schools and the right to choose among them does not complete the mission. Forces beyond the marketplace must help assure educational quality. Bruce Fuller and the "new decentralists" advocate seeking middle ground—a hybrid, really, between "centralized hierarchies" and "unfettered markets." Fuller writes: "The new decentralists rethink human interaction at two interwoven levels of social action. They consider how the firm is positioned in an organizational field, and then how the center enables more effective practice locally. The new social architects do not swerve between naïve notions of hierarchy or markets. Instead, they devise organizational forms that adapt to macro shifts in their field."[8]

Chartering is itself such an organizational form, an adaptation to the shortcomings of both centralized bureaucracies and free markets. But it's an adaptation that needs to keep adapting. Continuous improvement should be its watchword. That includes the development and deployment of multiple market facilitators and sources of support, from external standards and accountability to accurate consumer information for parents and help for them in making informed choices. A well-functioning education system balances the freedom and dynamism of the market with the shared obligation to ensure that needy children and hard-pressed taxpayers are both well served by what the market supplies.

As important as chartering's role in adding choices to the education marketplace and its emergence as a structural and governance breakthrough, its truly "disruptive innovation," to recall Clayton Christensen's term, has been what Kolderie calls the "withdrawal of the exclusive franchise" for delivering public education. It's akin to what Southwest Airlines, Uber, and Airbnb have meant to the airline, taxi, and hotel industries, respectively; what Zipcar and car2go have been to the auto-rental industry; and even perhaps what driverless cars and bike sharing may portend for the auto industry itself.

Yes, those are private-sector examples. Disruptive innovation in the public sector is rarer and usually emerges more gradually. Yet examples abound in the outsourcing of governmental functions to private operators, functions that range from collecting trash to securing buildings, from housing and feeding national-park visitors (and cleaning up behind them) to launching the rockets that put satellites into orbit and resupply the International Space Station. Plenty more can be found in the creation of quasi-public entities to run trains, airports, hospitals, convention centers, housing authorities, even community libraries.[9]

Aside, perhaps, from mayoral control, chartering is by far the most significant manifestation of structural and governance innovation in public education. And—as with every activity noted in the previous paragraph—disruption in this realm has caused heartburn among those who worry that more is being lost than gained and those into whose established systems this innovation has been implanted.

We cannot assuage all such concerns. But after twenty-five years, it's time to acknowledge that chartering is no firefly. It's here to stay, and anyone whose top priority is the education of children would do well to assist with its improvement and join in efforts to replicate its successes, address its shortcomings, and chart a future course that amplifies the good it can do for children in a society that has properly obligated itself to educate them all.

APPENDIX

THE TABLES AND FIGURES included here primarily augment the data and analyses in chapters 2 and 3.

STATE CHARTER LAWS

From the passage of the first charter law in Minnesota in 1991 through the late 1990s, the number of such laws grew quickly. Since the turn of the century, however, growth has slowed, with less than one new law per year. Today, forty-three states and the District of Columbia have charter-enabling legislation. Seven states are without a charter statute on their books (figure A.1).

FIGURE A.1   Number of states with charter laws, 1991–2015

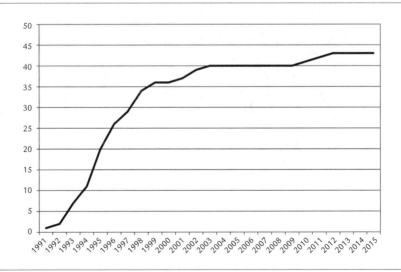

Sources: National Alliance for Public Charter Schools, "The Public Charter Schools Dashboard," accessed November 12, 2015, www.publiccharters.org/dashboard/home.

CHARTER CLOSURES

Figure A.2 shows charter school closures in 2014. Charter schools usually operate according to a time-limited contract that must be renewed at the end of the contract, most often after a five-year term. If a charter isn't renewed, that counts as a *closure*. But schools may also close or be closed before their charter is up. Both types of closures are included in figure A.2. It's a one-year snapshot, but it gives an idea of the reasons for school closures. Financial issues are the most common reason, followed by mismanagement and weak academic performance.

FIGURE A.2   Charter school closures by primary cause, nationwide, 2014

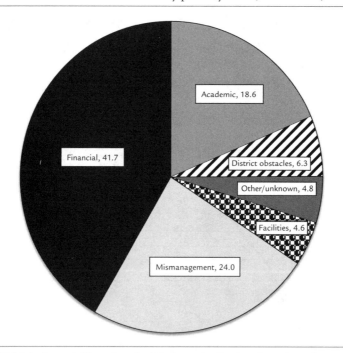

Source: Ted Rebarber and Alison Consoletti Zgainer, eds., "Survey of America's Charter Schools 2014," Center for Education Reform, Washington, DC, February 2014, www.edreform.com/wp -content/uploads/2014/02/2014CharterSchoolSurveyFINAL.pdf.

VIRTUAL CHARTERS

Figure A.3 gives, for each of twenty-five states with virtual charter schools, the percentage of all such schools in the country that operate within that state's borders, as well as the percentage (nationally) of virtual-charter attendees who reside in that state. As is evident, California has the most virtual schools, but Ohio has the largest enrollment.

Figure A.4 compares the average number of students per full-time teacher in virtual charter schools with both brick-and-mortar charters and district schools. Teachers at online charters educate, on average, 50 percent more kids than do their peers in brick-and-mortar charters, and 72 percent more than teachers in traditional public schools.

FIGURE A.3   Percentages of virtual charter schools within states' charter sector and their enrollments by state, 2013–2014

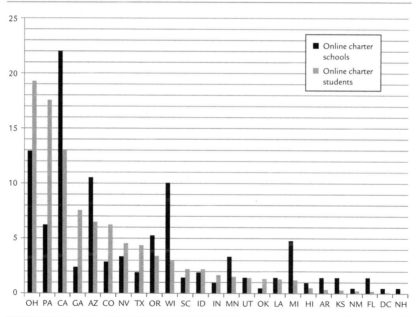

Source: Brian Gill et al., "Inside Online Charter Schools," Mathematica Policy Research, Cambridge, MA, October 2015, www.mathematica-mpr.com/~/media/publications/pdfs/education/inside_online_charter_schools.pdf.

FIGURE A.4   Students per full-time teacher by school type, 2013–2014

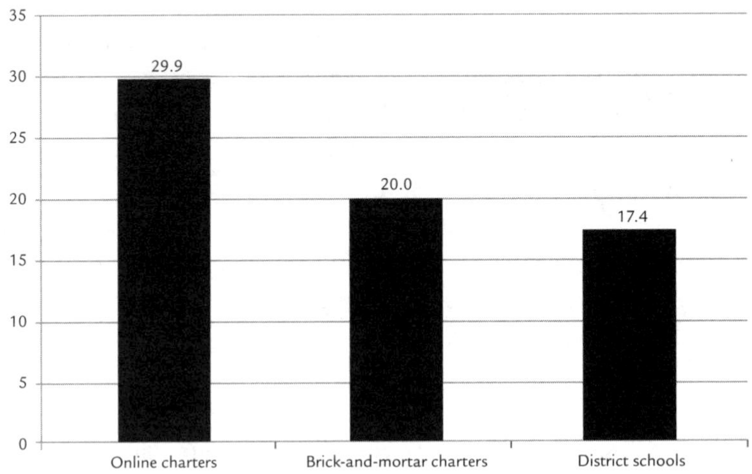

Source: Brian Gill et al., "Inside Online Charter Schools," Mathematica Policy Research, October 2015, www.mathematica-mpr.com/˜/media/publications/pdfs/education/inside_online_charter _schools.pdf.

CHARTER SCHOOLS
AND STUDENTS PER STATE

Figure A.5 lists, for each state and the District of Columbia, the number of charter schools in operation during the 2013–2014 school year and what percentage of its public schools that number represents. Figure A.6 shows charter enrollments for the 2013–2014 school year and the percentage of public school students who attend charters in each state (for those jurisdictions that had at least one charter school during that year).

The school figures in A.5 resemble the student data in figure A.6, but differ somewhat because charters vary in school size. Online charters, for example, enroll on average 1,000 students each, while the number for brick-and-mortar schools is approximately 375.

FIGURE A.5   Number of charter schools and percentage of public schools that are charter schools by state, 2013–2014

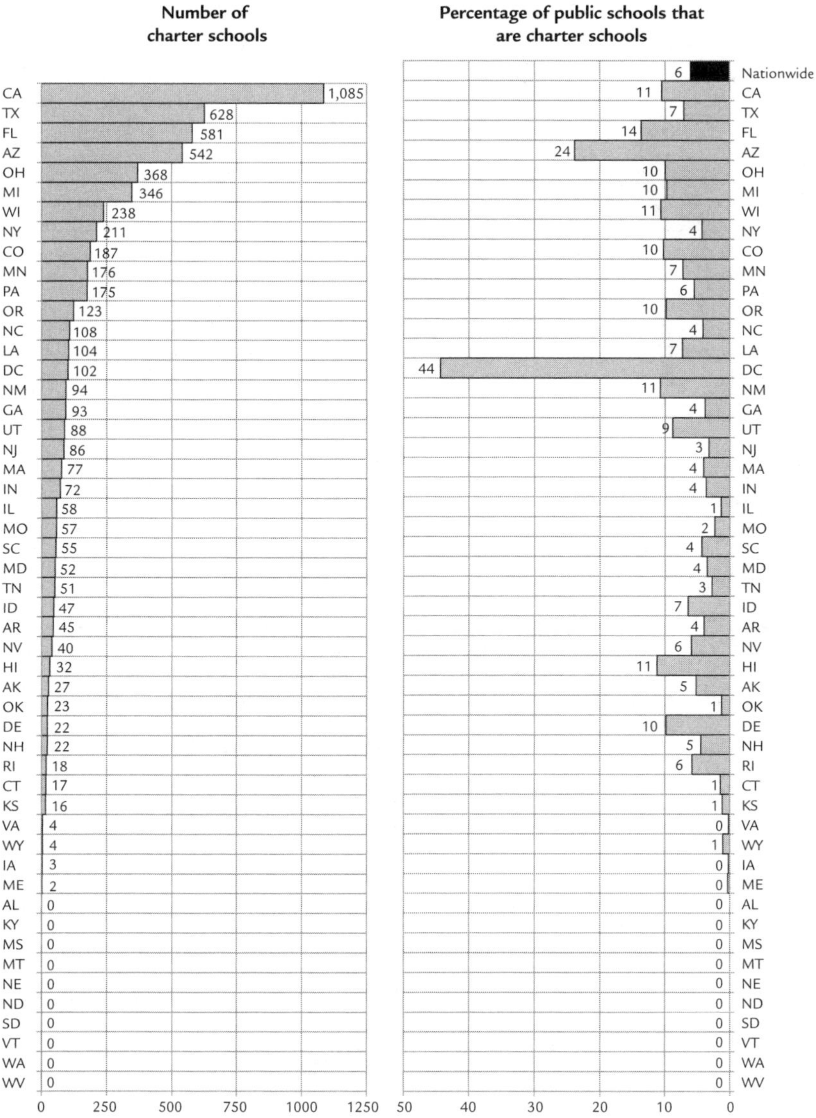

State	Number of charter schools	Percentage of public schools that are charter schools
Nationwide		6
CA	1,085	11
TX	628	7
FL	581	14
AZ	542	24
OH	368	10
MI	346	10
WI	238	11
NY	211	4
CO	187	10
MN	176	7
PA	175	6
OR	123	10
NC	108	4
LA	104	7
DC	102	44
NM	94	11
GA	93	4
UT	88	9
NJ	86	3
MA	77	4
IN	72	4
IL	58	1
MO	57	2
SC	55	4
MD	52	4
TN	51	3
ID	47	7
AR	45	4
NV	40	6
HI	32	11
AK	27	5
OK	23	1
DE	22	10
NH	22	5
RI	18	6
CT	17	1
KS	16	1
VA	4	0
WY	4	1
IA	3	0
ME	2	0
AL	0	0
KY	0	0
MS	0	0
MT	0	0
NE	0	0
ND	0	0
SD	0	0
VT	0	0
WA	0	0
WV	0	0

Source: National Alliance for Public Charter Schools, "The Public Charter Schools Dashboard," accessed November 12, 2015, www.publiccharters.org/dashboard/home.

FIGURE A.6 Charter school enrollments and percentage of public school students attending charter schools by state, 2013–2014

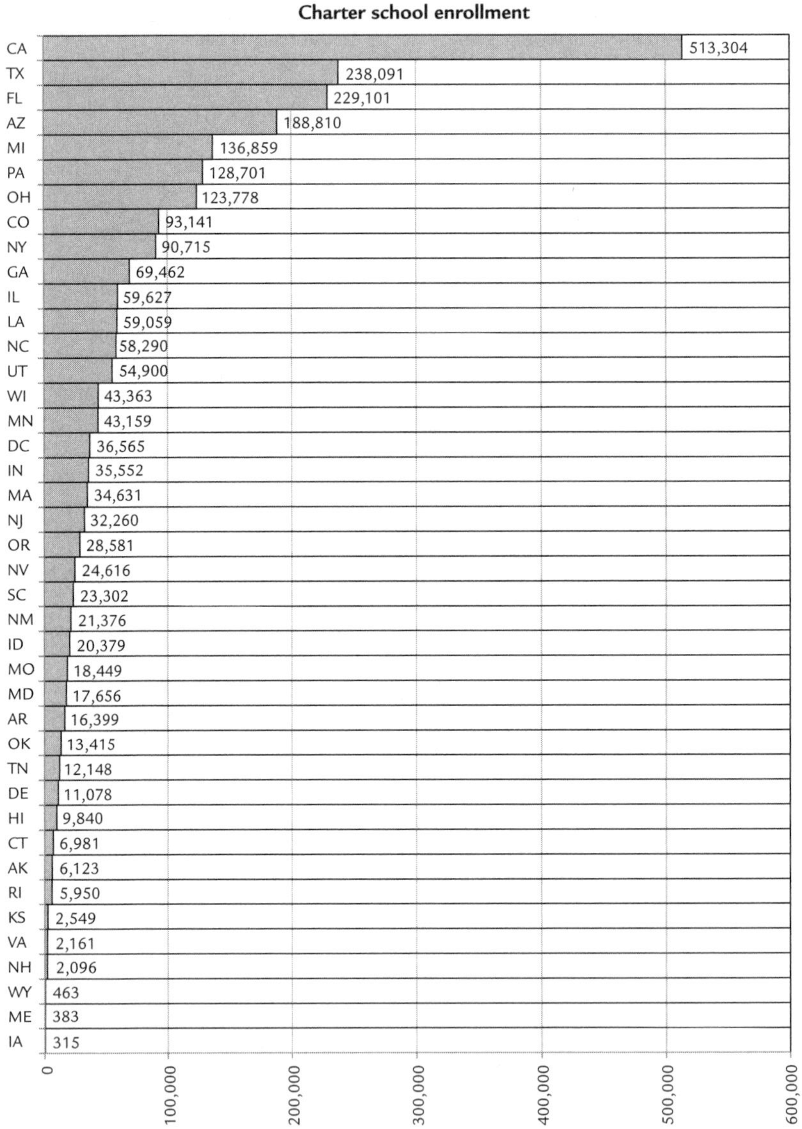
Charter school enrollment
CA 513,304
TX 238,091
FL 229,101
AZ 188,810
MI 136,859
PA 128,701
OH 123,778
CO 93,141
NY 90,715
GA 69,462
IL 59,627
LA 59,059
NC 58,290
UT 54,900
WI 43,363
MN 43,159
DC 36,565
IN 35,552
MA 34,631
NJ 32,260
OR 28,581
NV 24,616
SC 23,302
NM 21,376
ID 20,379
MO 18,449
MD 17,656
AR 16,399
OK 13,415
TN 12,148
DE 11,078
HI 9,840
CT 6,981
AK 6,123
RI 5,950
KS 2,549
VA 2,161
NH 2,096
WY 463
ME 383
IA 315
0
100,000
200,000
300,000
400,000
500,000
600,000

Sources: National Alliance for Public Charter Schools, "The Public Charter Schools Dashboard," accessed November 12, 2015, www.publiccharters.org/dashboard/home; and US Department of Education, Institute of Education Sciences, National Center for Education Statistics, "Elementary and Secondary Information System," accessed November 12, 2015, https://nces.ed.gov/ccd/elsi.

FIGURE A.6   *Continued*

Percentage of public school students attending charter schools

CA	8.1
TX	4.6
FL	8.4
AZ	17.1
MI	8.8
PA	7.3
OH	7.2
CO	10.6
NY	3.3
GA	4.0
IL	2.9
LA	8.3
NC	3.8
UT	8.8
WI	5.0
MN	5.1
DC	46.8
IN	3.4
MA	3.6
NJ	2.4
OR	4.8
NV	5.4
SC	3.1
NM	6.3
ID	6.9
MO	2.0
MD	2.0
AR	3.3
OK	2.0
TN	1.2
DE	8.4
HI	5.3
CT	1.3
AK	4.7
RI	4.2
KS	0.5
VA	0.2
NH	1.1
WY	0.5
ME	0.2
IA	0.1

Axis labels: 60.0, 50.0, 40.0, 30.0, 20.0, 10.0, 0.0

Sources: National Alliance for Public Charter Schools, "The Public Charter Schools Dashboard," accessed November 12, 2015, www.publiccharters.org/dashboard/home; and US Department of Education, Institute of Education Sciences, National Center for Education Statistics, "Elementary and Secondary Information System," accessed November 12, 2015, https://nces.ed.gov/ccd/elsi.

LOCAL DIFFERENCES

Table A.1 lists the districts where more than 30 percent of public school pupils attended charters in 2014–2015. For each district, the table displays the state in which the district is located, its total enrollment, its charter enrollment, and its charter enrollment share.

TABLE A.1   School districts with the largest percentage of charter students, 2014–2015

Rank	School district	State	Charter enrollment	Total enrollment	Charter enrollment share (%)
1	Orleans Parish School District	LA	42,860	46,200	93
2	Detroit City School District	MI	54,420	99,460	53
3	School District of the City of Flint	MI	5,660	12,150	47
4	District of Columbia Public Schools	DC	37,680	85,230	44
5	Kansas City School District	MO	9,980	24,210	41
6	Gary Community School Corporation	IN	5,010	12,580	40
7	The School District of Philadelphia	PA	64,090	194,750	33
8	Hall County Schools	GA	8,200	25,280	32
	Victor Valley Union High School District	CA	4,390	13,890	32
9	Indianapolis Public Schools	IN	13,830	43,920	31
	Grand Rapids Public Schools	MI	6,900	22,510	31
10	Dayton City School District	OH	6,220	20,440	30
	San Antonio Independent School District	TX	17,000	57,450	30
	Cleveland Municipal School District	OH	16,220	54,950	30

Source: National Alliance for Public Charter Schools, "A Growing Movement: America's Largest Charter School Communities," November 2015, www.publiccharters.org/wp-content/uploads/2014/12/2014_Enrollment_Share_FINAL.pdf.

FIGURE A.7   Percentages of charter and district schools by type of community, 2011–2012

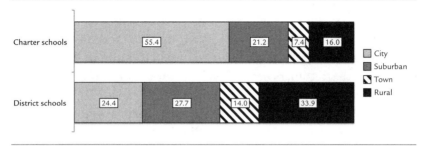

Source: Public Agenda, *Charter Schools in Perspective* (New York: Public Agenda, 2015), www.in -perspective.org/pages/download-the-guide.

Figure A.7 compares the presence of charter and district-run schools in city, suburban, town, and rural areas. The contrast is striking.

GRADE COMPOSITION

Figure A.8 compares charter and district schools by grade span. A little over half of all charters serve only elementary grades, while more than two-thirds of conventional public schools are elementary-only. High schools make up about a quarter of each sector, although combined schools—primarily K–8 and K–12 schools—are much more common in the charter sector.

FIGURE A.8   Grade spans of charter and district schools, 2011–2012

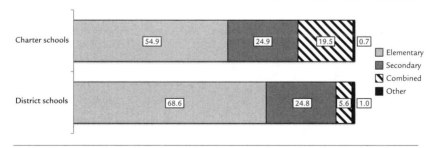

Source: Public Agenda, *Charter Schools in Perspective* (New York: Public Agenda, 2015), www.in -perspective.org/pages/download-the-guide.

Note: According to National Center for Education Statistics definitions, elementary schools begin with grade 6 or below and have no grade higher than 8. Secondary schools have no grade lower than 7. Combined schools begin with grade 6 or below and end with grade 9 or above.

DEMOGRAPHIC TRENDS

Figure A.9 tracks the racial composition of charter and all public schools over six recent years. As charter enrollments have risen, the number of students in each racial group has also increased, but not at the same rates. In 2012–2013, for example, Hispanic attendees overtook black charter-goers in total number for the first time.

FIGURE A.9   Racial demographics of charter and all public schools, nationwide, 2006–2007 to 2012–2013

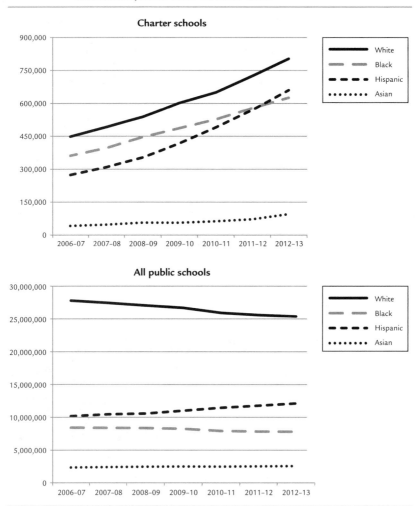

Source: National Alliance for Public Charter Schools, "The Public Charter Schools Dashboard," accessed November 12, 2015, www.publiccharters.org/dashboard/home.

FIGURE A.10   Percentage of total enrollments by race in charter and district schools in two cities, 2011–2012

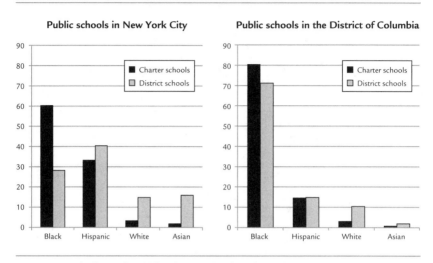

Source: National Alliance for Public Charter Schools, "The Public Charter Schools Dashboard," accessed November 12, 2015, www.publiccharters.org/dashboard/home.

In all public schools, the numbers of white and black students have actually declined as total enrollments have risen, while Hispanic numbers increased and Asian numbers remained mostly flat. Note that during the years shown here, Hispanic students have consistently outnumbered black pupils in public education as a whole, but didn't outnumber black children in charter schools until 2012.

Student demographics, however, vary considerably by district. Figure A.10 shows these data for New York City and Washington, DC.

TEACHERS

Table A.2 compares teachers in charter and traditional public schools on a number of metrics. *Teacher turnover* as shown is the combined percentage of teachers leaving a school to teach elsewhere and those leaving the profession altogether. In charter schools, 10.2 percent of teachers were movers, and 8.2 percent were leavers in 2011–2012; among district teachers, those percentages were 8.0 and 7.7, respectively (data not shown).

TABLE A.2   Teacher characteristics in charter and district schools, 2011–2012

Characteristic		Charter	District
Total number		115,600	3,269,500
Total percentage of all public school teachers		3.4	96.6
Average years teaching		8.7	14
Average years at current school		3.6	8.1
Teacher turnover (%)		18.4	15.7
Ethnicity (%)	*White*	13.1	7.6
	Hispanic	69.9	82.3
	Black	11.8	6.6
	Asian	2.8	1.8
Age (%)	Average	37.4	42.6
	Median	34.2	41.2
	Under 30	31	14.7
	30–39	51.5	54.1
	50–54	6.8	12.1
	55+	10.7	19.1
Gender (%)	Female	74.9	76.4
	Male	25.1	23.6
Highest degree (%)	Bachelor's	52.3	39.4
	Master's	37.3	48
	Higher than master's	6.3	8.8
Workload	Working full time (%)	91	92.8
	Hours per week	53.5	52.2
Compensation	Average full-time base salary	$44,500	$53,400
	Performance-based compensation (% of teachers)	15.8	4
Average student-to-teacher ratio	Self-contained classrooms	22.6	15.3
	Departmentalized instruction	22.7	18.2
Job satisfaction (%)	Strongly satisfied	53.5	59.6
	Somewhat satisfied	36.3	33.3

Sources: Rebecca Goldring, Lucinda Gray, and Amy Bitterman, "Characteristics of Public and Private Elementary and Secondary School Teachers in the United States: Results From the 2011–12 Schools and Staffing Survey, First Look," US Department of Education, Institute of Education Sciences, National Center for Education Statistics, August 2013, http://nces.ed.gov/pubs2013 /2013314.pdf; Rebecca Goldring, Soheyla Taie, and Minsun Riddles, "Teacher Attrition and Mobility: Results From the 2012–13 Teacher Follow-Up Survey, First Look," US Department of Education, Institute of Education Sciences, National Center for Education Statistics, September 2014, http://nces.ed.gov/pubs2014/2014077.pdf; and Public Agenda, Charter Schools in Perspective (New York: Public Agenda, 2015), www.in-perspective.org/pages/download-the-guide.

CHARTER SCHOOLS' IMPACT ON
STUDENT ACHIEVEMENT

Based on the 2015 CREDO study of charter schools in forty-one cities, table A.3 shows significant differences in achievement gains by race. Black and Hispanic pupils enjoyed the greatest gains, compared with their virtual twins in district schools. Asian charter-goer achievements were mostly flat, while white students fared worst. (See chapter 3 for an explanation of CREDO's virtual-twin method of matching charter and noncharter students.)

This table compares the effect of each student characteristic, all other factors being equal. Other factors include, for example, parental income, English language learner status, and grade level, each with effects that, in combination, make up the full effect on a student's achievement. That's why the plus-forty learning days that all combined charter pupils achieved in math (as explained in chapter 3) is greater than the effect of any sub-group membership alone.

Based on the same 2015 CREDO study, table A.4 shows that the longer a student is enrolled in a charter school, the greater his or her annual achievement gains, expressed in days of learning gained or lost, compared with a matched student in a district school.

TABLE A.3   Charter schools' average one-year impacts on reading and mathematics achievement in forty-one cities, expressed as days of learning, by race, 2006–2007 through 2011–2012

	Reading	Mathematics
Asian	0	9
Black	26	36
Hispanic	6	22
White	–14	–36

Source: Center for Research on Education Outcomes (CREDO), "Urban Charter School Study, 2015," CREDO, Stanford, CA, 2015, http://urbancharters.stanford.edu/download/Urban%20Charter%20School%20Study%20Report%20on%2041%20Regions.pdf.

TABLE A.4　Charter schools' comulative impacts on reading and mathematics achievement in forty-one cities, expressed as days of learning, by number of years enrolled, 2006–2007 through 2011–2012

	Reading	Mathematics
1st year	–7	7
2nd year	43	58
3rd year	43	86
4+ years	72	108

Source: Center for Research on Education Outcomes (CREDO), "Urban Charter School Study, 2015," CREDO, Stanford, CA, 2015, http://urbancharters.stanford.edu/download/Urban%20 Charter%20School%20Study%20Report%20on%2041%20Regions.pdf.

Note: This table depicts the difference in days of learning for charter students and students deemed virtual twins in district-operated schools using CREDO's methodology. See Center for Research on Education Outcomes, "National Charter School Study 2013," CREDO, Stanford, CA, 2013, http://credo.stanford.edu/documents/NCSS%202013%20Final%20Draft.pdf, 8.

NOTES

CHAPTER 1

1. Should they be called *chartered* or *charter* schools? Some argue that *charter* focuses too much on the school as created, whereas *chartered* and *chartering* suggest the broader strategy of creating a variety of different learning environments. We will use *charter* for the schools and *chartering* for the strategy.

2. A handful of schools in the public (or quasi-public) sector—magnet schools, lab schools, and so on—already possessed certain charter-like characteristics.

3. Charters that replace "failed" district schools are often obliged to retain the students who had been enrolled in the antecedent schools. Thus, strictly speaking, they are not schools of choice.

4. Particularly in states with weak charter laws, there are exceptions and partial exceptions that may, for instance, continue to include charter teachers in the district's collective-bargaining agreement, as in Maryland. *Conversion charters* that remain within the district also tend to enjoy less autonomy in these matters.

5. David Tyack and Elisabeth Hansot, *Managers of Virtue* (New York: Basic Books, 1982), 28-29.

6. David Tyack, Michael W. Kirst, and Elisabeth Hansot, "Educational Reform: Retrospect and Prospect," *Teachers College Record* 81, no. 3 (1980): 253-69.

7. David Tyack, *The One Best System* (Cambridge, MA: Harvard University Press, 1974), 7.

8. Albert Shanker, cited in *Wall Street Journal* (editorial), October 2, 1989.

9. US Department of Education, National Center for Education Statistics, *2014 Digest of Education Statistics*, April 2013, table 205.40, https://nces.ed.gov /programs/digest/d14/tables/dt14_205.40.asp; and US Department of Education, National Center for Education Statistics, *2015 Digest of Education Statistics*, September 2015, table 216.20, https://nces.ed.gov/programs/digest /d15/tables/dt15_216.20.asp. Many private, religiously affiliated schools (e.g., Catholic, Baptist, and Lutheran schools) operate within systems of their own, but these are generally much looser than public school districts.

10. As we observe the twenty-fifth anniversary of the nation's first charter law, we also note the fiftieth anniversary of *Equality of Educational Opportunity*— now referred to as "the Coleman report"—released in 1966.

11. James S. Coleman, "The Evaluation of 'Equality of Educational Opportunity,'" in *On Equality of Educational Opportunity*, ed. Frederick Mosteller and Daniel Patrick Moynihan (New York: Vintage Books, 1972), 149-50.

12. Debra Viadero, "Race Report's Influence Felt 40 Years Later," *Education Week*, June 21, 2006, www.edweek.org/ew/articles/2006/06/21/41coleman.h25.html,

notes: "When the report was done, it met with deafening silence. The lack of response was due in part to its release right before the July 4 weekend."

13. James S. Coleman, "Toward Open Schools," *Public Interest* 9 (fall 1967), www .nationalaffairs.com/public_interest/detail/toward-open-schools.

14. John B. Carroll, "A Model of School Learning," *Teachers College Record* 64 (1963).

15. See, for example, Marshall S. Smith and Stewart C. Purkey, "Effective Schools: A Review," *Elementary School Journal* 83 (March 1983): 427–52; Donovan F. Downer, "Review of Research on Effective Schools," *McGill Journal of Education* 26, no. 3 (fall 1991): 323–31; and Association for Effective Schools, "What Is Effective School Research?" Association for Effective Schools, Kinderhook, NY (1996), www.mes.org/esr.html.

16. Kenneth B. Clark, "Efficiency as a Prod to Social Action," *Monthly Labor Review* (August 1969): 55–56. While Clark wrote that sentence in 1969, it was echoed more than three decades later in George W. Bush's denunciation of the "soft bigotry of low expectations" as a key element of the rationale for No Child Left Behind.

17. Kenneth B. Clark, *An Intensive Program for the Attainment of Educational Achievement in Deprived Areas of New York City* (New York: MARC Education Groups, 1967), 6.

18. National Commission on Excellence in Education, "A Nation at Risk: The Imperative for Educational Reform," National Commission on Excellence in Education, April 1983, www2.ed.gov/pubs/NatAtRisk/index.html; and Thomas Toch, *In the Name of Excellence: The Struggle to Reform the Nation's Schools, Why It's Failing, and What Should Be Done* (Oxford: Oxford University Press, 1991).

19. "A Jeffersonian Compact," *New York Times*, October 1, 1989, 22.

20. Susan J. Bodilly, Susanna W. Purnell, Kimberly Ramsey, and Sarah J. Keith, *Lessons from New American Schools Development Corporation's Demonstration Phase* (Santa Monica, CA: RAND, 1996), www.rand.org/content/dam/rand/pubs /monograph_reports/2007/MR729.pdf; Mark Berends, Sheila Nataraj Kirby, Scott Naftel, and Christopher McKelvey, *Implementation and Performance in New American Schools Three Years into Scale-Up* (Arlington, VA: RAND, 2001), www.rand.org/content/dam/rand/pubs/monograph_reports/2009/MR1145 .pdf; and Jeffrey Mirel, "Unrequited Promise," *Education Next* (summer 2002), http://educationnext.org/unrequited-promise/.

21. Benno C. Schmidt, Jr., "The Edison's Project's Plan to Redefine Public Education," *Educational Leadership* 52, no. 1 (September 1994): 61–64.

22. Nathan Smith, "Competition and Free Thought: Friedman, Mill, and Educational Choice," Foundation for Economic Education, December 11, 2012, http://fee.org/freeman/competition-and-free-thought-friedman-mill-and -educational-choice/; and Milton Friedman, *Capitalism and Freedom* (Chicago: University of Chicago Press, 1962), 85–107.

23. James Forman, Jr., "The Secret History of School Choice: How Progressives Got There First," Yale Law School Faculty Scholarship Series, 93 GEO. L.J.

1287 (2005). See also Howard Fuller and Lisa Frazier Page, *No Struggle, No Progress: A Warrior's Life from Black Power to Education Reform* (Milwaukee: Marquette University Press, 2014); Ron Matus, "Meet the Voucher Left," *redefinED* (September 3, 2015), www.redefineonline.org/2015/09/meet-the -voucher-left-and-other-school-choice-progressives; and Matthew Miller, "A Bold Experiment to Fix City Schools," *Atlantic*, July 1999, www.theatlantic .com/magazine/archive/1999/07/a-bold-experiment-to-fix-city-schools /377683/.

24. Christopher Jencks, "Is the Public School Obsolete?" *Public Interest* (winter 1966): 18–27.

25. Theodore Sizer and Philip Whitten, "A Proposal for a Poor Children's Bill of Rights," *Psychology Today* (August 1968).

26. John E. Chubb and Terry M. Moe, *Politics, Markets, and America's Schools* (Washington, DC: Brookings Institution, 1990).

27. Harold Howe II, "Thoughts on Choice," *Teachers College Record* 93, no. 1 (fall 1991): 167–73. Beginning in 1970, the federal Office of Economic Opportunity undertook an initiative that led to a bobtailed voucher experiment in Alum Rock, California. See Eliot Levinson, *The Alum Rock Voucher Demonstration: Three Years of Implementation* (Santa Monica, CA: RAND, 1976).

28. John Brandl, *Money and Good Intentions Are Not Enough: Why a Liberal Democrat Thinks States Need Both Competition and Community* (Washington, DC: Brookings Institution, 1998), 116.

29. See, for example, David Osborne and Ted Gaebler, *Reinventing Government: How the Entrepreneurial Spirit Is Transforming the Public Sector* (New York: Penguin Books, 1993).

30. Charles Sabel and Jonathan Zetlin, "Experimentalist Governance," in *The Oxford Handbook of Governance*, ed. David Levi-Faur (Oxford: Oxford University Press, 2012); and Charles Sabel, "Rethinking the Street-Level Bureaucrat: Tacit and Deliberate Ways Organizations Can Learn," in *Economy in Society: Essays in Honor of Michael J. Poire*, ed. Paul Osterman (Cambridge, MA: MIT Press, 2013).

31. Peter L. Berger and Richard John Neuhaus, *To Empower People: The Role of Mediating Structures in Public Policy* (Washington, DC: American Enterprise Institute, 1977).

32. Upon Budde's death, the obituary headline in the *New York Times* described him as "first to propose charter schools." See Susan Saulny, "Ray Budde, 82, First to Propose Charter Schools, Dies," *New York Times*, June 21, 2005, www. nytimes.com/2005/06/21/us/ray-budde-82-first-to-propose-charter-schools -dies.html.

33. Ray Budde, "The Evolution of the Charter Concept," *Phi Delta Kappan* (September 1996): 72.

34. Ray Budde, *Education by Charter: Restructuring School Districts* (Andover, MA: Regional Laboratory for Educational Improvement of the Northeast and Islands, 1988).

35. Albert Shanker, National Press Club speech, Washington, DC, March 31, 1988, https://reuther.wayne.edu/files/64.43.pdf. Shanker never suggested that charter teachers should not be unionized, although this became a feature of many charter laws, a nontrivial reason that Shanker's own union has never truly supported this reform.

36. Albert Shanker, "Convention Plots New Course: A Charter for Change," *New York Times*, July 10, 1988.

37. Ibid.

38. For a detailed history of the passage of the Minnesota law, see Ember Reichgott Junge, *Zero Chance of Passage: The Pioneering Charter School Story* (Edina, MN: Beaver's Pond Press, 2012).

39. Joe Nathan, *Free to Teach: Achieving Equity and Excellence in Schools* (New York: Pilgrim Press, 1983).

40. These included options (1985) that permitted eleventh and twelfth graders to take courses at Minnesota postsecondary institutions, followed in 1987 and 1988 by an open-enrollment program that allowed children to attend any public school of their choice in Minnesota.

41. The League report not only talked about chartering but also developed proposals that would fashion cooperatively managed schools and broaden desegregation efforts.

42. The Progressive Policy Institute was affiliated with the center-left Democratic Leadership Council, a prominent member of which was Arkansas governor Bill Clinton.

43. Ted Kolderie, *Beyond Choice to New Public Schools* (Washington, DC: Progressive Policy Institute, 1990), 2.

44. Bryan C. Hassel, *The Charter School Challenge: Avoiding the Pitfalls, Fulfilling the Promise* (Washington, DC: Brookings Institution, 1999), 130–34. Kolderie termed charters "the R&D sector for public education." For his most recent formulation, see Ted Kolderie, *The Split Screen Strategy: Improvement + Innovation* (Edina, MN: Beaver's Pond Press, 2014).

45. That first law did not refer to these new schools as charters, opting instead for "outcome-based schools."

46. The 2016 federal appropriation for this program was $253.1 million, a 32 percent increase from 2015. It was reauthorized in 2015 with changes that encourage the replication of high-performing charters and allow governors and charter-support organizations to manage state grant programs in addition to a state's education department.

47. National Alliance for Public Charter School, home page, accessed January 21, 2016, www.publiccharters.org/.

48. National Association of Charter School Authorizers, home page, accessed January 21, 2016, www.qualitycharters.org/.

49. Andy Smarick, "Original Intent: What Legislative History Tells Us About the Purposes of Chartering," unpublished paper, July 27, 2005.

50. Kolderie, *Beyond Choice to New Public Schools*, 10.

CHAPTER 2

1. Throughout this chapter, for convenience we refer to the District of Columbia as a state.
2. National Alliance for Public Charter Schools (NAPCS), "A New Model Law for Supporting the Growth Of High-Quality Public Charter Schools," June 2009, www.publiccharters.org/wp-content/uploads/2014/01/ModelLaw _P7-wCVR_20110402T222341.pdf. As we show later in the book, the model law stresses fiscal and legal autonomy for charter schools, as well as their exemption from many statutes, regulations, and collective bargaining agreements.
3. No source known to us has charter school numbers before 1999.
4. Sara Mead, Ashley LiBetti Mitchel, and Andrew J. Rotherham, "The State of the Charter School Movement," Bellwether Education Partners, September 2015, http://bellwethereducation.org/sites/default/files/Charter%20 Research%200908%20FINAL.pdf, 10.
5. Although CMO *schools* outnumbered EMOs as early as 2007, CMO enrollments didn't match the EMO numbers until four years later, most likely because most large virtual schools are run by EMOs. See NAPCS, "The Public Charter Schools Dashboard,"accessed November 12, 2015, www.public charters.org/dashboard/home; and NAPCS, "A Closer Look at the Charter School Movement: Schools, Students, and Management Organizations, 2015–16," February 2016, www.publiccharters.org/wp-content/uploads/2016 /02/New-Closed-2016.pdf.
6. The year 2013 is the most recent one for which data were available. In that year, forty-three states had charter-enabling laws, but two of them—Mississippi and Washington State—had yet to open a charter school. That has changed since. Mississippi now has one school and Washington ten. In 2015, however, Alabama enacted a charter law and the Washington State Supreme Court voided that state's new law, which the legislature replaced the following year. See Stephanie Bell-Flynt, "Mississippi's First Charter School Is in Session," *MS News Now*, August 18, 2015, www.msnewsnow.com/story /29827573/charter-school-debuts-in-mississippi; Mike Cason, "Gov. Robert Bentley Signs Alabama Charter School Bill," *AL.com*, March 19, 2015, www .al.com/news/index.ssf/2015/03/gov_robert_bentley_signs_alaba.html; Steve Rosenfeld, "Washington Supreme Court Expels Charter Schools from State Public School System," *Salon*, September 10, 2015, www.salon.com/2015/09 /10/washington_charters_partner/; and Associated Press, "Washington Charter School System Gets Back To Work," *Education Week*, April 13, 2016, www.edweek.org/ew/articles/2016/04/13/washington-charter-school-system -gets-back_ap.html.
7. NAPCS, "A Closer Look at the Charter School Movement."
8. NAPCS, "Public Charter Schools Dashboard"; and US Department of Education, Institute of Education Sciences, National Center for Education Statistics, "Elementary and Secondary Information System," accessed November 12, 2015, https://nces.ed.gov/ccd/elsi/.

9. Public Agenda, *Charter Schools in Perspective* (New York: Public Agenda, 2015)9, www.in-perspective.org/pages/download-the-guide.

10. Andy Smarick, "A New Frontier: Utilizing Charter Schooling to Strengthen Rural Education," Bellwether Education Partners, January 2014, http://bell-wethereducation.org/sites/default/files/Bellwether_A_New_Frontier_Jan _2014.pdf.

11. Eleven states ban online charters (Alabama, Connecticut, Delaware, Maryland, Massachusetts, Mississippi, Missouri, New York, Tennessee, Virginia, and Washington), and thirteen allow them but currently have none (Alaska, Hawaii, Kentucky, Maine, Montana, Nebraska, New Jersey, North Carolina, North Dakota, Rhode Island, South Dakota, Vermont, and West Virginia). See Rosa Pazhouh, Robin Lake, and Larry Miller, "The Policy Framework for Online Charter Schools," Center on Reinventing Public Education, Seattle, October, 2015, www.crpe.org/sites/default/files/crpe-policy-framework -online-charter-schools-final_0.pdf.

12. Brian Gill et al., "Inside Online Charter Schools," Mathematica Policy Research, Cambridge, MA, October 2015, www.mathematica-mpr.com/~/media /publications/pdfs/education/inside_online_charter_schools.pdf; and NAPCS, "Public Charter Schools Dashboard." California puts geographic limits on where its e-schools can draw students from, while in Ohio, Pennsylvania, and several other states, enrollment can be statewide. See NAPCS, "The Health of the Public Charter School Movement: A State-by-State Analysis," October 2014, www.publiccharters.org/wp-content/uploads/2014/09 /health-of-the-movement-2014.pdf.

13. Michael Q. McShane and Jenn Hatfield, "Measuring Diversity in Charter School Offerings," American Enterprise Institute, July 2015, www.aei.org /wp-content/uploads/2015/07/Measuring-Diversity-in-Charter-School -Offerings.pdf. For an earlier analysis, see Dick Carpenter II, "Playing to Type? Mapping the Charter School Landscape," Thomas B. Fordham Institute, Washington, DC, May 2006, http://edexcellence.net/publications /playingtotype.html.

14. Ted Rebarber and Alison Consoletti Zgainer, eds., "Survey of America's Charter Schools 2014," Center for Education Reform, Washington, DC, February 2014, www.edreform.com/wp-content/uploads/2014/02/2014CharterSchool SurveyFINAL.pdf; and US Department of Education, Institute of Education Sciences, National Center for Education Statistics, "Elementary/Secondary Information System," accessed January 1, 2015, https://nces.ed.gov/ccd/elsi/.

15. Nationwide, at least 965 charter schools offer preschool in some thirty-three states. Yet in just eight of those states do more than twenty charters offer pre-K. In many jurisdictions, they are not allowed, or find it difficult, to get added to the list of providers. Even where a charter offers preschool, the children coming out of that program may not have direct access to the charter's own K–12 program unless they successfully navigate the admissions lottery. See Sara Mead and Ashley LiBetti Mitchel, "Pre-K and Charter Schools:

Where State Policies Create Barriers to Collaboration," Thomas B. Fordham
Institute, Washington, DC, July 2015, http://edex.s3-us-west-2.amazonaws
.com/publication/pdfs/fordham-prek_and_charters-complete_rev1.pdf.

16. US Department of Education, Institute of Education Sciences, National
Center for Education Statistics, *2014 Digest of Education Statistics*, November
2014, table 216.30, http://nces.ed.gov/programs/digest/d14/tables/dt14
_216.30.asp.

17. Ibid.

18. The charter student-teacher ratio is inflated by virtual schools, which have
a higher student-teacher ratio (29.9) than both brick-and-mortar charters
(20.0) and district-operated public schools (17.4). See Gill et al., "Inside Online Charter Schools."

19. Charter schools' median salary was $24,715 less than DCPS that year, and
their maximum was $36,062 less. See "Teacher Pay in the District," *Washing-
ton Post*, accessed November 14, 2015, www.washingtonpost.com/apps/g
/page/local/teacher-pay-in-the-district/403.

20. Leslie Brody, "Charter School Boasts Big Pay and Big Results," *Wall Street Journal*, October 24, 2014, www.wsj.com/articles/charter-school-study-finds
-high-teacher-pay-helps-students-1414123264; and Joshua Ferguson, Moria
McCullough, Clare Wolfendale, and Brian Gill, "The Equity Project Charter School: Impacts on Student Achievement," Mathematica Policy Research,
Cambridge, MA, October 24, 2014, www.mathematica-mpr.com/~/media
/publications/pdfs/education/tep_fnlrpt.pdf.

CHAPTER 3

1. "Best High Schools, National Rankings," *U.S. News & World Report*, www
.usnews.com/education/best-high-schools/national-rankings, accessed April
22, 2016.

2. NAPCS, *Measuring Charter Performance: A Review of Public Charter School Achievement Studies*, 6th ed. (Washington, DC: NAPCS, 2010), www.publiccharters
.org/wp-content/uploads/2014/01/NAPCS_AchvmntStdy_D8.pdf
_20110330T165151.pdf.

3. F. Howard Nelson, Bella Rosenberg, and Nancy Van Meter, "Charter School
Achievement on the 2003 National Assessment of Educational Progress,"
American Federation of Teachers, Washington, DC, August 2004, http://
nepc.colorado.edu/files/EPRU-0408-63-OWI.pdf.

4. Diana Jean Schemo, "Charter Schools Trail in Results, U.S. Data Reveals,"
New York Times, August 17, 2004, www.nytimes.com/2004/08/17/us/charter
-schools-trail-in-results-us-data-reveals.html?pagewanted=all; "Bad News
on the Charter Front," *New York Times*, August 18, 2004, www.nytimes.com
/2004/08/18/opinion/18wed1.html (no author given); Diana Jean Schemo,
"Education Secretary Defends Charter Schools," *New York Times*, August
18, 2004, www.nytimes.com/2004/08/18/education/18charter.html; and
Debra Viadero, "AFT Charter School Study Sparks Heated National Debate,"

Education Week, September 1, 2004, www.edweek.org/ew/articles/2004/09/01/01chartstudy.h24.html.

5. Nelson, Rosenberg, and Van Meter, "Charter School Achievement on the 2003 National Assessment of Educational Progress."

6. There weren't enough charter-school eighth graders in the sample to make valid comparisons.

7. Robert Bifulco and Helen F. Ladd, "The Impacts of Charter Schools on Student Achievement: Evidence from North Carolina," *Education Finance and Policy* 1, no. 1 (winter 2006): 50–90.

8. US Department of Education, National Center for Education Statistics, "National Assessment of Education Progress: America's Report Card: America's Charter Schools: Results from the NAEP 2003 Pilot Study," December 2014, http://nces.ed.gov/nationsreportcard/pdf/studies/2005456.pdf, 10. See also, Martin Carnoy, Rebecca Jacobsen, Lawrence Mishel, and Richard Rothstein, *The Charter School Dust-up: Examining the Evidence on Enrollment and Achievement* (Washington, DC: Economic Policy Institute, 2005).

9. Julian Betts and Paul Hill, "Key Issues in Studying Charter Schools and Achievement: A Review and Suggestions for National Guidelines," Center on Reinventing Public Education, Seattle, May 2006, www.crpe.org/sites/default/files/whp_ncsrp_wp2achiev_may06_0.pdf. See also Julian Betts and Richard C. Atkinson, "Better Research Needed on the Impact of Charter Schools," *Science* 335 (January 2012): 171–72.

10. Julian R. Betts and Paul T. Hill, eds., *Taking the Measure of Charter Schools: Better Assessment, Better Policymaking, Better Schools* (Lanham, MD: Rowman & Littlefield Education, 2010), 28–29. Emphasis in original.

11. NAPCS, *Measuring Charter Performance*. See also Priscilla Wohlstetter, Joanna Smith, and Caitlin C. Farrell, *Choice and Challenges: Charter School Performance in Perspective* (Cambridge, MA: Harvard Education Press, 2013), especially 51–67, "Have Charter Schools Increased Student Performance?"

12. NAPCS, *Measuring Charter Performance*.

13. Julian R. Betts and Y. Emily Tang, "Value-Added and Experimental Studies of the Effect of Charter Schools on Student Achievement: A Literature Review," Center on Reinventing Public Education, Seattle, December 2008, www.crpe.org/sites/default/files/pub_ncsrp_bettstang_dec08_0.pdf; Julian R. Betts and Y. Emily Tang, "The Effect of Charter Schools on Student Achievement: A Meta-analysis of the Literature," Center on Reinventing Public Education, Seattle, October 2011, www.crpe.org/sites/default/files/pub_NCSRP_BettsTang_Oct11_0.pdf; and Julian R. Betts and Y. Emily Tang, "A Meta-analysis of the Literature on the Effect of Charter Schools on Student Achievement," Center on Reinventing Public Education, Seattle, August 2014, www.crpe.org/sites/default/files/CRPE_meta-analysis_charter-schools-effect-student-achievement_workingpaper.pdf.

14. Julian R. Betts and Y. Emily Tang, "Charter School Achievement: A Review of the Evidence," in *Hopes, Fears, & Reality: A Balanced Look at American Charter*

Schools in 2008, ed. Robin J. Lake (Seattle: Center on Reinventing Public Education, 2008), 3.

15. Ibid., 4.

16. The virtual-twin approach builds on earlier efforts by others, especially the Northwest Evaluation Association, to use "synthetic control groups" in comparative research. The goal is to create a study where pairs of students are mirror images except that they attend different schools.

17. Beginning with its 2013 report, CREDO presented charter effects in two ways: first, using the familiar statistical description of growth in terms of standard deviations; second, for the benefit of nontechnical readers, converting a standard deviation score into estimated actual days of learning during a typical district school year. While the 2009 report did not include the latter metric, the 2013 report began using it and included a version for the earlier (2009) report. See Center for Research on Education Outcomes (CREDO), "National Charter School Study 2013," CREDO, Stanford, CA, 2013, http://credo.stanford.edu /documents/NCSS%202013%20Final%20Draft.pdf, 12–13.

18. Caroline M. Hoxby, "A Serious Statistical Mistake in the CREDO Study of Charter Schools," Stanford University and National Bureau of Economic Research, August 2009, http://credo.stanford.edu/reports/memo_on_the_credo _study.pdf, 1.

19. CREDO, "Fact vs. Fiction: An Analysis of Dr. Hoxby's Misrepresentation of CREDO's Research," CREDO, Stanford, CA, October 2009, http://credo .stanford.edu/reports/CREDO_Hoxby_Rebuttal.pdf; and CREDO, "CREDO Finale to Hoxby's Revised Memorandum," CREDO, Stanford, CA, November 2009, http://credo.stanford.edu/reports/CREDO%20Finale%20to%20 Hoxby.pdf. See also Devona H. Davis and Margaret E. Raymond, "Choices for Studying Choice: Assessing Charter School Effectiveness Using Two Quasi-Experimental Methods," *Economics of Education Review* 31, no. 2 (April 2012): 225–36.

20. See, for example, Liv Finne, *Guide to Major Charter School Studies: Methodological Flaws Undermine CREDO's Study Findings* (Seattle: Washington Policy Center, 2012); "Reviewing the Conclusions of CREDO's National Charter School Study 2013," Center for Education Reform, Washington, DC, June 2013, www.edreform.com/2013/06/reviewing-the-conclusions-of-credos-national -charter-school-study-2013/; Andrew Maul and Abby McClelland, "Review of Charter School Study of 2013," National Education Policy Center, University of Colorado, July 2013, http://nepc.colorado.edu/thinktank/review-credo -2013; Derek Black, "Charter School Study of Student Achievement Draws Criticism from All Sides," *Education Law Prof Blog*, July 17, 2013, http://law professors.typepad.com/education_law/2013/07/charter-school-study-of -student-achievement-draws-criticism-from-all-sides.html; CREDO, "National Charter School Study," Technical Appendix, https://credo.stanford.edu /documents/NCSS2013_Technical%20Appendix.pdf; Andrea Gabor, "New CREDO Study, New Credibility Problems," Andrea Gabor web page, April 28,

2015, http://andreagabor.com/2015/04/28/new-credo-study-new-credibility-problems-from-new-orleans-to-boston/; and CREDO, "CREDO Response to Maul and Gabor," CREDO, Stanford, CA, June 2015, http://credo.stanford.edu/pdfs/CREDOResponsetoMaulandGabor.pdf.

21. Tom Troy, "Charters Fail to Deliver, Analysis Shows," *Toledo Blade*, August 7, 2001, www.toledoblade.com/Education/2001/08/07/Charters-fail-to-deliver-analysis-shows.html; and Chester E. Finn, Jr., Terry Ryan, and Michael B. Lafferty, *Ohio's Education Reform Challenges: Lessons from the Frontlines* (New York: Palgrave Macmillan, 2010).

22. Scott Stephens, "Charter Schools Don't Do Well on State Exams; and Passage Rates Are Worse Than Public Schools," *Cleveland Plain Dealer*, June 27, 2000.

23. For a full account, see Finn, Ryan, and Lafferty, *Ohio's Education Reform Challenges*, especially ch. 4.

24. Building Charter School Quality, "About BCSQ," http://charterschoolquality.org/about-bcsq, accessed November 14, 2015.

25. Building Charter School Quality, "A Framework for Academic Quality," June 2008, http://charterschoolquality.org/media/1186/FrameworkForAcademicQuality.pdf; and Building Charter School Quality, "A Framework for Operational Quality," May 2009, http://charterschoolquality.org/media/1187/FrameworkForOperationalQuality.pdf.

26. National Association of Charter School Authorizers, "Principles & Standards," www.qualitycharters.org/for-authorizers/principles-and-standards, accessed November 14, 2015; and National Alliance for Public Charter Schools, "National Public Charter Schools Commitment to Quality," www.publiccharters.org/national-public-charter-schools-commitment-quality, accessed November 14, 2015.

27. Emily H. Peltason and Margaret E. Raymond, *Charter School Growth and Reception*, vol. 1 (Stanford, CA: CREDO, January 2013), https://credo.stanford.edu/pdfs/CGAR%20Growth%20Volume%20I.pdf. Beginning with the 2013 CREDO report, the analysis included both mathematics and reading data.

28. CREDO, "National Charter School Study 2013."

29. This refers to students who are deemed virtual twins using CREDO's methodology. Ibid., 8.

30. CREDO, "Urban Charter School Study, 2015," CREDO, Stanford, CA, 2015, http://urbancharters.stanford.edu/download/Urban%20Charter%20School%20Study%20Report%20on%2041%20Regions.pdf.

31. Chapter 4 contains a brief comparison of Massachusetts and Ohio, illustrating the variability in student achievement among states (and cities)—variability that has often been noted by CREDO and other analysts.

32. CREDO, "Urban Charter School Study, 2015."

33. Studies conducted using admission lotteries are called *randomized controlled trials* and are often referred to as the gold-standard research method.

34. Philip Gleason, Melissa Clark, Christina Clark Tuttle, and Emily Dwyer, "The Evaluation of Charter School Impacts: Final Report," National Center

for Education Evaluation and Regional Assistance, US Department of Education, 2010, www.mathematica-mpr.com/~/media/publications/PDFs/education/charter_school_impacts.pdf.

35. The school sample was not nationally representative, so the study's findings ought not be generalized to all charter middle schools.

36. Great Lakes Center for Education Research & Practice, home page, http://greatlakescenter.org, accessed November 14, 2015; and National Education Policy Center, home page, http://nepc.colorado.edu, accessed November 14, 2015.

37. Gary Miron, Chris Coryn, and Dawn M. Mackety, "Evaluating the Impact of Charter Schools on Student Achievement: A Longitudinal Look at the Great Lakes States," Great Lakes Center for Education Research & Practice, East Lansing, MI, June 2007, http://greatlakescenter.org/docs/Research/Miron_Charter_Achievement/Miron_Charter%20Achievement.pdf.

38. National Education Policy Center, "Publications," http://nepc.colorado.edu/publications, accessed November 14, 2015; and National Education Policy Center, "NEPC Think Twice Think Tank Reviews," http://nepc.colorado.edu/think-tank-reviews, accessed November 14, 2015.

39. Francesca López, "Review of a Meta-analysis of the Literature on the Effect of Charter Schools on Student Achievement," National Education Policy Center, September 2014, http://nepc.colorado.edu/files/nepc-ttr-chartermeta.pdf. For Betts and Tang's response, see Julian R. Betts and Y. Emily Tang, "Review of a Meta-analysis of the Literature on the Effect of Charter Schools on Student Achievement," Center on Reinventing Public Education, August 2014, www.crpe.org/sites/default/files/CRPE_meta-analysis_charter-schools-effect-student-achievement_workingpaper.pdf.

40. Andrew Maul, "Review of Urban Charter School Study 2015," National Education Policy Center, April 2015, http://nepc.colorado.edu/files/ttr-urbancharter-credo.pdf.

41. The Harlem Children's Zone became the inspiration for President Obama's Promise Neighborhoods initiative. See US Department of Education, "Programs: Promise Neighborhoods," www2.ed.gov/programs/promiseneighborhoods/index.html, accessed November 14, 2015.

42. Promise Academy Charter Schools, "Our Schools," accessed January 21, 2016, www.hczpromise.org/our-schools.

43. Will Dobbie and Roland G. Fryer, Jr., "Are High Quality Schools Enough to Close the Achievement Gap? Evidence from a Social Experiment in Harlem," Working Paper 15473, National Bureau of Economic Research, November 2009, www.nber.org/papers/w15473.pdf.

44. Will Dobbie and Roland G. Fryer, Jr., "The Medium-Term Impacts of High-Achieving Charter Schools," paper, January 6, 2014, http://scholar.harvard.edu/files/fryer/files/dobbie_fryer_hcz_01062015_1.pdf.

45. Patrick L. Baude, Marcus Casey, Eric A. Hanushek, and Steven G. Rivkin, "The Evolution of Charter School Quality," Working Paper 20645, National Bureau of Economic Research, October 2014, www.nber.org/papers/w20645.

46. Texas has revoked or nonrenewed the charters of an usually large percentage of problematic schools. See, for example, Texas Education Agency, Division of Charter School Administration, "Summary of Charter Awards and Closures," updated December 9, 2015, http://tea.texas.gov/Texas_Schools /Charter_Schools/Charter_Schools_-_Reports/.

47. Matthew M. Chingos and Martin R. West, "The Uneven Performance of Arizona's Charter Schools," *Educational Evaluation and Policy Analysis* 37, no. 1S (May 2015): 120S–134S.

48. Mark Berends, "Sociology and School Choice: What We Know After Two Decades of Charter Schools," *Annual Review of Sociology* 41, no. 159 (2015), www.annualreviews.org/doi/pdf/10.1146/annurev-soc-073014-112340.

49. Ron Zimmer et al., *Charter Schools in Eight States: Effects on Achievement, Attainment, Integration, and Competition* (Santa Monica, CA: RAND, 2009), www.rand.org/content/dam/rand/pubs/monographs/2009/RAND _MG869.pdf. A follow-up analysis found further evidence that charter high school students in the Sunshine State were likelier than others to persist in college, and that charter high school attendance is associated with greater annual earnings among young adults than among comparable students who attended charter middle schools but went on to district high schools. See Kevin Booker, Brian Gill, Tim Sass, and Ron Zimmer, "Charter High Schools' Effects on Long-Term Attainment and Earnings," Working Paper 29, Mathematica Policy Research, Cambridge, MA, January 2014.

50. Berends, "Sociology and School Choice."

51. Susan Dynarski, "Urban Charter Schools Often Succeed; and Suburban Ones Often Don't," *New York Times*, November 20, 2015, www.nytimes.com /2015/11/22/upshot/a-suburban-urban-divide-in-charter-school-success -rates.html?_r=0.

52. Booker et al., "Charter High Schools' Effects on Long-Term Attainment and Earnings," 28.

CHAPTER 4

1. KIPP Foundation, "KIPP: 2014 Report Card," 2014, www.kipp.org/files /dmfile/2014KIPPReportCard.pdf.

2. The primary analytic method used a matched comparison-group design that produced impact estimates for forty-one KIPP schools. The study also used a lottery-based experimental design for thirteen of these schools.

3. Christina Clark Tuttle et al., "KIPP Middle Schools: Impact on Achievement and Other Outcomes: Final Report," Mathematica Policy Research, Cambridge, MA, February 2013, www.mathematica-mpr.com/~/media/publications/PDFs /education/KIPP_middle.pdf. For the other Mathematica reports, see KIPP Foundation, "Mathematica Research on KIPP Schools," 2015, www.kipp.org /results/mathematica-study.

4. There were also gains in science and social studies. Three to four years after enrollment, students had achieved (respectively) fourteen and eleven more months of learning than if they had not enrolled in a KIPP school.
5. Tuttle et al., "KIPP Middle Schools," xvii.
6. Christina Clark Tuttle et al., "Understanding the Effect of KIPP as It Scales: Volume I, Impacts on Achievement and Other Outcomes," Mathematica Policy Research, Cambridge, MA, September 2015, www.mathematica-mpr.com /˜/media/publications/pdfs/education/kipp_scale-up_vol1.pdf; and Virginia Knechtel et al., "Understanding the Effect of KIPP as It Scales: Volume II, Leadership Practices at KIPP," Mathematica Policy Research, Cambridge, MA, September 2015, www.mathematica-mpr.com/˜/media/publications /pdfs/education/kipp_scale-up_vol2.pdf.
7. Caroline M. Hoxby, Sonali Murarka, and Jenny King, "How New York City's Charter Schools Affect Student Achievement," New York City Charter School Evaluation Project, Cambridge, MA, September 2009, http://users.nber .org/˜schools/charterschoolseval/how_NYC_charter_schools_affect _achievement_sept2009, IV, 8–9.
8. Caroline M. Hoxby and Sonali Murarka, "New York City Charter Schools: How Well Are They Teaching Their Students?" *Education Next* (summer 2008): 54–61. The investigators note that findings from this study may not apply to other charter students who are substantially different from those studied. For a critique, see Sean F. Reardon, "Review of How New York City's Charter Schools Affect Achievement," National Education Policy Center, University of Colorado, 2009, http://nepc.colorado.edu/thinktank/review -how-New-York-City-Charter.
9. There have been smaller-scale studies of virtual schools, focused on specific providers or states. See, for example, Stephanie Saul, "Profits and Questions at Online Charter Schools," *New York Times*, December 12, 2011, www .nytimes.com/2011/12/13/education/online-schools-score-better-on-wall -street-than-in-classrooms.html?_r=0; and John Hechinger, "K12 Backed by Milken Suffers Low Scores as States Resist," *BloombergBusiness*, November 14, 2014, www.bloomberg.com/news/articles/2014-11-14/k12-backed-by-milken -suffers-low-scores-as-states-resist.
10. See Brian Gill et al., "Inside Online Charter Schools," Mathematica Policy Research, Cambridge, MA, October 2015, www.mathematica-mpr.com/˜ /media/publications/pdfs/education/inside_online_charter_schools.pdf.
11. Rosa Pazhouh, Robin Lake, and Larry Miller, "The Policy Framework for Online Charter Schools," Center on Reinventing Public Education, October 2015, www.crpe.org/publications/policy-framework-online-charter-schools.
12. A total of thirty-four states permit online schools, either explicitly or because the state charter law is silent on the issue.
13. National Alliance for Public Charter Schools, "Measuring Up: 1. No Caps," accessed April 15, 2016, www.publiccharters.org/law-database/caps/.

14. For example, K12—a firm active in multiple states—spent over $1.25 million lobbying the Pennsylvania legislature between 2007 and 2015. See Pazhouh, Lake, and Miller, "Policy Framework for Online Charter Schools," 4.

15. While this sector is dominated by EMOs, some places also have many small virtual charters affiliated with, and sponsored by, their own districts, either because this improves learning options for students or because federal start-up funds were available for new charter schools.

16. James L. Woodworth et al., "Online Charter School Study 2015," CREDO, October 2015, https://credo.stanford.edu/pdfs/OnlineCharterStudyFinal2015 .pdf. This analysis excluded students who take online courses while also enrolled in brick-and-mortar schools, and it omitted blended-learning schools.

17. We see the oddity of saying that charter students achieve 180 fewer days of learning per year, mindful that most district schools are in session for only that many days. Still, following the CREDO methodology, which converts differences in standard deviations to days per year of learning, the standard deviation is –0.25 for math, which equates to 180 fewer days.

18. The well-known Florida Virtual School is not a charter; hence its results are not included here.

19. James L. Woodworth et al., "Online Charter School Study 2015," CREDO, October 2015, https://credo.stanford.edu/pdfs/OnlineCharterStudyFinal 2015.pdf, 63.

20. National Alliance for Public Charter Schools, press release, October 27, 2015, www.publiccharters.org/press/national-alliance-responds-credos-virtual -charter-schools-report/.

21. National Association of Charter School Authorizers, press release, October 28, 2015, www.qualitycharters.org/news-commentary/press-releases/nacsa -urges-authorizers-to-act-on-online-charter-schools/.

22. CREDO, "Charter School Performance in Ohio," December 2014, https:// credo.stanford.edu/pdfs/OHReport12182014_FINAL.pdf.

23. Ibid.

24. CREDO, "Charter School Performance in Massachusetts," February 2013, https://credo.stanford.edu/documents/MAReportFinal_000.pdf.

25. Thirteen percent had results that were significantly worse in reading, and 17 percent in math; 43 percent were similar to district schools in reading, 37 percent in math.

26. See chapter 9 for a comparison of Boston's Commonwealth charter schools (which operate quite independently) with the Pilot Schools created by the district, which have less autonomy.

27. National Alliance for Public Charter Schools, "Measuring up to the model: A ranking of state charter school laws," January 2016, www.publiccharters.org /wp-content/uploads/2016/01/Model-Law-Final_2016.pdf.

28. DC Public Charter School Board, "Performance Management Framework: Guidelines and Technical Guide," November 2011, www.dcpcsb.org/sites /default/files/data/images/2010-2011%20pmf%20guidelines%2011_1_11

.pdf; and DC Public Charter School Board, "2015 Annual Report," 2015, www.dcpcsb.org/blog/2015-annual-report.

29. Jeff Cohen, Alex Doty, and Florian Schalliol, "Transforming Public Education in the Nation's Capital," FSG 2014, www.fsg.org/publications/transforming-public-education-nations-capital.

30. Josephine C. Baker, *The Evolution & Revolution of DC Charter Schools* (self-published, 2014), especially 73–96.

31. Fifty-four schools were not tiered, because they were in their first year of operation or did not have tested grades. DC Public Charter School Board, "2015 Annual Report."

32. CREDO, "National Charter School Study 2013," 2013, http://credo.stanford.edu/documents/NCSS%202013%20Final%20Draft.pdf, 52.

33. Ted Kolderie, *Beyond Choice to New Public Schools* (Washington, DC: Progressive Policy Institute, 1990), 2, ch. 2.

CHAPTER 5

1. Erica Frankenberg, Genevieve Siegel-Hawley, and Jia Wang "Choice Without Equity: Charter School Segregation and the Need for Civil Rights Standards," Civil Rights Project, Los Angeles, 2010, https://civilrightsproject.ucla.edu/research/k-12-education/integration-and-diversity/choice-without-equity-2009-report/frankenberg-choices-without-equity-2010.pdf.

2. Gary Ritter, Nathan Jensen, Brian Kisida, and Joshua McGee, "A Closer Look at Charter Schools and Segregation: Flawed Comparisons Lead to Overstated Conclusions," *Education Next* (summer 2010), http://educationnext.org/a-closer-look-at-charter-schools-and-segregation/. Their methodological criticism of the Civil Rights Project report is also worth nothing. They point to "a critical flaw," namely, that "in every case, whether the authors examine the numbers at the national, state, or metropolitan level, they compare the racial composition of *all* charter schools to that of *all* traditional public schools. . . . As the authors themselves point out . . . : 'the concentration of charter schools in urban areas skews the charter school enrollment towards higher percentages of poor and minority students.'" See also Brian Gill, "School Choice and Integration," in *Getting Choice Right: Ensuring Equity and Efficiency in Education Policy*, ed. Julian R. Betts and Tom Loveless (Washington, DC: Brookings Institution, 2005), 130–145.

3. For a list of the one hundred largest districts, see US Department of Education, *2014 Digest of Education Statistics*, table 215.10, accessed January 21, 2016, https://nces.ed.gov/programs/digest/d14/tables/dt14_215.10.asp.

4. Sara Mead, Ashley LiBetti Mitchel, and Andrew J. Rotherham, "The State of the Charter School Movement," Bellwether Education Partners, September 2015, http://bellwethereducation.org/sites/default/files/Charter%20Research%200908%20FINAL.pdf.

5. Susan Pendergrass and Nora Kern, "Waiting for Their Chance: A Closer Look at Wait Lists in Urban Public Charter Schools," National Alliance for Public

Charter Schools, May 2015, www.publiccharters.org/wp-content/uploads /2015/05/waitlist_web.pdf.

6. *Waiting for Superman*, directed by Davis Guggenheim (Electric Kinney Films, Participant Media, and Walden Media, 2010), DVD.

7. Christensen Institute, home page, accessed November 14, 2015, www .christenseninstitute.org.

8. There are effective inner-city schools in the district sector as well, but, to our knowledge, no urban district has managed to scale success in anything like the way that Eva Moskowitz, for example, has replicated her Success Academies in New York City.

9. See, for example, Richard Whitmire, *On the Rocketship: How Top Charter Schools Are Pushing the Envelope* (San Francisco: Jossey-Bass, 2014); and David Osborne, "Schools of the Future: California's Summit Public Schools," Progressive Policy Institute, January 2016, www.progressivepolicy.org/slider/schools -of-the-future-californias-summit-public-schools/.

10. B. C. Hassel, G. Locke, J. Kim, and N. Losoponkul, "Raising the Bar: Why Public Charter Schools Must Become Even More Innovative," The Mind Trust, 2015, www.themindtrust.org/raising-the-bar.

11. Charter school diversity in seventeen cities was tallied in Michael Q. McShane and Jenn Hatfield, "Measuring Diversity in Charter School Offerings," American Enterprise Institute, July 2015, www.aei.org/wp-content /uploads/2015/07/Measuring-Diversity-in-Charter-School-Offerings.pdf.

12. Abigail Thernstrom and Stephan Thernstrom, *No Excuses: Closing the Racial Gap in Learning* (New York: Simon & Schuster, 2003). See also Jay Mathews, *Work Hard; Be Nice* (Chapel Hill, NC: Algonquin Books, 2009).

13. See, for example, Jay Mathews, *Escalante: The Best Teacher in America* (New York: Henry Holt & Co., 1988).

14. Valerie Strauss, "Why No Excuses Charter Schools Mold Very Submissive Students Starting in Kindergarten," *Washington Post*, September 19, 2014, www.washingtonpost.com/blogs/answer-sheet/wp/2014/09/19/why-no -excuses-charter-schools-mold-very-submissive-students-starting-in -kindergarten/.

15. Sarah Reckhow and Jeffrey W. Snyder, "The Expanding Role of Philanthropy in Education Policy," *Education Researcher* 43, no. 4 (May 2014), http://edr .sagepub.com/content/43/4/186.short, 1-10; and Sarah Reckhow and Megan Tompkins-Stange, "'Singing from the Same Hymnbook' at Gates and Broad," in *The New Education Philanthropy: Politics, Policy, and Reform*, ed. Frederick M. Hess and Jeffrey R. Henig (Cambridge, MA: Harvard Education Press, 2015), 55–78.

16. This occurred even as the amount of inflation-adjusted grant dollars distributed by the top fifteen funders to these newer line jurisdictional challengers grew 73 percent.

17. Reckhow and Snyder, "The Expanding Role of Philanthropy"; and Reckhow and Tompkins-Stange, "'Singing from the Same Hymnbook.'"

18. The Philanthropy Roundtable has chronicled many examples of this giving in a series of donor guidebooks. See, for example, Julie Kowal, Bryan Hassel, and Sarah Crittenden, with Dana Brinson and Jacob Rosch, *Investing in Charter Schools: A Guide for Donors* (Washington, DC: Philanthropy Roundtable, 2009); and Karl Zinsmeister, *From Promising to Proven: A Wise Giver's Guide to Expanding on the Success of Charter Schools* (Washington, DC: Philanthropy Roundtable, 2014). See also Hess and Henig, eds., *The New Education Philanthropy*.

19. Joanne Barkan, "Got Dough? How Billionaires Rule Our Schools," *Dissent* (winter 2011), www.dissentmagazine.org/article/got-dough-how-billionaires-rule-our-schools; and Kevin K. Kumashiro, "When Billionaires Become Education Experts," *Academe* (May–June 2012), www.aaup.org/article/when-billionaires-become-educational-experts#.ViFS9MeFPcs. While these two pieces are politically left-leaning, some on the right are also critical of recent shifts in philanthropy. See, for example, William Schambra, "The Problem of Strategic Philanthropy," *Non Profit Quarterly* (August 12, 2013), http://nonprofitquarterly.org/2013/08/12/the-problem-of-strategic-philanthropy/.

20. Match Education is the shared brand name of Match Charter Public School, The Match Foundation, Inc., and The Charles Sposato Graduate School of Education, Inc.

21. Relay has approval to operate in seven states and has been accredited by the Middle States Commission and the National Council for Accreditation of Teacher Education.

22. Steven Adamowski, "The Autonomy Gap," Thomas B. Fordham Institute, Washington, DC, April 2007, http://edexcellence.net/publications/autonomygap.html.

23. Ash Center for Democratic Governance and Innovation, Kennedy School, Harvard University, "Charter School Law," accessed November 14, 2015 www.innovations.harvard.edu/charter-school-law; and Ash Center for Democratic Governance and Innovation, Kennedy School, Harvard University, "Mayor's Charter School Initiatives," accessed November 14, 2015, www.innovations.harvard.edu/mayors-charter-schools-initiative.

24. Nelson Smith, "Redefining the School District in America," Thomas B. Fordham Institute, Washington, DC, June 2015, http://edexcellence.net/publications/redefining-the-school-district-in-america.

25. Center on Reinventing Public Education, "Portfolio Strategy," accessed November 14, 2015, www.crpe.org/research/portfolio-strategy.

CHAPTER 6

1. For a history of the school district, see Roald F. Campbell, Luvern L. Cunningham, Raphael O. Nystrand, and Michael D. Usdan, *The Organization and Control of American Schools*, 6th ed. (New York: Merrill, 1990), especially ch. 5, "The Local School District"; Michael Kirst, "The Political and Policy Dynamics of K–12 Education Reform from 1965 to 2010: Implications for

Changing Postsecondary Education," Research Priorities for Broad-Access Higher Education, Stanford University, 2010, http://cepa.stanford.edu /content/political-and-policy-dynamics-12-education-reform-1965-2010 -implications-changing; Paul T. Hill, "Recovering from an Accident: Repairing Education Governance with the Principle of Comparative Advantage" in *Who's in Charge Here? The Tangled Web of School Governance*, ed. Noel Epstein (Washington, DC: Brookings, 2004); and Paul T. Hill et al., "Big City School Boards: Problems and Options," Center on Reinventing Public Education, Seattle, December 2002, www.crpe.org/publications/big-city-school-boards -problems-and-options.

2. Ted Kolderie, "The States Will Have to Withdraw the Exclusive," Public Services Redesign Project, July 1990, www.educationevolving.org/pdf/States WillHavetoWithdrawtheExclusive.pdf, 1.

3. David L. Kirp, "How to Fix the Country's Failing Schools. And How Not To," *New York Times*, January 9, 2016, www.nytimes.com/2016/01/10/opinion /sunday/how-to-fix-the-countrys-failing-schools-and-how-not-to.html; David L. Kirp, *Improbable Scholars: The Rebirth of a Great American School System and a Strategy for America's Schools* (Oxford, UK: Oxford University Press, 2013); and Michael Q. McShane, "Improbable Scholars, Inappropriate Conclusions," *Education Next* (June 13, 2013), http://educationnext.org/improbable -scholars-inappropriate-conclusions.

4. "The Counterfeit High School Diploma," editorial, New York Times, December 31, 2015, www.nytimes.com/2015/12/31/opinion/the-counterfeit-high -school-diploma.html?_r=0.

5. Milton Friedman, personal correspondence with the authors, November 25, 1998, cited in Chester E. Finn, Jr., Bruno V. Manno, and Gregg Vanourek, *Charter Schools in Action: Renewing Public Education* (Princeton, NJ: Princeton University Press, 2000), 182.

6. Anthony Cody, "15 Months in Virtual Charter Hell: A Teacher's Tale," *Education Week*, January 6, 2014, http://blogs.edweek.org/teachers/living-in -dialogue/2014/01/15_months_in_virtual_charter_h.html. This blog was posted by an aggrieved former teacher in a virtual charter school describing her own disillusioning experience.

7. Ohio's website, for example, makes you look in one place for district-operated schools and then separately for "community" (i.e., charter) schools not authorized by the district in which they're located. Once you find them, the school reports are hard to interpret—and completely useless in determining which *other* schools might be located within striking distance and how to compare them. See Ohio Department of Education, *Ohio School Report Cards*, "Select a School," accessed November 27, 2015, http://reportcard.education .ohio.gov/Pages/School-Search.aspx.

8. Chester E. Finn, Jr., and Brandon L. Wright, *Failing Our Brightest Kids: The Global Challenge of Educating High-Ability Students* (Cambridge, MA: Harvard Education Press, 2015).

9. See, for example, Harvard Graduate School of Education, Making Caring Common Project, "Turning the Tide: Inspiring Concern for Others and the Common Good Through College Admissions," Harvard Graduate School of Education, January 2016, http://mcc.gse.harvard.edu/files/gse-mcc/files/20160120_mcc_ttt_report_interactive.pdf?m=1453303517.

10. Marc J. Holley, Anna J. Egalite, and Martin F. Lueken, "Competition with Charters Motivates Districts," *Education Next* (fall 2013), http://education next.org/competition-with-charters-motivates-districts/.

CHAPTER 7

1. For an excellent review, see Joey Gustafson, "Charter Authorizers Face Challenges," *Education Next* (summer 2013), http://educationnext.org/charter -authorizers-face-challenges.

2. Chicago International Charter School, home page, accessed November 27, 2015, www.chicagointl.org.

3. There's an important distinction between vendors that supply services—accounting, payroll, lunch, transport, IT, speech therapy, etc.—to a school and those that shoulder responsibility for operating the entire school. In both cases, the school's governing board is the purchaser, but in the latter case, it is really hiring an outside organization to do the whole thing, from teaching to sweeping—and to deliver academic results.

4. National Association of Charter School Authorizers, "Authorizer Contact Information," accessed November 27, 2015, https://public.tableau.com/profile /nacsa#!/vizhome/NACSAAuthorizerContactInformation9315/Map.

5. The Thomas B. Fordham Foundation, with which all three of us have been associated, is one of Ohio's 501(c)3 authorizers and, by 2016, had eleven schools around the Buckeye State in its sponsorship portfolio.

6. National Association of Charter School Authorizers, "Principles & Standards," accessed February 6, 2016, www.qualitycharters.org/for-authorizers /principles-and-standards.

7. This problem is less common when a publicly financed state or local agency is the authorizer, but it can turn into a full-fledged conflict of interest for universities, nonprofits, and others that cover their authorizing costs with enrollment-based fees levied on the schools in their stables. On the other hand, state and local agencies may face different conflicts of interest, such as the desire to minimize the competition that charters pose to traditional schools.

8. Michael Q. McShane, Jenn Hatfield, and Elizabeth English, "The Paperwork Pile-Up: Measuring the Burden of Charter School Applications," American Enterprise Institute, May 2015, www.aei.org/wp-content/uploads/2015/05 /Paperwork-Pileup-final.pdf.

9. Mila Koumpilova, "Minnesota Wants More Oversight from Charter School Authorizers," *TwinCities.com*, January 9, 2014, www.twincities.com/education /ci_24880924/minnesota-wants-more-oversight-from-charter-school -authorizers.

10. Michigan has some forty authorizers, but adequate state accountability data were available only for a subset of them. See Amber Arellano, Sarah Lenhoff, and Sunil Joy, "Accountability for All: The Need for Real Charter School Authorizer Accountability In Michigan," Education Trust–Midwest, February 2015, http://midwest.edtrust.org/resource/accountability-for-all.

11. Patrick L. Baude, Marcus Casey, Eric A. Hanushek, and Steven G. Rivkin, "The Evolution of Charter School Quality," Working Paper 20645, National Bureau of Economic Research, October 2014, www.nber.org/papers /w20645. For an analysis of the relationship between type of authorizer and charter school effectiveness in Ohio, see Ron Zimmer, Brian Gill, Jonathon Attridge, and Kaitlin Obenauf, "Charter Authorizers and Student Achievement," Education Finance and Policy 9, no. 1 (winter 2014), www.mit pressjournals.org/doi/abs/10.1162/EDFP_a_00120?journalCode=edfp# .VliPEN-rTdQ, 50–85.

12. Bellwether Education Partners estimate that there have been approximately eleven hundred closures in just the past five years. See Sara Mead, Ashley Li-Betti Mitchel, and Andrew J. Rotherham, "The State of the Charter School Movement," Bellwether Education Partners, September 2015, http://bell wethereducation.org/publication/state-charter-school-movement.

13. Ibid.

14. "Measuring Up to the Model: A Ranking of State Charter School Laws," National Alliance for Public Charter Schools, January 2016, www.publiccharters .org/wp-content/uploads/2016/01/Model-Law-Final_2016.pdf.

15. Personal communication with staff of the California Charter Schools Association.

16. Friendship Public Charter School, "Meet Our Leaders," accessed January 14, 2016, www.friendshipschools.org/apps/pages/index.jsp?uREC_ID=205526 &type=d&pREC_ID=467223.

17. Josh Sweigart, "Charter Operator Accused of Fraud Given Probation," Dayton Daily News, December 18, 2013, www.daytondailynews.com/news/news/local /charter-operator-accused-of-fraud-given-probation/ncPJC/.

18. Pansophic Learning, for example, operates private schools in Switzerland and the Middle East, while Arizona-based Basis Schools recently opened its first international school—also private—in Shenzhen, China.

CHAPTER 8

1. Other complexities include funds that must or must not be spent during certain periods. Some activities are advance-funded, others treated as after-the-fact reimbursements. Some jurisdictions allocate dollars to charters on a monthly basis, according to enrollments, while others prepay for the full year but may expect reimbursement by the school if fewer children than expected attend all year. A further complexity arises when districts retain some of the funding "owed" to a charter school in order to provide

various services to the school and its pupils—services that may range from bus transportation to special education to simple overhead for the superintendent's office.

2. Meagan Batdorff et al., "Charter School Funding: Inequity Expands," School Choice Demonstration Project, Department of Education Reform, University of Arkansas, April 2014, www.uaedreform.org/wp-content/uploads /charter-funding-inequity-expands.pdf.

3. Ibid. "Weighted funding" assumes that "districts have the same urban/ metro vs. suburban/rural proportion of enrollment as charter schools." The funding is weighted because charters are more likely to be urban, and urban schooling costs more than suburban and rural schooling.

4. Ibid.

5. Ibid. "Weighted disparity" also assumes that "districts have the same urban/ metro vs. suburban/rural proportion of enrollment as charter schools." The calculation is weighted because charters are more likely to be urban, and urban schooling costs more than suburban and rural schooling.

6. Scott Hiaasen and Kathleen McGrory, "Florida Charter Schools: Big Money, Little Oversight," *Miami Herald*, September 19, 2011, www.miamiherald.com /news/special-reports/cashing-in-on-kids/article1939199.html.

7. Most charters are also relatively new and thus likely to employ a newer, younger teaching force at the outset. The fiscal crunch worsens as those teachers become veterans (and probably more effective in the classroom) and expect reasonable raises.

8. Portland (Oregon) Public Schools, "What Is the Difference Between Capital Funds and Operating Funds?" accessed November 25, 2015, www.pps.k12 .or.us/files/buildings-and-learning/Capop-factsheet-D3.pdf.

9. When charters can tap publicly backed bond revenues, the arrangement is more often the kind used for business development, such as the District of Columbia's revenue-bond program, than the kind commonly used for school construction and renovation. See, for example, Friendship Public Charter School, "Meet Our Leaders," accessed January 14, 2016, www.friendshipschools.org /apps/pages/index.jsp?uREC_ID=205526&type=d&pREC_ID=467223; and District of Columbia Charter Schools, "Facilities Funding for DC Public Charter Schools," accessed January 14, 2016, http://dcps.dc.gov/service /facilities-financing-dc-public-charter-schools.

10. Lisa Grover, "State Policy Snapshot: Facilities Funding for Public Charter Schools," National Association for Public Charter Schools, May 2015, www .publiccharters.org/wp-content/uploads/2015/05/facilities_funding _snapshot_final.pdf.

11. Adam Emerson, "How Facility Funding Fails Charter Schools," Thomas B. Fordham Institute, Washington, DC, May 3, 2013, http://edexcellence.net /commentary/education-gadfly-daily/choice-words/2013/how-facility -funding-fails-charter-schools.html.

12. Charter School Facilities Initiative, "Charter School Facilities Initiative: Initial Findings from Ten States," April 2013, http://facilitiesinitiative.org/media/1013/csfinationalsummary-fnl_april2013_.pdf; and Emerson, "How Facility Funding Fails Charter Schools."

13. Turner-Agassi Charter School Facilities Fund, "What We Do," accessed November 25, 2015, www.turneragassi.com/What-We-Do.

14. Turner-Agassi Charter School Facilities Fund, "Portfolio," accessed November 25, 2015, www.turneragassi.com/Portfolio.

15. Local Initiatives Support Coalition, "Education Programs: Charter School Financing," accessed November 25, 2015, www.lisc.org/section/ourwork/national/education.

16. Laura Arenschield, "KIPP Columbus Charter-School Campus Blossoms," *Columbus Dispatch*, October 27, 2014, www.dispatch.com/content/stories/local/2014/10/27/charter-school-campus-blossoms.html.

17. National Charter School Resource Center, "April 2015 Newsletter: Finding Space: Analyzing Charter School Facilities," April 22, 2015, www.charterschoolcenter.org/newsletter/april-2015-finding-space-analyzing-charter-school-facilities; and Jim Griffin, Leona Christy, and Jody Ernst, "Finding Space: Charter Schools in District-Owned Facilities," National Charter School Resource Center, 2015, www.charterschoolcenter.org/sites/default/files/Finding%20Space.pdf.

18. New York City Charter School Center, "Facilities," accessed November 25, 2015, www.nyccharterschools.org/facilities; National Alliance for Public Charter Schools, "The Public Charter Schools Dashboard," accessed November 25, 2015, www.publiccharters.org/dashboard/home; and New York City Department of Education, "School Budget Overview," accessed November 25, 2015, http://schools.nyc.gov/AboutUs/funding/schoolbudgets/default.htm.

19. Private money doesn't always mean philanthropic dollars. Schools may, for example, own property that brings in rent or charge fees for before- and after-school activities, adult education, and more. Jay P. Greene, "Buckets into the Sea: Why Philanthropy Isn't Changing Schools, and How it Could," in *With the Best of Intentions: How Philanthropy Is Reshaping K-12 Education*, ed. Frederick M. Hess (Cambridge, MA: Harvard Education Press, 2005); and Batdorff et al., "Charter School Funding: Inequity Expands."

20. Michael Alison Chandler, "KIPP D.C. Receives $4 Million Gift from Private Donor," *Washington Post*, September 11, 2015, www.washingtonpost.com/local/education/kipp-dc-receives-4-million-gift-from-private-donor/2015/09/11/387db1b0-5899-11e5-abe9-27d53f250b11_story.html.

21. Michael Alison Chandler, "Some D.C. Charter Schools Get Millions in Donations; Others, Almost Nothing," *Washington Post*, August 26, 2015, www.washingtonpost.com/local/education/some-charter-schools-get-millions-in-donations-others-almost-nothing/2015/08/22/b1fdaef0-4804-11e5-8e7d-9c033e6745d8_story.html?hpid=z2.

22. See these two chapters in Frederick M. Hess and Jeffrey R. Henig, eds., *The New Education Philanthropy: Politics, Policy, and Reform* (Cambridge, MA: Harvard Education Press, 2015): Michael McShane and Jenn Hatfield, "The Backlash Against 'Reform' Philanthropy," 125–42; and Larry Cuban, "A Critique of Contemporary Edu-Giving," 143–62.

23. Frederick M. Hess, "The New Educational Philanthropy," American Enterprise Institute, December 21, 2015, www.aei.org/publication/interview-education-expert-the-new-educational-philanthropy.

24. University of Arkansas, College of Education and Health Professionals, Education Reform, "Faculty," accessed February 6, 2016, http://edre.uark.edu/people/faculty.php; and Batdorff et al., "Charter School Funding: Inequity Expands."

25. "The i3 grant competition is the Obama Administration's signature education innovation initiative. To date, the Department has received more than 4,300 applications and awarded more than $1.2 billion matched by $200 million in private sector funding." From US Department of Education, "U.S. Department of Education Announces Highest-Rated Applications for the 2015 Investing in Innovation Competition," November 13, 2015, www.ed.gov/news/press-releases/us-department-education-announces-highest-rated-applications-2015-investing-innovation-competition.

26. For the types of schools and other projects that are supported, see, for example, Charter School Growth Fund, "Our Portfolio," accessed November 25, 2015, http://chartergrowthfund.org/portfolio; and NewSchools Venture Fund, "Our Ventures," accessed November 25, 2015, www.newschools.org/ventures.

27. Analyzing the fifteen largest K–12 grant makers in 2010, Reckhow and Snyder found that three of their top five gift recipients were charter related: Charter School Growth Fund ($46 million from six funders); KIPP ($24 million from nine funders); and NewSchools Venture Fund ($18 million from ten funders). Sarah Reckhow and Jeffrey W. Snyder, "The Expanding Role of Philanthropy in Education Policy," *Educational Researcher* 43, no. 4 (May 2014), http://edr.sagepub.com/content/43/4/186.short.

28. See these sources by National Alliance for Public Charter Schools: "A Closer Look at the Charter School Movement: Schools, Students, and Management Organizations, 2015–16," February 2016, www.publiccharters.org/wp-content/uploads/2016/02/New-Closed-2016.pdf; "FAQs," accessed November 12, 2015, www.publiccharters.org/get-the-facts/public-charter-schools/faqs/; and "The Public Charter Schools Dashboard," accessed November 12, 2015, www.publiccharters.org/dashboard/home.

29. To our knowledge, only Arizona allows for-profit entities to hold school charters directly from the state.

30. Alex Molnar, Gary Miron, and Jessica L. Urschel, "Profiles of For-Profit Education Management Organizations: Twelfth Annual Report, 2009–2010," National Education Policy Center, Research and Technology, Western

Michigan University, December 2010, www.wmich.edu/sites/default/files
/attachments/u246/2014/EMO-FP-09-10.pdf; and National Alliance for
Public Charter Schools, "Public Charter Schools Dashboard."

31. Frederick M. Hess, "The Future of Educational Entrepreneurship," American
Enterprise Institute, November 20, 2008, www.aei.org/publication/the-future
-of-educational-entrepreneurship-2/.

32. See, for example, Steven R. Strahler, "Textbook Case of a Dying Biz," *Crain's
Chicago Business*, March 3, 2012, www.chicagobusiness.com/article/20120303
/ISSUE01/303039966/textbook-case-of-a-dying-biz.

33. Laura Owen, "What Apple Is Wading Into: A Snapshot of the K-12 Textbook
Business," *Gigaom*, January 21, 2012, https://gigaom.com/2012/01/21/419
-the-abcs-and-123s-of-apple-and-the-K–12-textbook-market/.

34. See, for example, Public Broadcasting System, "The Testing Industry's Big
Four," accessed November 25, 2015, www.pbs.org/wgbh/pages/frontline
/shows/schools/testing/companies.html.

35. Such vendors "provide specific services for fee, such as accounting, payroll
and benefits, transportation, financial and legal advice, personnel recruitment, professional development, and special education." Molnar et al., "Profiles of For-Profit Education Management Organizations."

36. Rosetta Stone, Inc., "Annual Report for Year Ending December 31, 2014,
United States Securities and Exchange Commission, Form 10-K, Commission File Number 1-34283," http://globaldocuments.morningstar.com
/documentlibrary/Document/d5ab359318379df8ba4b51ceb0f052b2.msdoc
/original.

37. California Charter Schools Association, "Find a Vendor: A Service for CCSA
Member Schools," accessed November 25, 2015, https://ccsa.force.com/apex
/VendorBase.

38. K12 Inc., "Annual Report for The Fiscal Year Ending June 30, 2015, United
States Securities and Exchange Commission, Form 10-K, Commission File
Number 001-33883," http://globaldocuments.morningstar.com/document
library/Document/0f0f49a78308aed7ff1f9d0227294933.msdoc/original.

39. National Alliance for Public Charter Schools, "CMO and EMO Public Char-
ter Schools: A Growing Phenomenon in the Charter School Sector," accessed
November 25, 2015, www.publiccharters.org/wp-content/uploads/2014/01
/NAPCS-CMO-EMO-DASHBOARD-DETAILS_20111103T102812.pdf.

40. Catherine Candisky, "North Side Charter School Board Quits Amid Concerns," *Columbus Dispatch*, June 2, 2015, www.dispatch.com/content/stories
/local/2015/06/02/imagine-charter-school-board.html.

41. Ibid.

42. Valerie Strauss, "Reports on Charter Schools Expose New Problems," *Washington Post*, November 9, 2011, www.washingtonpost.com/blogs/answer
-sheet/post/reports-on-charter-schools-expose-new-problems/2011/10/31
/gIQAcMye3M_blog.html. See also Elisa Crouch, "Imagine Schools' Real Estate Deals Fuel Company Growth," *St. Louis Post-Dispatch*, October 30, 2011,

www.stltoday.com/news/local/education/article_dbf9b959-0c73-586c-97e7
-6fca3a729b39.html.

43. Department of Justice, US Attorney's Office, Eastern District of Pennsylvania, "Additional Charges Filed Against Charter School Founder and
Co-Defendants," January 22, 2013, www.justice.gov/usao-edpa/pr/additional
-charges-filed-against-charter-school-founder-and-co-defendants; Office
of the Controller, City of Philadelphia, "Appendix C to Review of Charter
School Oversight by the School District of Philadelphia: Information Con-
cerning Dr. Dorothy June Hairston-Brown Associated Entities," accessed
November 25, 2015, www.philadelphiacontroller.org/publications/audits
/CharterSchoolAudit_JuneBrown.pdf; and Martha Woodall, "Pa. Sues
Devon Cyber Charter the Education Dept. Accused Agora Cyber Charter
School of Misusing Public Dollars [sic]," *Philly.com*, May 1, 2009, http://
articles.philly.com/2009-05-01/news/25274248_1_agora-cyber-charter
-school-taxpayer-money-michael-race.

44. Michael Alison Chandler, "Charter School Founder, Company Agree to Pay
$3 Million to Settle Lawsuit," *Washington Post*, May 4, 2015, www.washington
post.com/local/education/charter-school-founder-company-agree-to-pay
-3-million-to-settle-lawsuit/2015/05/04/ccdd6ddc-f269-11e4-84a6
-6d7c67c50db0_story.html

45. Ibid.

46. Ibid.

47. See, for example, Mitch Smith, "U.S. Investigates Possible Misconduct in
Chicago Public Schools," *New York Times*, April 16, 2015, www.nytimes.com
/2015/04/17/us/us-investigates-possible-misconduct-in-chicago-public
-schools.html; and Mackinac Center for Public Policy, "Financial Scandals
Exposed in Michigan School Districts," November 12, 2002, www.mackinac
.org/4835.

48. In a robust market, producers of shoddy goods eventually lose customers,
profits decline, and shareholders balk. An example in the for-profit charter sector occurred in late 2015, when distraught K12 shareholders voted
down a generous compensation package for managers of this controversial virtual-school operator. Molly Hensley-Clancy, "Investors Rebel Against
Controversial Online School Operator K12," *BuzzFeed News*, December 16,
2015, www.buzzfeed.com/mollyhensleyclancy/investors-rebel-against
-controversial-online-school-operator#.pnAwN0Zz3.

49. Batdorff et al., "Charter School Funding: Inequity Expands."

50. SEED Foundation, "FAQs," accessed November 25, 2015, www.seedfoundation
.com/index.php/about-seed/faqs; and Vilsa E. Curto and Roland G. Fryer,
Jr., "The Potential of Urban Boarding Schools for the Poor: Evidence from
SEED," paper, October 14, 2012, http://scholar.harvard.edu/files/fryer/files
/seed23.pdf.

51. For an explanation of how charter school laws could better handle financing see, for example, National Alliance for Public Charter Schools, "A New

Model Law for Supporting the Growth of High-Quality Public Charter Schools," June 2009, www.publiccharters.org/wp-content/uploads/2014/01/ModelLaw_P7-wCVR_20110402T222341.pdf.

52. US Department of Education, National Center for Education Statistics, 2014 Digest of Education Statistics, table 236.55, accessed January 14, 2016, https://nces.ed.gov/programs/digest/d14/tables/dt14_236.55.asp.

CHAPTER 9

1. John Herbers, "Governors Seek Greater Authority Over Operation of Public Schools," *New York Times*, August 24, 1986, www.nytimes.com/1986/08/24/us/governors-seek-greater-authority-over-operation-of-public-schools.html.

2. Ohio Laws and Rules, "Display of National and Ohio Mottoes," Section 3313.801, effective date October 12, 2006, http://codes.ohio.gov/orc/3313.801.

3. National Alliance for Public Charter Schools, "Measuring Up to the Model: A Ranking of State Charter School Laws," January 2016, www.publiccharters.org/wp-content/uploads/2016/01/Model-Law-Final_2016.pdf.

4. A few charters were attached to other governmental bodies—and some states have more than one arrangement, such as retaining "conversion" schools within districts while start-ups operate independently.

5. US Department of Education, National Center for Education Statistics, "States with Charter School Caps, Automatic Exemptions, Required Teacher Certification, and Identification of Special Education Responsibilities for Charter Schools: 2014–15," table 3.3, accessed November 29, 2015, http://nces.ed.gov/programs/statereform/tab3_3.asp. The teacher-certification requirement has many nuances. Some states permit individual schools to seek waivers. In some states, part-time and volunteer teachers need not be certified. In other places, schools may select part of their instructional staff from uncertified individuals. In several states, some charters have obtained the authority to train and certify their own teachers and administrators. Whether the charter is a start-up or a converted district school often affects certification issues. Whether the charter is treated as its own district or as part of a traditional district is sometimes another factor in certification requirements. And until the recent revision to federal law, the No Child Left Behind Act's "highly qualified teacher" requirement generally overrode state-conferred flexibility for charter schools in regard to who might be employed as instructors.

6. Eric A. Hanushek and Finis Welch, eds., *Handbook of the Economics of Education*, vol. 2 (Philadelphia: Elsevier, 2006), ch. 18, esp. pp. 1064–65, http://hanushek.stanford.edu/sites/default/files/publications/Hanushek%2BRivkin%202006%20HbEEdu%202.pdf); and Thomas J. Kane, Jonah E. Rockoff, and Douglas O. Staiger, "What Does Certification Tell Us About Teacher Effectiveness? Evidence from New York City," *Economics of Education Review* 27 (2008), www0.gsb.columbia.edu/faculty/jrockoff/certification-final.pdf, 615–31.

7. Any district can "convert" a traditional school to charter status—though this practice is all but unheard of in Ohio—and virtual charters can operate statewide.

8. The Frederick Classical Charter School in Maryland wanted to hire nine instructors suited to its education model. But the state offers charters no exemption from district policies, so the school had to select teachers from among those already employed by the district but—for whatever reason—not yet assigned elsewhere. Classical Charter head Tom Neumark commented: "It's not that we don't want [them], it's that we don't know them. We want to talk to them and assess if they're a good fit for the school." Under Maryland law, however, the district is responsible for charter staffing. See Adam Emerson, "One Maryland Charter Highlights Half-Broken Promise of Autonomy," Thomas B. Fordham Institute, Washington, DC, June 10, 2013, http://edexcellence.net/commentary/education-gadfly-daily/choice-words/2013/one-maryland-charter-highlights-half-broken-promise-of-autonomy.html.

9. Exceptions or modifications may be made for schools serving specific populations, such as former dropouts or children with disabilities.

10. The 2015 ESEA reauthorization gives states considerably greater freedom from federal regulation when designing their student- and school-accountability regimes.

11. Michael Q. McShane, Jenn Hatfield, and Elizabeth English, "The Paperwork Pile-Up: Measuring the Burden of Charter School Applications," American Enterprise Institute May 2015, www.aei.org/wp-content/uploads/2015/05/Paperwork-pile-up-embargoed.pdf.

12. *Commonwealth charters* is the term used in Massachusetts law to describe schools authorized exclusively by the state board of education and distinct from several other kinds of charter and quasi-charter schools that are also subject to district approval. See James A. Peyser, "Boston and the Charter School Cap," *Education Next* 14, no. 1 (winter 2014), http://educationnext.org/boston-and-the-charter-school-cap.

13. Atila Abdulkadiroglu et al., "Accountability and Flexibility in Public Schools: Evidence from Boston's Charters and Pilots," *Quarterly Journal of Economics* 126, no. 2 (2011): 669–748 (quote from p. 699), http://qje.oxfordjournals.org/content/126/2/699.full.

14. Hiren Nisar, "Do Charter Schools Improve Student Achievement?" National Center for the Study of Privatization in Education, May 2012, www.ncspe.org/publications_files/OP216.pdf.

15. Colorado, however, allows first come, first served.

16. National Alliance for Public Charter Schools, "Clear Student Recruitment, Enrollment, and Lottery Procedures: How Well Do States' Laws Align to This Component of the Model Law?" accessed November 29, 2015, www.publiccharters.org/law-database/clear-student-recruitment-enrollment-lottery-procedures/.

17. We're not aware of any source of national data on charters that focus on special populations. But an online search of the database maintained by the Colorado League of Charter Schools shows six schools in the Rocky Mountain State for gifted and talented pupils, and a search for "alternative" charters in Florida yields sixty-one hits, including schools for children with disabilities, dropouts, and various other at-risk populations. Colorado League of Charter Schools, "Member Search Results," accessed February 6, 2016, http://coloradoleague.org/search/newsearch.asp; and Florida Department of Education, "Florida Charter School List by District," accessed February 6, 2016, www.floridaschoolchoice.org/Information/charter_schools/Directory.

18. Maya Angelou Schools, "Maya Angelou Academy at New Beginning," accessed February 6, 2016, www.seeforever.org/maya-angelou-public-charter-schools/maya-angelou-academy-at-new-beginnings; and Five Keys Charter, "Community Partners and School Locations," accessed February 6, 2016, www.fivekeyscharter.org/community-partners.

19. See, for example, Seattle Public Schools, "List of Seattle Public Schools," accessed November 29, 2015, www.seattleschools.org/directory/option; and Seattle Public Schools, "Profile of Marshall Alternative High School," accessed November 29, 2015,www.seattleschools.org/UserFiles/Servers/Server_543/File/Migration/General/marshall,john.pdf?sessionid=10a38be9b7fb56b73592d194b0db4043.

20. Paul Hill, "The Obligations of High-Output Charter High Schools," Center on Reinventing Public Education, August 26, 2015, www.crpe.org/thelens/obligations-high-output-charter-high-schools.

21. Robin Lake, "An Alternative View on Charter Schools and Backfill," Center on Reinventing Public Education, August 26, 2015, www.crpe.org/thelens/alternative-view-charter-schools-and-backfill.

22. Foundation for Excellence in Education, "Competency-Based Education," accessed December 15, 2015, http://excelined.org/competency-based-education.

23. See, for example, Foundation for Excellence in Education, "Idaho Agrees: Flexible Pace > Seat Time," March 27, 2015, http://excelined.org/2015/03/27/idaho-agrees-flexible-pace-seat-time; and State of Georgia, Education Reform Commission, "Recommendation from Sub-committees to Full Commission," November 19, 2015, http://gov.georgia.gov/sites/gov.georgia.gov/files/related_files/site_page/Sub%20Committee%20Final%20Recommendations%20Working%20Document%20111815%20%282%29.pdf, 57–59.

24. See, for example, Chester E. Finn, Jr., Andrew J. Rotherham, and Charles R. Hokanson, Jr., *Rethinking Special Education for a New Century*, Thomas B. Fordham Institute, October 2001, http://edexcellence.net/publications/rethinkingsped.html.

25. The Los Angeles district, for example, operates several separate schools for significantly disabled children. See, for example, A. B. Perez Special

Education Center, home page, accessed December 15, 2015, www.lausd.k12 .ca.us/Perez_School/school.html; Los Angeles Unified School District, School Information Branch, "Ernest P. Willenberg Special Education Center," accessed December 14, 2015, http://search.lausd.k12.ca.us/cgi-bin /fccgi.exe?w3exec=geninfo&which=1957; and Lowman School, home page, accessed December 14, 2015, www.lausd.k12.ca.us/Lowman_School /lowman1.html.

26. Excluding or "counseling out" a child who does not meet a school's academic or behavioral standards is not the same as discriminating on grounds of race, religion, and so forth. Preventing and rectifying the latter is the proper work of innumerable civil-rights enforcers.

27. Lauren Morando Rhim, Jesse Gumz, and Kelly Henderson, "Key Trends in Special Education in Charter Schools: A Secondary Analysis of the Civil Rights Data Collection 2011–2012," National Center for Special Education in Charter Schools, 2015, http://static1.squarespace.com/static/52feb326 e4b069fc72abb0c8/t/567b0a3640667a31534e9152/1450904118101/crdc _full.pdf, 18, 20.

28. Ibid, 23.

29. Ibid, 3. See also Arianna Prothero, "Special Education Charters Renew Inclusion Debate," *Education Week*, September 16, 2014, www.edweek.org /ew/articles/2014/09/17/04specialneedscharters.h34.html, which discusses the Arizona Autism Charter School.

30. Rhim et al., "Key Trends in Special Education in Charter Schools," 24.

31. Robert A. Garda, Jr., "Culture Clash: Special Education in Charter Schools," *North Carolina Law Review* 90, no. 3 (2012), http://papers.ssrn.com/sol3/papers .cfm?abstract_id=1791780.

32. Ibid.

33. See, for example, Arianna Prothero, "In Denver, Charters and District Team Up on Special Education," *Education Week*, November 30, 2015, www.edweek .org/ew/articles/2015/12/02/in-denver-charters-and-district-team-up.html.

34. In 2010, the Southern Poverty Law Center filed a special education lawsuit that alleged that these students were not receiving services under federal law. After extensive negotiation, the center withdrew its suit and the RSD put in place a new system for dealing with special education. See Recovery School District, "Serving Children with Special Needs in New Orleans," accessed January 3, 2016, www.rsdla.net/apps/news/show_news.jsp?REC_ID =363991&id=0.

35. ReNEW Schools is the name of the network that includes among its charters one that focuses on severely disabled students.

36. Lynn Schnaiberg and Robin Lake, "Special Education in New Orleans: Juggling Flexibility, Reinvention, and Accountability in the Nation's Most Decentralized School System," Center on Reinventing Public Education, Seattle, January 2015, www.crpe.org/publications/special-education-new -orleans-juggling-flexibility-reinvention-and-accountability.

37. Jacob L. Rosch and Dana Brinson, "Charter School Autonomy: A Half-Broken Promise," Thomas B. Fordham Institute, Washington, DC, October 2011, http://edexcellence.net/publications/charter-school-autonomy-a .html, 5.

38. Ashley Hirtzel, "Union Leader Calls for Level Playing Field with Charter Schools," WBFO 88.7, Buffalo's NPR News Station, May 1, 2014, http://news .wbfo.org/post/union-leader-calls-level-playing-field-charter-schools.

39. Darrel Rowland, "Kasich to Revamp Ohio Laws on Charter Schools," *Columbus Dispatch*, December 19, 2014, www.dispatch.com/content/stories/local /2014/12/18/kasich-to-revamp-ohio-laws-on-charter-schools.html.

40. Julie Corbett, "Chartering Turnaround: Leveraging Public Charter School Autonomy to Address School Failure," National Alliance for Public Charter Schools, August 2015, www.publiccharters.org/wp-content/uploads/2015 /08/turnaround_web.pdf.

41. Summarized from National Alliance for Public Charter Schools, "A New Model Law for Supporting the Growth of High-Quality Public Charter Schools," NAPCS Research and Publications, June 22, 2009, www.public charters.org/publications/model-law-supporting-growth-high-quality -public-charter-schools.

CHAPTER 10

1. Paul T. Hill and Ashley Jochim, "The Street-Level Politics of School Reform," Center on Reinventing Public Education, Seattle, November 2015, www .yumpu.com/en/document/view/54768159/the-street-level-politics-of -school-reform.

2. In 2015, Democratic presidential candidate front-runner Hillary Clinton, who joined her husband as a multidecade charter booster, distanced herself from this reform, with some observers noting that her timing coincided with her endorsement by both national teachers unions. See Kimberly Hefling, "Hillary Clinton Rebukes Charter Schools," *Politico*, November 9, 2015, www. politico.com/story/2015/11/hillary-clinton-charter-schools-education -215661.

3. Total US public school enrollments have been rising, but essentially all of the recent increase is accounted for by the charter sector—and by increasing numbers of Hispanic students. Private school enrollments, however, fell by 11 percent between 1997 and 2011. See William J. Hussar and Tabitha M. Bailey, *Projections of Education Statistics to 2022*, National Center for Education Statistics, Institute of Education Sciences, US Department of Education, February 2014, https://nces.ed.gov/pubsearch/pubsinfo.asp?pubid=2014051.

4. Examples include the Alliance for School Choice, the Center for Education Reform, the Policy Innovation in Education Network, the Thomas B. Fordham Institute, Democrats for Education Reform, the Center on Reinventing Public Education, Education Post, the Lynde and Harry Bradley Foundation, the Walton Family Foundation, the Doris & Donald Fisher Fund, the Eli and

Edythe Broad Foundation, the Laura and John Arnold Foundation, and the Foundation for Excellence in Education.

5. Diane Ravitch, "The Billionaire Boys Club," in *The Death and Life of the Great American School System: How Testing and Choice are Undermining Education* (New York: Basic Books, 2010), 195–222.

6. Daniel Bergner, "The Battle for New York Schools: Eva Moskowitz vs. Mayor Bill de Blasio," *New York Times*, September 3, 2014, www.nytimes.com/2014 /09/07/magazine/the-battle-for-new-york-schools-eva-moskowitz-vs-mayor -bill-de-blasio.html?_r=0.

7. "Thousands Of Charter Schools Supporters Rally In Brooklyn," CBSNew York/Associated Press, October 7, 2015, http://newyork.cbslocal.com/2015 /10/07/brooklyn-charter-schools-rally/.

8. Monica Disare, "This Time, Teachers Take the Political Stand in Charter School Battle," *Chalkbeat New York*, October 21, 2015, http://ny.chalkbeat.org /2015/10/21/this-time-teachers-take-the-political-stand-in-charter-school -battle/#.VliTA9-rTdQ.

9. Andrew P. Kelly, "Turning Lightning into Electricity: Organizing Parents for Education Reform," American Enterprise Institute, December 2014, www.aei.org/wp-content/uploads/2014/12/Kelly_Turning-Lightning-Into -Electricity.pdf. See also Bruno V. Manno, "Not Your Mother's PTA," *Education Next* (winter 2012), http://educationnext.org/not-your-mothers-pta.

10. See, for example, Caprice Young's interview of former California Assembly speaker Fabian Nunez regarding the role of "parent power" in reversing a legislative action that would have made school facilities harder for charters to access in Los Angeles. Fabian Nunez, interview by Caprice Young, n.d., video, accessed November 27, 2015, https://drive.google.com/a/edexcellence.net /file/d/0BwZ67BBZCMA6VFlzZHprQmM0ZGc/view (relevant comments start around minute 11).

11. See, for example, David Scharfenberg, "Cap on Charter Schools Wrong, Baker Tells Rally," *Boston Globe*, September 22, 2015, www.bostonglobe.com /metro/2015/09/22/baker-lift-charter-school-cap/pWLQnrofqH6EmpAFs5gSeN /story.html; and Massachusetts Teachers Association, "MTA President: Charter Initiative Would Undermine Public Schools and Communities," 2015, www.google.com/search?q=Massachusetts+charter+ballot +initiative&ie=utf-8&oe=utf-8. On the lawsuit, see Peter Balonon-Rosen, "Group Sues to Lift Massachusetts Charter Cap," Learning Lab, September 15, 2015, http://learninglab.wbur.org/2015/09/15/lawsuit-filed-to-lift -massachusetts-charter-cap.

12. They have a point. Although the total exodus of pupils from a district school into charters might justify eliminating one classroom and teaching position, it's hard to do that when, say, nineteen departures are scattered across different grades and may occur at different times during the year. Nor do the sending school's heating and electric bills decline, or its need for custodians, security guards, and buses.

13. Rachel M. Cohen, "When Charters Go Union," *American Prospect* (summer 2015), http://prospect.org/article/when-charters-go-union.

14. For examples, see Maisie McAodd, "Do Charters 'Cream' Students? You Bet!" United Federation of Teachers, March 5, 2015, www.uft.org/news-stories/do-charters-cream-students-you-bet; Laura McKenna, "Why Don't Suburbanites Want Charter Schools?" *Atlantic*, October 1, 2015, www.theatlantic.com/education/archive/2015/10/why-dont-suburbanites-want-charter-schools/408307/; and Diana Ravitch, "Charter Schools Vs. Catholic Schools," *Diane Ravitch's Blog*, May 21, 2012, http://dianeravitch.net/2012/05/21/charter-schools-vs-catholic-schools.

15. Abraham M. Lackman, "The Collapse of Catholic School Enrollment: The Unintended Consequence of the Charter School Movement," *Albany Government Law Review* 6, no. 1 (2012), www.albanygovernmentlawreview.org/archives/pages/article-information.aspx?volume=6&issue=1&page=001. Going forward, Lackman estimates that each new charter will draw about a hundred students from the Catholic school system. See also Adam B. Schaeffer, "The Charter School Paradox," Cato Institute, Washington, DC, August 28, 2012, www.cato.org/blog/charter-school-paradox. For an analysis of this effect in Michigan, see Eugene F. Thomas, Ron Zimmer, and John T. Jones, "Beyond Achievement, Enrollment Consequences of Charter Schools in Michigan," *Advances in Applied Microeconomics* 14 (2006), 241–255, www.rand.org/pubs/external_publications/EP20060020.html.

16. Cardinal Newman Society, "Catholic Schools 'Switching' to Charter Schools, Study Finds," May 19, 2014, www.cardinalnewmansociety.org/CatholicEducationDaily/DetailsPage/tabid/102/ArticleID/3290/Catholic-Schools-%E2%80%98Switching%E2%80%99-to-Charter-Schools-Study-Finds.aspx; Michael Q. McShane and Andrew P. Kelly, "Sector Switchers," Friedman Foundation, April 29, 2014, www.edchoice.org/research/sector-switchers; and Seton Education Partners, "Charter School Initiative," accessed November 27, 2015, www.setonpartners.org/what-we-do/charter-school-network/.

17. Sarah Yatsko, Elizabeth Cooley Nelson, and Robin Lake, "District-Charter Collaboration Compact: Interim Report," Center on Reinventing Public Education, Seattle, June 2013, www.crpe.org/publications/district-charter-collaboration-compact-interim-report, 2.

18. Daniela Doyle, Christen Holly, and Bryan C. Hassel, "Is Detente Possible? District-Charter School Relations in Four Cities," Thomas B. Fordham Institute, Washington, DC, November 2015, http://edexcellence.net/publications/is-detente-possible-district-charter-school-relations-in-four-cities.

19. Ohio Department of Education, "Community School Directory," accessed January 14, 2016, http://education.ohio.gov/Topics/Quality-School-Choice/Community-Schools/Forms-and-Program-Information-for-Community-School/Directory-of-Community-Schools-and-Sponsors (listing 373

charter schools); Public School Review, "Ohio Charter Public Schools," accessed January 14, 2016, www.publicschoolreview.com/ohio/charter-public-schools (stating that 120,224 Ohio students attend charter schools); and Ohio Department of Education, "Fall Enrollment (Headcount)—October 2014 Public Districts and Buildings," accessed January 14, 2016, http://education.ohio.gov/Topics/Data/Frequently-Requested-Data/Enrollment-Data (stating that approximately 1.8 million K–12 students attend Ohio public schools).

20. By statute, start-up charters in Ohio, except for the virtual kind, are confined to cities and low-performing districts. Any district may convert an extant school into a charter, but few have done so.

21. When these divorces succeeded, White Hat attorneys insisted that the school's assets still belonged to White Hat, the former school operator, and with some reluctance, the Ohio Supreme Court agreed, noting that the company had a valid contract that specified such ownership. See Valerie Strauss, "Ohio Supreme Court Sides with For-Profit Company over Charter Schools," *Washington Post*, September 16, 2015, www.washingtonpost.com/news/answer-sheet/wp/2015/09/16/ohio-supreme-court-sides-with-for-profit-company-over-charter-schools.

22. Jim Siegel, "Charter-School Reform Is Tabled in Ohio House Until September," *Columbus Dispatch*, July 1, 2015, www.dispatch.com/content/stories/local/2015/07/01/charter-law-reform-is-tabled-until-september.html?fb_comment_id=739014976220834_739075022881496#f371e93c58.

23. Jim Siegel, "Former Batchelder Staffers Lobby for Charter School," *Columbus Dispatch*, February 2015, www.dispatch.com/content/blogs/the-daily-briefing/2015/02/02-16-15-charter-lobby.html.

24. Matt Barnum, "Ohio Fixed Its Scandal-Plagued Charter Schools, Right? Not So Fast," The Seventy Four, January 4, 2016, www.the74million.org/article/ohio-fixed-its-scandal-plagued-charter-schools-right-not-so-fast.

25. Richard Whitmire, "New Report Shows Surging Charter Enrollment, But Could Breakthroughs Be the Prelude to a Backlash?" The Seventy Four, November 15, 2015, www.the74million.org/article/whitmire-new-report-shows-surging-charter-enrollment-but-could-breakthroughs-be-the-prelude-to-a-backlash.

26. According to Bellwether Education Partners, the proportion of low-income students in Colorado and Utah charter schools is as low as 17 and 19 percent, respectively. See Sara Mead, Ashley LiBetti Mitchel, and Andrew J. Rotherham, "The State of the Charter School Movement," Bellwether Education Partners, September 2015, http://bellwethereducation.org/sites/default/files/Charter%20Research%200908%20FINAL.pdf.

27. As of autumn 2015, there were 34 such schools operating in every borough except Staten Island. See Success Academies, "Schools," accessed January 14, 2016, www.successacademies.org/schools (website that allows users to browse schools by New York City borough).

28. Priscilla Wohlstetter, "A New Solution to an Old Problem: School Integration," *Huffington Post*, November 23, 2015, www.huffingtonpost.com/priscilla
-wohlstetter/a-new-solution-to-an-old_b_8630760.html.
29. Amanda Ulrich, "New Coalition Promotes Diverse Student Populations in Charter Schools," *Education Week*, July 1, 2014, http://blogs.edweek.org
/edweek/charterschoice/2014/07/new_coalition_promotes_diverse_student
_populations_in_charter_schools.html.
30. Richard Whitmire, "More Middle-Class Families Choose Charters," *Education Next* (summer 2015), http://educationnext.org/middle-class-families
-choose-charters.

CHAPTER 11

1. Arguably, of course, these are the children who derive the greatest benefit because the schools they attend were explicitly designed to benefit them.
2. "The No-Excuses Charter School Movement," *Dewey to Delpit* (blog), accessed November 14, 2015, http://edcommentary.blogspot.com/p/no-excuses
-charter-movement.html.
3. Albert Cheng, Collin Hitt, Brian Kisida, and Jonathan N. Mills, "The Impact of 'No Excuses' Charter Schools on Academic Achievement," National Center for the Study of Privatization in Education, accessed February 6, 2016, www.ncspe.org/publications_files/OP226.pdf. The authors note that their quest for experimental studies meant they were, in effect, looking only at oversubscribed schools with lottery-based admission. Other studies have shown that such schools are typically—and understandably—more effective than those with too few or just enough pupils.
4. When visiting DC's laid back "School Without Walls," a selective-admission public high school for high-achieving students, one of us was told that kids entering ninth grade there from DC's several KIPP middle schools were even "less able to handle the independence we expect of all our pupils" than those coming from the most buttoned-down private schools in the area.
5. Ariel Sacks, "Guest Post: A Day in the Life of a No Excuses Charter School Student," Center for Teaching Quality, February 10, 2014, www.teaching
quality.org/content/blogs/ariel-sacks/guest-post-day-life-no-excuses
-charter-school-student.
6. KIPP, "The Promise of College Completion," April 2011, www.kipp.org
/results/college-completion-report/2011-college-completion-report.
7. Robert Pondiscio, "'No Excuses' Kids Go to College," *Education Next* (spring 2013), http://educationnext.org/no-excuses-kids-go-to-college.
8. David Whitman, *Sweating the Small Stuff* (Washington, DC: Thomas B. Fordham Institute, 2008).
9. Foundation for Excellence in Education, "Old Standards v. Common Core," accessed December 14, 2015, http://excelined.org/common-core-toolkit
/old-standards-v-common-core-a-side-by-side-comparison-of-english
-language-arts-2/.

10. Doug McCurry, "Achievement First Fully Embraces the Common Core!" *The Chalkboard: Life @ Achievement First*, May 3, 2013, www.achievementfirst.org /chalkboard/post/article/achievement-first-embraces-the-common-core.

11. Aspire Public Schools, "Approach: College for Certain," accessed December 14, 2015, http://aspirepublicschools.org/approach/college-for-certain/.

12. Charter School Growth Fund, home page, accessed December 14, 2015, http://chartergrowthfund.org/.

13. Joanne W. Golann, "The Paradox of Success at a No-Excuses School," *Sociology of Education* (January 14, 2015), http://soe.sagepub.com/content/early /2015/01/13/0038040714567866.

14. Intensity, of course, isn't the only reason for teacher turnover. In Los Angeles, for example, Bruce Fuller concludes, "We see a lot of teachers who are super-bright, super-committed to the kids, but don't necessarily see teaching as a long-term career." See Stephen Sawchuk, "Charters Look to Change Perceptions on Teacher Turnover" *Education Week*, June 3, 2015, www.edweek .org/ew/articles/2015/06/03/charters-look-to-change-perceptions-on -teacher.html.

CHAPTER 12

1. Bruce Fuller ed., *Inside Charter Schools: The Paradox of Radical Decentralization* (Cambridge, MA: Harvard University Press, 2000). For other illustrations of charter-school diversity, see Joe Nathan, *Charter Schools: Creating Hope and Opportunity for American Education* (San Francisco: Jossey-Bass, 1996); Bryan Hassel, *The Charter School Challenge: Avoiding the Pitfalls, Fulfilling the Promise* (Washington, DC: Brookings Institution, 1999); Katherine K. Merseth et al., *Inside Urban Charter Schools: Promising Practices and Strategies in Five High-Performing Schools* (Cambridge, MA: Harvard Education Press, 2009); and Peter Frumkin, Bruno V. Manno, and Nell Edgington, *The Strategic Management of Charter Schools: Frameworks and Tools for Educational Entrepreneurs* (Cambridge, MA: Harvard Education Press, 2011).

2. Great Hearts Academies, "Philosophical Pillars," accessed December 14, 2015, www.greatheartsaz.org/about-us-mainmenu-26/philosophical-pillars.

3. Springs Charter Schools, "Our Approach," accessed December 14, 2015, http://springscharterschools.org/about-us/our-approach.

4. Cornville Region Charter School, "Agriculture Education," accessed December 14, 2015, http://cornvilleregionalcharterschool.org/agriculture -education/.

5. Alexis de Tocqueville, *Democracy in America*, ed. and trans. Harvey C. Mansfield and Delba Winthrop (Chicago: University of Chicago Press, 2000), excerpt accessed December 14, 2015 and available at www.press.uchicago.edu /Misc/Chicago/805328.html.

6. The same firm also operates Christian private schools in the Milwaukee area. Eagle College Preparatory Schools, home page, accessed February 6, 2016, http://eagleprep.org.

7. Chartering could go further, if state laws were amended, to include schools with a religious orientation. That's beyond reach today because of statutes requiring that charters be secular and, in some places, because of constraints in state constitutions. There would also be challenges under the First Amendment of the US Constitution, but such schools may pass Supreme Court muster on the same basis as parochial schools receiving voucher-bearing students. See *Zelman v. Simmons-Harris*, 536 U.S. 639 (2002), opinion available at www.law.cornell.edu/supct/html/00-1751.ZS .html. One of us has suggested for years that these constraints should be eased where possible. See Chester E. Finn, Jr., "Why Not Religious Charter Schools?" *Education Week*, December 10, 2003, www.edweek.org/ew/articles /2003/12/10/15finn.h23.html.

8. Public School Review, "California Vocational Public Charter Schools," accessed December 14, 2015, www.publicschoolreview.com/california/vocational-public -schools/charter.

9. Naomi Schaefer Riley, "How a Bronx Charter School Is Revolutionizing Education," *New York Post*, September 21, 2014, http://nypost.com/2014/09/21 /how-a-bronx-charter-school-is-revolutionizing-education/; Seton Education Partners, "El Camino Faith Foundation," accessed December 14, 2015, www.setonpartners.org/what-we-do/el-camino-faith-formation; and El Camino NYC Facebook page, accessed December 14, 2015, www.facebook .com/ElCaminoNYC.

10. Greg Bluestein, "Georgia Opens First Prison Charter School," *Atlanta Journal-Constitution*, September 17, 2015, www.myajc.com/news/news/state -regional-govt-politics/georgia-opens-first-prison-charter-school/nnhJN. See also "Georgia Expands Educational Opportunities for Inmates," *Correctional News*, September 22, 2015, www.correctionalnews.com/articles/2015/09/22 /georgia-expands-educational-opportunities-inmates.

11. Carlos Rosario International Public Charter School, home page, accessed February 6, 2016, www.carlosrosario.org.

12. Of the ten most racially diverse public schools in the District of Columbia in 2014–2015, six were charters. The National Coalition of Diverse Charter Schools and author Richard Kahlenberg are working to promote more like them. See Michael Alison Chandler, "As D.C. Gentrifies, Some Charter Schools Aim to Reach Broader Spectrum," *Washington Post*, December 4, 2015, www.washingtonpost.com/local/education/charter-schools-appealing-to -more-diverse-families-as-dc-gentrifies/2015/12/03/1d79c3f8-8dab-11e5 -acff-673ae92ddd2b_story.html; National Coalition of Diverse Charter Schools, home page, accessed December 14, 2015, www.diversecharters.org; and Richard D. Kahlenberg and Halley Potter, *A Smarter Charter: Finding What Works for Charter Schools and Public Education* (New York: Teachers College Press, 2014).

13. Khan Academy, home page, accessed December 14, 2015, www.khanacademy .org/.

14. Khan Academy, "About LASD," accessed January 14, 2016, www.khanacademy
.org/coach-res/reference-for-coaches/lasd/a/about-lasd; and David Osborne,
"Schools of the Future: California's Summit Public Schools," Progressive
Policy Institute, January 2016, www.progressivepolicy.org/slider/schools-of
-the-future-californias-summit-public-schools/. For a sampling of more
schools using Khan Academy offerings, see "12 Inspiring Schools Using
Khan Academy," *OnlineUniversities.com* (blog), April 23, 2012, www.online
universities.com/blog/2012/04/12-inspiring-schools-using-khan-academy.

15. Kevin Bronk, "Richard Whitmire on Rocketship, Parent Advocates and a
Movement Towards Equity," *Beyond* (Rocketship Education blog), accessed
December 14, 2015, http://blog.rsed.org/2014/05/27/richard-whitmire-on
-rocketship-parent-advocates-and-a-movement-towards-equity.

16. Tom Vander Ark, "8 Ways Machine Learning Will Improve Education," *Getting Smart*, November 26, 2015, http://gettingsmart.com/2015/11/8-ways
-machine-learning-will-improve-education/.

17. Launa Hall, "I Gave My Students iPads—Then Wished I Could Take Them
Back," *Washington Post*, December 2, 2015, www.washingtonpost.com
/opinions/i-gave-my-students-ipads--then-wished-i-could-take-them-back
/2015/12/02/a1bc8272-818f-11e5-a7ca-6ab6ec20f839_story.html; and
Sherry Turkle, *Reclaiming Conversation: The Power of Talk in a Digital Age* (London: Penguin Press, 2015).

18. See, for example, Digital Learning Now, "About," accessed December 14,
2015, www.digitallearningnow.com/about; International Association for
K–12 Online Learning, home page, accessed December 14, 2015, www.inacol
.org; and Digital Learning Institute, home page, accessed December 14, 2015,
www.digitallearninginstitute.org.

19. Minnesota New Country School, "MNCS Design Elements," accessed February 6, 2016, www.newcountryschool.com/about-mncs/mncs-design
-elements.

20. Sarah Sparks, "Teachers Say They Have Less Autonomy, Fed. Data Show," *Education Week*, December 7, 2015, http://blogs.edweek.org/edweek/teacherbeat
/2015/12/teachers_say_they_have_less_au.html.

21. Teacher-Powered Schools, "List of Teacher-Powered Schools," accessed December 14, 2015, www.teacherpowered.org/inventory/list. See also National
Resource Center on Charter School Finance and Government, "Involving
Teachers in Charter School Governance," October 2008, www.charterschool
center.org/sites/default/files/files/field_publication_attachment/Involving
_Teachers_v2_0.pdf; and School Redesign, "How a Teacher Partnership Manages a Public School," Center for Teacher Quality, March 27, 2015, www
.teachingquality.org/content/how-teacher-partnership-manages-public-school.

22. Paul Manna and Patrick McGuinn, eds., *Education Governance for the Twenty-
First Century* (Washington, DC: Brookings Institution, 2013), 123–24, 382–83.

23. In this account, we borrow liberally—and appreciatively—from David Osborne, "A Tale of Two Systems: Education Reform in Washington D.C.,"

Progressive Policy Institute, September 2015, www.progressivepolicy.org
/slider/tale-of-two-systems-education-reform-in-washington-d-c.

24. Daniela Doyle, Christen Holly, and Bryan C. Hassel, "Is Détente Possible?
District-Charter School Relations in Four Cities," Thomas B. Fordham Institute, Washington, DC, November 2015, 72–80, http://edexcellence.net
/publications/is-detente-possible-district-charter-school-relations-in-four-cities.

25. Much else was going on at the same time, of course, including sizable demographic shifts in the nation's capital, new academic standards, and No Child
Left Behind.

26. DCPS no longer has an elected board of its own. Instead, the District of Columbia has an elected state board of education and a state superintendent,
both of which work closely with the mayor and deputy mayor for education,
but neither of which actually runs schools.

27. Emma Brown, "D.C.'s Hospitality High to Convert from Charter to Traditional School," *Washington Post*, April 9, 2014, www.washingtonpost.com
/local/education/dcs-hospitality-high-to-convert-from-charter-to-traditional
-school/2014/04/29/76087bd8-cfc3-11e3-a6b1-45c4dffb85a6_story.html;
and Daniel J. Sernovitz, "Academy for Construction and Design to Uproot
from Its Longtime Home at Cardozo," *Washington Business Journal*, May 15,
2015, www.bizjournals.com/washington/breaking_ground/2015/05
/academy-for-construction-and-design-on-the-move.html.

28. Scott Pearson, John H. McKoy, and Neerav Kingsland, "How Many Charter
Schools Is Just Right?" *Education Next* (summer 2015), http://educationnext
.org/how-many-charter-schools-just-right.

29. David Osborne, "Tale of Two Systems," iii–iv.

30. Paul T. Hill and Ashley E. Jochim, *A Democratic Constitution for Public Education*
(Chicago: University of Chicago Press, 2015).

31. Paul T. Hill and Christine Campbell, "Growing Number of Districts Seek
Bold Change with Portfolio Strategy," Center on Reinventing Public Education, June 2011, www.crpe.org/publications/growing-number-districts-seek
-bold-change-portfolio-strategy.

32. Paul Hill, Ashley Jochim, and Christine Campbell, "Portfolio Strategies, Re-
linquishment, The Urban School System of the Future, and Smart Districts,"
Center on Reinventing Public Education, Seattle, February, 2013, 1–2, www
.crpe.org/publications/portfolio-strategies-relinquishment-urban-school
-system-future-and-smart-districts.

33. Quoted in Melanie Asmar, "Why Denver superintendent Tom Boasberg Landed
an Unprecedented Six-Month Break," *Chalkbeat Colorado*, November 18, 2015,
http://co.chalkbeat.org/2015/11/18/why-denver-superintendent-tom-boasberg
-landed-an-unprecedented-six-month-break/#.Vm1_KcdIjIU.

34. In the early years of chartering, Denver was generally hostile, even filing a
constitutional challenge to the law after an application that DPS denied was
approved by the Colorado State Board of Education. The charter law was
unanimously upheld in 1999 by the Colorado Supreme Court. Eventually,

the legislature created the Colorado Charter Schools Institute to enable pro-spective school operators to bypass district opposition. See Jim Griffin, "Col-orado's Charter Schools: Their History and Their Future," *Denver Post*, May 19, 2013, www.denverpost.com/ci_23261474/colorados-charter-schools-their-history-and-their-future.

35. Burt Hubbard, Nancy Mitchell, "Leaving to Learn," National Neighborhood Indicators Partnership, April 2007, www.neighborhoodindicators.org/library/catalog/leaving-learn-series.

36. Ibid., 21.

37. The "Denver Plan" had additional elements, among which probably the best known is ProCom, a performance-based compensation scheme for teachers. See Denver Public Schools, "The Denver Plan 2020," accessed December 16, 2015, http://denverplan.dpsk12.org.

38. Michael Bennet and the Denver School Board, "A Vision for a 21st Century School District," *Rocky Mountain News*, April 26, 2007, www.greateducation.org/news/2007/04/bennet-a-vision-for-a-21st-century-school-district/.

39. Colorado Department of Education, "Options for Autonomous Schools in Colorado: A Handbook for School and District Leaders," August 2009, www.cde.state.co.us/sites/default/files/documents/choice/download/autonomous schoolshandbook.pdf. The first was approved in April 2016.

40. Doyle, et al., "Is Détente Possible?," 62–69.

41. Julie Poppen, "Denver Lands $4 million for 'Chanter Compact,'" *Chalkbeat Colorado*, December 5, 2012, http://co.chalkbeat.org/2012/12/05/denver-lands-4-million-for-charter-compact.

42. Richard Whitmire, "Inside Successful District Charter Compacts," *Education Next* (fall 2014), http://educationnext.org/inside-successful-district-charter-compacts.

43. "Start with the Facts 2014: At the Base of a Climb," *A + Denver* (September 2014), www.aplusdenver.org/_docs/SWTF-Final1.pdf.

44. Doyle, et al., "Is Détente Possible?," 62–69.

45. Sarah Yatsko, Elizabeth Cooley Nelson, and Robin Lake, "District-Charter Collaboration Compact: Interim Report," Center on Reinventing Public Education, Seattle, June 2013, www.crpe.org/sites/default/files/compact_interim_report_6_2013_0.pdf (Appendix VI).

46. Paul T. Hill. Christine Campbell, and Bethany Gross, *Strife and Progress: Portfolio Strategies for Managing Urban Schools* (Washington, DC: Brookings Institution, 2013) 13–14.

47. Louisiana is complicated, as it has five types of charters. See Louisiana Department of Education, "Louisiana Charter Schools At-A-Glance," accessed December 16, 2015, www.louisianabelieves.com/schools/charter-schools.

48. Christen Holly et al., "Ten Years in New Orleans: Public Resurgence and the Path Ahead," New Schools for New Orleans, June 2015, 25–29, www.new schoolsforneworleans.org/wp-content/uploads/2015/06/Public-School-Resurgence-Full-Report-FINAL.pdf.

49. As of 2014–2015, the RSD also had six charter schools in East Baton Rouge and one in Shreveport. See Louisiana Department of Education, "Recovery School District 2014 Annual Report," accessed December 16, 2015, www .louisianabelieves.com/docs/default-source/katrina/2014-rsd-annual -report-print-version.pdf?sfvrsn=2.

50. See, for example, Neerav Kingsland, "The Hidden Connection in City-wide Reform: How Charter Schools Can Bring Equity to Public Education," National Alliance for Public Charter Schools, June 2015, www.publiccharters .org/wp-content/uploads/2015/06/NPC035_NolaPaper_F1.pdf.

51. Holly et al., "Ten Years in New Orleans," 54.

52. An attorney by training, Pastorek had served as general counsel of the National Aeronautics and Space Administration . He hired both Vallas and White. Vallas had led the Chicago and Philadelphia school systems before coming to Louisiana as RSD superintendent. White had served as Joel Klein's deputy in New York before coming to Louisiana, first as RSD head, then as Pastorek's successor in the state superintendent post.

CHAPTER 13

1. National Alliance for Public Charter Schools, "Measuring Up to the Model: A Ranking of State Charter School Laws," January 2015, www.publiccharters .org/wp-content/uploads/2015/01/model_law_2015.pdf.

2. Ibid.

3. US Department of Education, Office of Innovation and Improvement, "Charter Schools Program (CSP) Grant Competitions," accessed November 27, 2015, www2.ed.gov/about/offices/list/oii/csp/about-cs-competitions.html.

4. Charter School Growth Fund, home page, accessed November 27, 2015, http://chartergrowthfund.org.

5. Examples include New Schools for New Orleans, The Mind Trust (in Indianapolis), the DC Schools Fund (affiliated with the national NewSchools Venture Fund), and the Philadelphia School Partnership. See Education Cities, "Building Education Cities," December 2014, http://education-cities.org /wp-content/uploads/Report-Building-Education-Cities.pdf.

6. Caroline M. Hoxby, "The Supply of Charter Schools," in *Charter Schools Against the Odds*, ed. Paul T. Hill (Stanford, CA: Education Next Books, 2006), 15–44.

7. National Alliance for Public Charter Schools, "Measuring Up to the Model," 7, 109, 111–112.

8. Paul Hill, "Defining and Organizing for School Autonomy," Center on Reinventing Public Education, Seattle, June 2013, www.crpe.org/publications /defining-and-organizing-school-autonomy.

9. National Association of Charter School Authorizers, "2014 Overview of the State of Charter Authorizing," 2014, www.qualitycharters.org/wp-content /uploads/2015/08/NACSA_2014-SOCA.pdf.

10. Marguerite Roza, *Educational Economics: Where Do School Funds Go?* (Washington, DC: Urban Institute Press, 2010).

11. See, for example, Education Resource Strategies, "Transforming School Funding: A Guide to Implementing Student-Based Budgeting," January 2014, www.erstrategies.org/library/implementing_student-based_budgeting. For a description of the version under consideration in Indianapolis, see Dylan Peers McCoy, "Rich School, Poor School: IPS Push to Even Out Funding Could Bring Big Changes," *Chalkbeat Indiana*, December 10, 2015, http://in.chalkbeat.org/2015/12/10/rich-school-poor-school-ips-push-to-even-out-funding-could-bring-big-changes/#.VrZLZ5MrLdQ. For an excellent overview of this approach to education funding, see Lisa Snell, *A Handbook for Student-Based Budgeting, Principal Autonomy and School Choice* (Los Angeles: Reason Foundation, 2013).

12. Lisa Grover, "State Policy Snapshot: Facilities Funding for Public Charter Schools," National Association for Public Charter Schools, May 2015, www.publiccharters.org/wp-content/uploads/2015/05/facilities_funding_snapshot_final.pdf.

13. Thomas Stewart and Patrick J. Wolf, *The School Choice Journey: School Vouchers and the Empowerment of Urban Families* (London: Palgrave Macmillan, 2014).

14. Learn DC, home page, accessed November 27, 2015, www.learndc.org; and My School DC, home page, accessed November 27, 2015, www.myschooldc.org.

15. Ashley Jochim, Michael DeArmond, Betheny Gross, and Robin Lake, "How Parents Experience Public School Choice," Center on Reinventing Public Education, Seattle, December 2014, 2, www.crpe.org/sites/default/files/crpe_how-parents-experience-public-school-choice_1_1.pdf.

16. Dale Russakoff, *The Prize: Who's in Charge of America's Schools?* (New York: Houghton Mifflin, 2015). See also Juli Kim et al., "Early Lessons from Newark's Experience with Charter Schools," Public Impact, accessed January 19, 2016, http://publicimpact.com/web/wp-content/uploads/2015/08/Early_Lessons_from_Newarks_Experience_With_Charter_Schools-Public_Impact.pdf.

17. Paul T. Hill. Christine Campbell, and Betheny Gross, *Strife and Progress: Portfolio Strategies for Managing Urban Schools* (Washington, DC: Brookings Institution, 2013); and Paul T. Hill and Ashley Jochim, "The Street-Level Politics of School Reform," Center on Reinventing Public Education, Seattle, November 2015, www.yumpu.com/en/document/view/54768159/the-street-level-politics-of-school-reform.

18. Alex Kotlowitz, "'The Prize' by Dale Russakoff," *New York Times*, August 19, 2015, www.nytimes.com/2015/08/23/books/review/the-prize-by-dale-russakoff.html?_r=0.

19. Hill and Jochim, "Street-Level Politics of School Reform."

20. Mary Moran, "Howard Fuller Explains What's Happening in New Orleans," *Education Post*, August 7, 2015, https://educationpost.org/howard-fuller-explains-whats-happening-in-new-orleans (blog post with embedded video in which Fuller discusses the ups and downs of New Orleans school reform).

See also Paul Schmitz, "Educating Reformers and Activists: Dr. Howard Fuller's Powerful Example and Lessons," *Huffington Post*, November 4, 2014, www.huffingtonpost.com/paul-schmitz/educating-reformers-and-a_b _6096460.html?utm_hp_ref=books&ir=Books; and Howard Fuller and Lisa Frazier Page, *No Struggle No Progress: A Warrior's Life from Black Power to Education Reform* (Milwaukee: Marquette University Press, 2014).

21. Lyndsey Layton, "GOP-Led States Increasingly Taking Control from Local School Boards," *Washington Post*, February 1, 2016, www.washingtonpost.com /local/education/gop-led-states-increasingly-taking-control-from-local -school-boards/2016/02/01/c01a8e4e-bad3-11e5-b682-4bb4dd403c7d_story .html. When the Thatcher government in England removed many schools from the control of local authorities in the 1980s and made them answerable directly to Whitehall, this was widely interpreted in Britain as an attempt to strengthen the Tory party by weakening many Labour (and union) strongholds.

22. Charter School Growth Fund, "Our Portfolio," accessed December 15, 2015, http://chartergrowthfund.org/portfolio/#Emerging_CMO_Fund.

23. Equitas Academy, home page, accessed December 15, 2015, www.equitas academy.org.

24. Capital Preparatory Schools, home page, accessed December 15, 2015, http:// wearecapitalprep.org/index.html.

25. For an approach to this issue, see, for example, Rebecca Kisner, "The Parent Engagement Continuum in High-Performing Charter Schools: A Guide for Schools," Donnell-Kay Foundation, May 2013, http://dkfoundation.org/sites /default/files/files/DK%20Parent%20Engagement%20Paper%20FINAL%205 %2017%2013.pdf, which describes three organizations that illustrate this engagement continuum.

26. A language-centric high school, for example, may be ill suited to students who don't already have a grounding in the relevant language, just as a STEM -focused school may reasonably expect entering pupils to have some proficiency—as well as interest—in science and math.

27. For a description of the DC arrangement, see My School DC, "About My School DC," accessed November 27, 2015, www.myschooldc.org/about/about -my-school-dc. For a description of the Denver system, see Denver Public Schools, "How to Choose a School," accessed November 27, 2015, http:// schoolchoice.dpsk12.org/how-to-choose-a-school. See also Betheny Gross, Michael DeArmond, and Patrick Denice, "Common Enrollment, Parents, and School Choice: Early Evidence from Denver and New Orleans," Center on Reinventing Public Education, Seattle, May 2015, www.crpe.org/sites /default/files/crpe-brief-common-enrollment-denver-nola.pdf; and Sara Mead, Ashley LiBetti Mitchel, and Andrew J. Rotherham, "The State of the Charter School Movement," Bellwether Education Partners, September 2015, http://bellwethereducation.org/sites/default/files/Charter%20Research %200908%20FINAL.pdf 88.

28. The District of Columbia School Transit Subsidy Program offers free or reduced fares for students who use public transit to travel to and from DC public, public charter, private, and parochial schools.

29. Denver Public Schools, "Success Express," accessed February 6, 2016, http://transportation.dpsk12.org/successexpress; and Jeffrey M. Vincent et al., "Beyond the Yellow Bus: Promising Practices for Maximizing Access to Opportunity Through Innovations in Student Transportation," Center for Cities + Schools, University of California, Berkeley, 2014, http://citiesandschools.berkeley.edu/reports/CC+SYellowBus2014.pdf.

30. Michael J. Petrilli, "The School Choice Movement's Schisms, Explained," Thomas B. Fordham Institute, Washington, DC, January 27, 2016, http://edexcellence.net/articles/the-school-choice-movements-schisms-explained.

31. Cami Anderson, "Resolving the Charter School Debate," *Education Week*, January 26, 2016, www.edweek.org/ew/articles/2016/01/27/resolving-the-charter-school-debate.html.

CHAPTER 14

1. David Tyack and Larry Cuban, *Tinkering Toward Utopia: A Century of Public School Reform* (Cambridge, MA: Harvard University Press, 1995), 1, 7.

2. Ted Kolderie, *Beyond Choice to New Public Schools* (Washington, DC: Progressive Policy Institute, 1990), 2, ch. 2.

3. David L. Kirp, "How to Fix the Country's Failing Schools. And How Not To," *The New York Times*, January 9, 2016, www.nytimes.com/2016/01/10/opinion/sunday/how-to-fix-the-countrys-failing-schools-and-how-not-to.html. See also David L. Kirp, *Improbable Scholars: The Rebirth of a Great American School System and a Strategy for America's Schools* (Oxford, UK: Oxford University Press, 2013). For a criticism of this book, see Grover J. Whitehurst, "Deconstructing Union City," Brookings Institution, October 16, 2013, www.brookings.edu/research/papers/2013/10/16-education-nation-union-city-reform-critique-whitehurst.

4. Tennessee Achievement School District, "Building the Possible," accessed January 14, 2016, http://achievementschooldistrict.org/about; and Nelson Smith, "Redefining the School District in America," Thomas B. Fordham Institute, Washington, DC, June 2015, http://edexcellence.net/publications/redefining-the-school-district-in-america.

5. For an excellent review of different governance models and their transition challenges, see Paul Manna and Patrick McGuinn, eds., *Education Governance for the Twenty-First Century* (Washington, DC: Brookings Institution, 2013), especially essays by Paul T. Hill and Kenneth J. Meier.

6. Philip B. Kurland and Ralph Lerner, eds., *The Founders' Constitution* (Chicago: University of Chicago Press, 1987), Volume 3, Article 1, Section 8, Clause 8, Document 4, Massachusetts Constitution of 1780, CH. 5, SEC. 2, accessed December 15, 2015, http://press-pubs.uchicago.edu/founders/documents/a1_8_8s4.html.

7. Washington State Constitution, Article IX, accessed December 15, 2015, https://ballotpedia.org/Article_IX_Washington_State_Constitution.

8. Bruce Fuller, *Organizing Locally: How the New Decentralists Improve Education, Health Care, and Trade* (Chicago: University of Chicago Press, 2015), 186, 196.

9. See, for example, Sandra Norman-Eady, "Quasi-Public Agencies," OLR Research Report, September 8, 2006, www.cga.ct.gov/2005/rpt/2005-R-0772 .htm; Home Forward, home page, accessed December 15, 2015, www.home forward.org; and Library Systems & Services, "Communities List," accessed December 15, 2015, www.lssi.com/communities/communities-list.

ABOUT THE AUTHORS

CHESTER E. FINN, JR. is distinguished senior fellow and president emeritus at the Thomas B. Fordham Institute and a senior fellow at Stanford's Hoover Institution. His previous positions include Professor of Education and Public Policy at Vanderbilt University, counsel to the US ambassador to India, legislative director for Senator Daniel Patrick Moynihan, and Assistant US Secretary of Education for Research and Improvement. He has also been on the research staffs of the Brookings Institution, the Hudson Institute, and the Manhattan Institute and has taught high school social studies in Massachusetts. Author, coauthor, or editor of more than twenty books, he published his most recent book, *Failing Our Brightest Kids: The Global Challenge of Educating High-Ability Students* (coauthored with Brandon L. Wright), in 2015. He has written more than four hundred articles in a wide array of scholarly and popular publications. Finn is a regular contributor to Fordham's *Education Gadfly Weekly*, a contributing editor of *Education Next*, and a contributor to such online outlets as *NationalReview.com*, *Politico*, and *Atlantic.com*. He serves on the boards of the National Council on Teacher Quality, the Core Knowledge Foundation, and the Maryland State Board of Education and has spoken at hundreds of conferences and symposia across the United States and in many other countries. He is the recipient of awards from the Educational Press Association of America, the National Association for Gifted Children, the National Alliance for Public Charter Schools, and the Education Writers Association. Finn holds three degrees from Harvard University and an honorary doctorate from Colgate University.

BRUNO V. MANNO is senior advisor for K–12 Education with the Walton Family Foundation. His previous positions include Senior Program Associate for Education with the Annie E. Casey Foundation; Senior Fellow in the Education Policy Studies Program at the Hudson Institute; Executive Director of the congressionally created National Commission on the Cost of Higher Education; the Director of Planning for the Office of Educational Research and Improvement; and the Assistant Secretary of Education for Policy and Planning in the US Department of Education. He is also the author, coauthor, or editor of seven books and has written more than two hundred articles in such publications as *Education Next, National Affairs, Education Week, The Public Interest,* the *Wall Street Journal, Washington Post,* the *Weekly Standard, Journal of School Choice,* and *Wilson Quarterly.* He is a former member of the President's Commission on White House Fellowships, a past member and chair of the Presidential Scholars Commission, a former chair of the boards of the National Alliance for Public Charter Schools and Education Sector, and a past board member of the Thomas B. Fordham Foundation and Institute, The Mind Trust, and Grantmakers for Education. He holds two degrees from the University of Dayton (BA and MA) and a PhD from Boston College. Manno undertook postdoctoral studies, which included appointments as Visiting Senior Lecturer at Catholic Teachers College in Sydney, Australia (now the Catholic University of Australia), Visiting Research Associate at the National Opinion Research Center at the University of Chicago, and Visiting Lecturer at the Institute for Catholic Educational Leadership at the University of San Francisco.

BRANDON L. WRIGHT is the editorial director of the Thomas B. Fordham Institute. He is the coauthor (with Chester E. Finn, Jr.) of the book *Failing Our Brightest Kids: The Global Challenge of Educating High-Ability Students.* His writing has appeared in places like the *Wall Street Journal,* the *New York Post, Newsweek, Education Next, Education Week,* and *National Review.* He holds a Juris Doctor from American University Washington College of Law and a bachelor's degree from the University of Michigan.

INDEX

burnout, 97
Bush, George H. W., 12, 137
busing systems, 200

California, 17, 25, 26, 27, 33, 57, 94, 170
California Charter Schools Association, 142
capital funding, 105–107, 193
Capitalism and Freedom (Friedman), 13
Capital Prep, 197
career-technical schools, 170
Carlos Rosario International Public
    Charter School, 170
Carlson, Arne, 17
Carpe Diem Schools, 172
Carroll, John B., 10
Catholic schools, 137, 144, 164
Center for Research on Education Out-
    comes (CREDO), 41–46, 48, 56–61
Center on Reinventing Public Education
    (CRPE), 39–41, 56, 57, 72, 199
centralization, 78
Charles Sposato Graduate School of
    Education, 70
Charter Board Partners, 94
Charter Friends National Network, 18
charter management organizations
    (CMOs), 8, 25, 70–72, 95, 110, 131, 189
charters, 88
Charter School Achievement Consensus
    Panel, 39–41
Charter School Growth Fund, 108, 140,
    162, 189, 205
charter-school laws, 1, 17–19, 21–22, 118,
    142, 177, 188–190
charter schools
    accomplishments of, 63–73
    caps on, 23, 81, 118, 142, 188–189
    changes needed in, 187–202
    collaboration between districts and, 144
    as competition, 84–85, 137, 138, 167
    competition among, 146–147
    current state of, 25–33
    debates over, 1, 43–44, 135–141
    demand for, 64–65, 122, 146
    diversity of, 168–171
    efficiency of, 113–114
    enrollment statistics, 24–26, 64–65,
        121–124
    evolution of, 21–33
    examples of, 53–62
    features of, 7–8
    funding of, 7–8, 101–114, 142–143, 146, 189
    future of, 149–150, 153–154

goals of, 18
governance of, 8, 71–73, 87–99
growth of, 1, 33, 159–160
information on, 82–84
market-based model of, 79–85, 90, 138,
    188–190, 209
national support system for, 17–18
number of, 22–23
online, 24, 27, 46, 56–59, 111, 172–173
openings and closings of, 22–24, 92–93,
    146
origins of, 7–20
performance of, 1, 37–51, 54–61, 82
potential of, 2
problems with, 81–84
promises of, 167–185
public education and, 203–210
quality approach to, 43–44
regulation of, 115–133, 190–191
at-risk students in, 31–32
role of, 1–2
services for, 200–201
special education and, 125–130
teachers in, 32–33, 70–71, 104–105
types of, 24–25, 27–28
Charter Schools USA, 109, 140
Chicago, 49–50, 118
Chicago International Charter School, 88
children with disabilities, 31, 58, 123,
    125–130, 154
Chingos, Matthew, 48–49
Christensen, Clayton, 65, 210
Chubb, John, 13
Citizens League, 16
Civic Builders, 73
civil rights advocates, 143
civil society, 14, 97
Clark, Kenneth B., 11, 19
Cleveland, 195–196
Clinton, Bill, 12, 17, 19
Coleman, James S., 10, 19, 116
collective bargaining agreements, 78, 104,
    118, 132, 137, 143, 190
college attendance, 49–50, 51, 54, 156, 158,
    162, 164
college preparatory curriculum, 157, 159
co-location, 107
Colorado, 17, 176–180
Common Core State Standards, 11, 160
common schools, 8–9, 19, 171, 207–208
community engagement, 196–198
community schools, 43
community values, 157